ESCAPE FROM BERKELEY

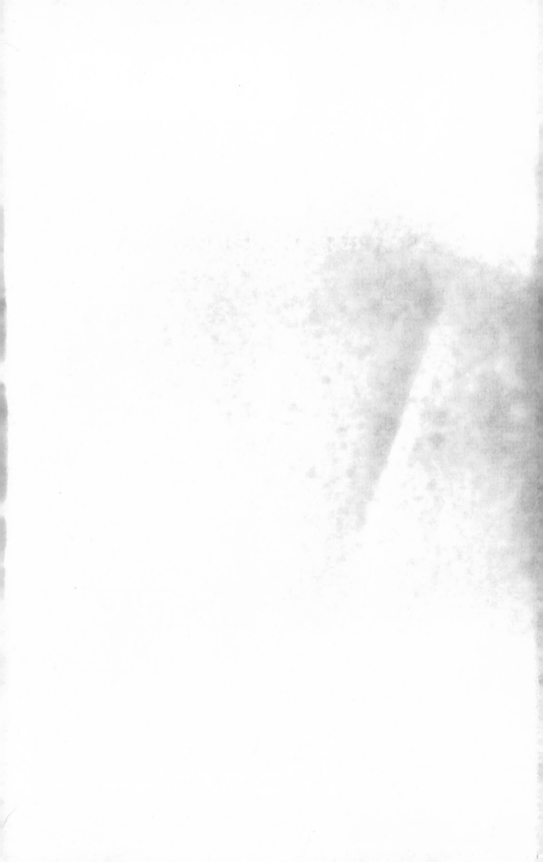

ESCAPE FROM BERKELEY

An Ex-liberal progressive socialist
embraces America (and doesn't apologize).

Howard Hyde

CitizenEcon.com
Pacific Palisades, California
2016

First Printing: 2016

ISBN-13: 978-0692667477
ISBN-10: 0692667474

CitizenEcon.com
Pacific Palisades, CA 90272
HHCapitalism@gmail.com

Cover design by Yves Lajoie, yapmedia.net

Cover photo credit: H97.1.140
Chris Kjobech, untitled (Free Speech Movement Leader Mario Savio Leading Student Protestors at U.C. Berkeley), November 20, 1964. Gelatin silver photograph, 10.25 x 13 in. Collection of Oakland Museum of California. The Oakland Tribune Collection. Gift of ANG Newspapers.

To Ginger and Laura

Acknowledgments

I am indebted to many people for making this book possible, not least of whom the authors named in the bibliography and in the chapter "The Curriculum". I cannot express enough my gratitude to those individuals who recognized the value and importance of this work and contributed financially through the website www.CitizenEcon.com. You make the impossible possible.

Special Thanks to Kimberly Benning for her incomparable copy editing.

CONTENTS

SPECIAL FOREWORD TO THE MILLENNIAL GENERATION V

Part I: From Berkeley Leftist to Republican Club President . 1

CHAPTER NOUGHT: THEN AND NOW 3
BERKELEY, CALIFORNIA: MY HOME SWEET HOME 7
    SLATE..7
    The Free Speech Movement..8
    Vietnam 9
    People's Park 11
    The 70s..12
    Growing Up 13
    The Void 19
A SEED AND A DEPARTURE 21
    Milton Friedman, "Free to Choose"....................................21
    Leaving Berkeley 26
LA BELLE FRANCE 29
    Le Bohemien 29
    Le Contrôle de Loyers et le Chômage...................................33
    Touche Pas à Mon Pote..35
COMING HOME (ALMOST)..37
    Move In Today!...37
    The Ultimate Resource 39
    The Daughter of a Shahid 43
    A High-Tech Lynching 44
    A Formal Introduction..49
    A Conservative Libertarian Blog and a Republican Club.............50
THE CURRICULUM..53
    Econ 101, 102, 103 54
    "Great Economic Thinkers"...55
    "Giants of Political Thought"...60
    More Giants...61
BERKELEY REDUX..75
    Radical Left vs. Liberal Left..75

Red-Baiting Redux *76*

The Road to Serfdom *78*

The Failures of Liberalism *79*

The Content of Our Character *80*

We Had a Dream *83*

My Idols Reconsidered *86*

Aftermath *113*

The Cashing-In (Excerpted) *114*

Part II: Citizen Economics **121**

THE TEA PARTY FOR DOCTORS 123

WHERE DO JOBS COME FROM? 130

WHY DOES THE PAY SUCK? 134

HOW DOES PROSPERITY HAPPEN? 137

THE ENTREPRENEURIAL CYCLE: FROM SCARCITY TO
ABUNDANCE 140

"HUMAN NEEDS BEFORE PROFITS!" 143

WHY WE DON'T NEED TRADE WARS 147

Trade Facts and Stats *148*

WHY WE DON'T NEED A NEW NEW NEW DEAL 152

A Crisis of Intervention *153*

Roosevelt to the Rescue *156*

So what would you have done, smarty-pants? *157*

Conclusions *161*

UNDERSTANDING THE FINANCIAL CRISIS OF 2008 163

Wilderness Preservation *164*

Affordable Housing *165*

WHY OBAMACARE WILL FAIL 169

Part III: Socialized Medicine and Obamacare **173**

POST-OBAMACARE REFORM 175

THE UNAFFORDABLE MANDATE ACT 183

HEALTH CARE SOLUTIONS: PATIENTS IN COMMAND 186

HOW DARE WE CLAIM AMERICA IS #1 IN HEALTH CARE? ... 189

FIRE THE REAL BOSS OF THE VA 191

OBAMACARE: AND THEN A MIRACLE HAPPENS 194

Part IV: Politics and Foreign Policy **199**

TOWNHALL ROOT CANAL 201

INDIA GETS IT - BUT AMERICA DOESN'T 203

THROW THE BUMS...IN!..206
LIBERTARIANISM AND REPUBLICANS..208
OUR INTOLERABLE SUCCESS IN IRAQ..211
ANSWERING THE LIBERTARIAN INDICTMENTS ON IRAQ 213
HILLARY'S PATH TO 9/11 219
CONSERVATIVE FUNDRAISING: WHAT ME WORRY? 225

Part V: Global Warning..229

CLIMATE CHANGE: WHERE IS THE SCIENCE?..........................231
BACK TO THE FUTURE   AND THE SOLUTION TO CLIMATE
CHANGE..236
WE HAVE A LOT OF WEATHER TODAY!....................................240
Transcript of Interview on "The Larry Elder Show," June 12, 2015   240

Part VI: America 249

DÍA DE INDEPENDENCIA 251
John Adams and the American Revolution 252
YEARNING TO BREATHE FREE: IMMIGRATION REDUX..........257
The Only Resource That Counts...257
The Case for Closing the Border: Real and Present Dangers............262
Unfair Competition 262
Sayonara, California?...270
Crime and Demographics..271
Media Disinformation 278
Federal Bureaus of Missing Data 281
Economic Collateral Damage...284
Culture Matters...286
Democrat Party Political Gamesmanship 291
Invasion: "La Reconquista"..295
Islamic Sharia Law...297
Choices..298
COMPREHEN*SIBLE* IMMIGRATION REFORM............................299
JOHN HENRY'S AMERICA...307

Bibliography...311

About the Author 318

Special Foreword to the Millennial Generation

A few years back I was giving a speech to a Republican club in the Glendale/Eagle Rock area of Los Angeles. I introduced myself with, "Hello, I am Howard Hyde and I am an ex-liberal socialist progressive Democrat from Berkeley." I had used this line a few times before at various groups, and among middle-aged and older conservatives it was usually received with knowing smiles and, occasionally, applause.

This time it was slightly different. In addition to the usual (i.e., greying and balding) suspects in attendance, a local high school teacher had sent a contingent of young people to attend this meeting as part of a civics lesson (they were equally encouraged to attend Democratic Party political meetings). It occurred to me for the first time that—duh!—these kids probably had no clue as to the significance of that expression in general, or Berkeley in particular. And so I decided that instead of leaving the significance of "Berkeley in the Sixties" as an assumed and understood part of our common heritage, I would be prepared to explain it to those unfamiliar, and to clarify the details for those who may have only a superficial understanding. As someone who grew up in the social aftermath of the radical upheavals of Berkeley in the sixties, and who survived and overcame the pernicious ideological as well as psychological effects of that era, I feel a special responsibility that my particular perspective makes possible.

Any part of this book, including this one, may be the only one you are willing to read, so I am at pains to make it count. This book is for the general public, but it is especially intended as a wake-up call to young people, in particular those who may not have been exposed to perspectives like this before. The urgency is founded in the main on two fears: 1) that crises of a magnitude of those of the twentieth century, or worse, are nearly inevitable in the not-distant future, and 2) that the next generation will have less ability to cope with them than the prior two or three generations had, in spite of all of the historical information available at the swipe of a smartphone screen.

Study history. It sucks, and no one is immune or exempt. Those who are ignorant of history are condemned to repeat it (thank you, George Santayana), to which I would add: those who are ignorant of political economy might just as well not have opposable thumbs. And so I present here my offering of a token of economic and historical enlightenment.

When the inevitable crisis hits you—whether personally, as in the loss of a job with dim prospects of finding another, or impersonally, as in the awareness of unexpected misfortune of large numbers of others—please remember what you read here. When the market crashes, when the next trillion-dollar bailout gets bipartisan approval and yet never seems quite to put things back to "normal" (the experience of which you can't even remember anymore), when hyperinflation robs you of your savings and renders the economy dysfunctional, when an unavoidable war or civil unrest overruns your sheltered world, remember.

Will you have the intellectual tools necessary to cope with the crisis? Have you been given adequate instruction in principles and methodologies to figure out why it is happening and what to do about it? Have you learned the lessons especially of the last hundred years, so that you may be confident in knowing how to avoid the misfortunes of that tragic century, for yourself, your family, your country?

The majority of you have been taught for most of your lives, from kindergarten or even pre-school through college and/or graduate school, by members of a narrowly prescribed club. For all the diversity of skin color, ethnicity, and sexual preference or gender identity, there is a remarkable homogeneity of social philosophy, of world view based on a certain prejudicial understanding of history, law and economics. The decisive quality of the members of this club is not so much that they are liberal, progressive, Leftist, Marxist or radical per se, but that they have spent the majority of their adult and professional lives in institutions protected and removed by degrees from "real world" market forces: in public schools, universities, unions, subsidized crony-socialist businesses and government. They have spent far less time than the average American working either as an employee or owner in a business or farm that is neither subsidized nor favored by the government, which survives only by virtue of its ability to provide products and services of satisfactory quality to customers who voluntarily give up their hard-earned dollars in exchange but are free to take their business elsewhere if another company does it better;

businesses staffed by employees who are free to work for someone else if the conditions of employment don't meet their expectations. Collectively by historical standards they have a feeble understanding— through lack of experience—of property ownership, personal risk, responsibility, accountability, production and customer or client service. Political humorist Evan Sayet might call them the graduates of the Kindergarten of Eden (if indeed they have yet graduated).

You may read what I have to say in this book and still conclude that you disagree and are determined to follow a different philosophy or someone else, which of course is your prerogative in a free country (don't try this in an un-free one). But this much I guarantee: you will not be able to stay within your "safe space" forever, enjoying your (NOT!) God-given right to go through life without ever being offended. Your trigger-warning Maginot Line will be breached by the Panzer tanks of inevitable reality[1]. You will eventually have to read authors and listen to speakers that you haven't before, that none of your teachers or professors ever assigned to you, that you are inclined to disagree with, indeed that you have in large part been programmed to reject outright before their third word. Putting your fingers in your ears and humming isn't going to be adequate to solving the problems that are headed your way.

Conservative Millennials, you are not off the hook! You will have to read John Maynard Keynes, John Kenneth Galbraith, Paul Krugman, Immanuel Kant and Karl Marx in order to cope with the challenges that you will face.

So, on those cheerful notes, let's get started—the sooner to prove me wrong.

---

1   Maginot Line: The military fortifications that France built on the German border in the 1930s. The German army made an end-run around it through Belgium in 1940, and France capitulated in six weeks. Panzers were prominently used by the German army during WWII.

Part I: From Berkeley Leftist to Republican Club President

In which our hero presents the key milestones and outcomes of his personal intellectual and philosophical journey.

Chapter Nought: Then and Now . . .

If you want to understand how a candidate for President of the United States could repudiate the American Revolution, the Declaration of Independence and the Constitution and then win two consecutive elections by resounding majorities, Berkeley in the 1960s provides some key insights.

But I'm getting ahead of myself; permit me to start over.

At the crest of thousands of years of barbarism and feeble attempts at civilization, there emerged in the last two hundred and fifty years in North America a nation that would surpass all others, past and contemporary, in general prosperity, scientific, medical and technological advancement, justice, artistic creativity and liberty, such that it became the premier destination for immigrants worldwide, the most desirable place for most human beings, rich and poor, to live. This came about due to the serendipitous confluence of independent-minded, self-governing peoples, mostly practicing religious traditions grounded in Judeo-Christian theology, who recognized and fought to defend private property rights and the most highly circumscribed and constrained role that has ever prevailed in any complex society, of the authority to punish for offenses other than those recognized as most fundamental by a diversity of sects. The principles of this society and system of governance are set forth in the legacy and text of the founding documents the Declaration of Independence and the Constitution, together with its Bill of Rights, and the dynamic and superlatively productive economic system that emerged from this framework has been given (by its enemies, intended as a pejorative) the name "Capitalism." This nation is the United States of America, affectionately known simply as "America"[2].

To be sure, this nation, like all human endeavors, being neither of Heaven nor of the Garden of Eden but rather of Earth, is far from

---

[2]   Most South/Latin Americans have a different idea when they use the word "America". Who knew?

perfect, and injustices and travesties that appall any compassionate person, regardless of party, religion or faction, have occurred throughout this nation's history up to the present day. But judging a nation requires standards by which to judge, and the standards by which we judge the United States hardly existed prior to its founding. Conquest and slavery were universally "normal". Nobody wanted to be conquered, but no one saw conquest as an immoral aberration. Nobody wanted to be a slave, but almost nobody effectively objected to the institution of slavery. Other nations that lack America's ideals do not fall short of what they lack in the first place. Only by its own extraordinary standards does America fail.

Closely associated with this nation, and sharing (and in some cases, surpassing by degrees) its liberties and prosperity is the nation from which it emerged, Great Britain, derived from its own founding document of the year 1215, the Magna Carta Libertatum—the Great Charter of the Liberties—and those within Britain's enduring sphere of influence, law and language. Put simply, the great majority of the most prosperous and free nations that exist today are those where the English language is spoken and English constitutional and common law reign. Most of the people who have achieved this are native sons and daughters of Anglo-Saxon tribes, but this is not required; freedom and prosperity are available to all who would embrace their principles and responsibilities.

May these principles and their results endure, be nurtured and propagated to the uttermost ends of the Earth forevermore, for the benefit of humanity.

- - - - - - - - - - - - -

That is more or less how I have seen the world for the past twenty-four years or so. But since I'm a little older than twenty-four, that wasn't always the case. Thirty years ago, my philosophy could be summarized by the following emotions:

- Capitalism is a system of exploitation of the poor for the benefit of the rich.
- Businessmen are greedy and don't pay enough taxes.

4

- Corporations are evil, pollute the environment and don't pay enough taxes.
- America is a racist, unjust and imperial/colonial nation.
- America's military is a malignant force for murder and genocide in the world.
- Republican leaders are rich, white, old racist pigs who hate the poor, minorities, women and gays, don't care if sick people die in the streets, and want tax cuts for the rich at the expense of the down-trodden. And that goes (went) triple for Ronald Reagan.
- The Republican rank-and-file are uncivilized, intellectually retarded and sexually repressed Neanderthals.
- Helping the poor, preserving the environment, conserving wildlife habitat, protecting endangered species and supporting education and the arts and sciences are the proper domain and should be the primary task of government, preferably at the federal level, through adequate taxation and regulation.
- Our unsustainable exploitation of the world's natural resources and poor nations can only end in well-deserved exhaustion, shortage and destruction.

In other words, thirty years ago my worldview was perfectly conformed to that of the majority of college professors, Hollywood stars, radical leftists and Democratic Party power brokers today.

In this book I will tell the story of my evolution from liberal socialist to evangelist for Capitalism, describing a few key life experiences and influences; I will expose and refute the categorical charges against Capitalism, businessmen, corporations, the military and America in general, implicit in my emotions listed above; and I will apply the principles of what I have come to call **Citizen Economics** to a variety of contemporary problems. It is my hope that I may challenge superficially held beliefs (such as the emotions just enumerated), educate people about principles I consider critical to the understanding of the world which are poorly taught (when they are taught at all) in our schools and universities, and provide tools for like-minded citizens, officials, political candidates, teachers and journalists to better communicate, persuade, and exercise their influence.

Berkeley, California: My Home Sweet Home

And gentlemen in England now a-bed
Shall think themselves accursed they were not here,
And hold their manhoods cheap whiles any speaks
That fought with us upon Saint Crispin's day.
"Henry V" by William Shakespeare

Berkeley, California, has long been associated with left-wing causes, politics and agitation. It was the site in the 1960s and early 1970s of dozens of protest demonstrations and riots. Those events and many related ones at other university campuses around the country during that era, and the ideology that fueled them, have had a powerful influence on the generation of political leaders who now hold the reins of power in the twenty-first century in a plurality of sectors and levels, including the current (2009-2017) occupant of the White House. They shaped my world view from my youth through my young adulthood. The radical movements' leaders successfully instilled in me and others like me a sense of holding my manhood cheap for having missed out on participating in their noble causes. Their heirs may be found on hundreds of college campuses today.

SLATE

Liberal and Leftist politically-minded students at the University of California, Berkeley came together in the late 1950s to form an on-campus organization they called SLATE, which presented candidates for election to student government. They agitated against the activities of the anti-communist House Un-American Activities Committee (HUAC) and in support of civil rights and other causes, and above all, challenged university policies intended to keep "off-campus" politics away from the university. They picketed Bay Area businesses which discriminated on the basis of race. Their major triumph in this campaign came when they were able, by means of mass disruption at the Sheraton Palace Hotel, to compel the entire industry to begin hiring minorities at all levels of the organization. And in the summer of 1964,

7

a number of Berkeley students travelled to the Southern states to support civil rights demonstrations there[3].

The Free Speech Movement

In the fall of 1964, a few dozen students set up tables and booths for distributing political literature at the edge of the University of California, Berkeley campus. The campus police ordered them to take their tables down, as their activity was a violation of (recently made more restrictive) university policy. In late September and early October, the students openly defied the ban, manning their posts and refusing to move when ordered; perhaps after facing down police dogs and the Ku Klux Klan in Mississippi, they weren't going to be intimidated by any wimpy college deans. On October 1 in the midst of confrontation over this activity, student activist leader Jack Weinberg was arrested and placed in the back seat of a police car. This police action drew a crowd of students, who surrounded the car, preventing it from moving, sat down and refused to leave . . . for over thirty hours. During the standoff, students used the roof of the police car as a stage, complete with microphone and loudspeakers, from which to make political speeches (afterward they took up a collection to pay for any incidental damage to the car: $455.01). Behind the scenes student leaders negotiated campus policies related to political activity in general, and the disposition of Jack Weinberg in particular, with the faculty and the administration, the latter led by university president Clark Kerr.

Thus was born the Berkeley Free Speech Movement, or FSM, framed in the noble terms of the First Amendment to the Constitution of the United States of America.

The students continued to push the envelope, holding frequent rallies on the campus, complete with microphones and loudspeakers, and the administration struggled to maintain control. Things came to a head again in late November when the administration announced disciplinary action against the movement leaders. On December 2 the students responded by staging a mass sit-in, over 1,000 occupying one

---

[3] Rorabaugh p. 19

of the campus's most prominent buildings, Sproul Hall, for over twenty-four hours. More than 700 student demonstrators were arrested; it was the largest mass arrest to date in California history.

On December 4, the student leaders called a strike. Approximately half of the students at the university skipped classes. On the 7th, President Kerr convened a public convocation at the outdoor Greek Theatre[4], where he announced revised university policies, mostly amounting to compromise with (if not capitulation to) the movement's demands. That might have been the end of it, but immediately as the meeting was being adjourned, FSM leader Mario Savio mounted the stage and attempted to avail himself of the microphone. He was tackled and dragged away by cops, creating a spectacle that re-inflamed all of the passions that had almost died out.

Early in 1965 some students decided to push the envelope further in what became known as a new FSM, the *Filthy* Speech Movement, agitating for their right to mouth and display in public words not normally permitted on television during prime time (Crossword puzzle hint: four letters signifying reproductive copulation, beginning with the letter "F").

From May to August 1965, the leaders of the Sproul Hall sit-in were put on trial, convicted and given sentences ranging from fines of $50 to 120 days in jail. Those sentenced to be locked up were offered two years' probation in lieu of incarceration, but some refused the offer because they had plans to participate in more protests, which, per the terms of probation, would land them directly in jail anyway.

Vietnam

What other protests did they have in mind? Well, the Vietnam War, of course. It was in the spring of 1965 that President Lyndon Johnson announced escalation of the American presence in Southeast Asia, with a commensurate increase in draft calls for young men, many of whom were enrolled as college students (and many more who enrolled

---

[4]   The Greek Theatre is one of Berkeley's treasures, designed by legendary architect Julia Morgan.

in college and graduate school for the purpose of obtaining deferments, an option recently provided by an act of Congress). Teach-ins led to public debates, then to demonstrations, defiant draft-card burnings and eventually to riots.

The Vietnam Day Committee held its first major rally in Berkeley in May 1965. In the fall of that year, protesters attempted to stop troop trains passing through Berkeley. On October 15 the students, led by (among others) Frank Bardacke, attempted to lead a march from the Berkeley campus to the military induction center in neighboring Oakland. The City of Berkeley had granted a parade permit but Oakland had not, and the ten thousand-plus marchers were turned away at the border of the city, where they were met by four hundred Oakland policemen. Rather than risk violence, Bardacke led the marchers in retreat. The next day they tried again, with fewer but more committed demonstrators. Hell almost broke loose when a group of Hell's Angels motorcycle gangsters attacked some of the demonstrators and their banners. The march stalled again. Finally, on November 20, a march larger than the prior two was completed to Oakland without significant incidents.

By 1967, the political center of gravity in Berkeley had shifted definitively leftward. While a majority of Berkeleyans had initially been slow to oppose the Vietnam War, opposition only increased with time, even including some conservatives. *The Berkeley Barb*, a radical newspaper started by student movement leader Max Sherr, overtook in circulation the traditional conservative newspaper *The Berkeley Daily Gazette* (for which I would work a deliverer ('paper boy') in the early 70s). The counterculture of the hippies (long, unkempt hair, drop-out attitude, colorful handmade garments and trinket jewelry, marijuana-smoking, folk-rock singing), originated in the Haight-Ashbury district of San Francisco and was an outgrowth of the prior "Beat," or "Beatnik," counter-culture generation. It had arrived in Berkeley in force during a student strike of the fall of 1966. Prior to this time the students protesting had appeared mostly clean-cut and all-American, with the men in short hair, jackets and ties, and the women well-groomed and prudent, if not prudish. That appearance "evolved" as the decade progressed.

The week of October 16, 1967, was designated "Stop the Draft" week. Multiple events and demonstrations were held; hundreds of young men publicly burned their draft cards. That Tuesday 2,000 to 4,000 protesters converged on the induction center in Oakland, this time resulting in open street-fighting with riot police, and a few days later again, on an even greater scale. Although there were hundreds of police, they were outnumbered by the protesters, who dominated downtown Oakland for most of the day and successfully shut down the induction center.

The leaders of the marches that had led to the riots were put on trial in 1969 in what became known as the Trial of the Oakland Seven.

January 1968 became the turning point for American public opinion on the Vietnam War. The North Vietnamese communists staged simultaneous attacks on U.S. troops and their allies in several cities and locations throughout Vietnam during the holiday known as Tet. The Tet Offensive was a complete military defeat and failure for the North Vietnamese, but political perceptions trumped "mere" military outcomes. CBS News anchor Walter Cronkite declared Tet a defeat for the U.S., and that became the political reality. American support for the war never recovered.

People's Park

And then, in 1969, came People's Park. A group of hippies, drop-outs, students, runaways and Vietnam War protesters commandeered, landscaped and gardened a vacant lot near—and owned by—the university, close to Telegraph Avenue, the mecca of coffee houses, record and book stores just south of the university campus. When the university attempted to reclaim their property, erecting fencing to keep the squatters out, a confrontation ensued which rapidly escalated into violence; tear gas, Billy clubs, and eventually shotguns were deployed. University buildings were again occupied. James Rector, a student, was shot and killed by police; another was blinded. California Governor Ronald Reagan called out the National Guard, which occupied the city like an invading army for two and a half weeks. Reagan made a personal appearance on the campus, at which he dressed down professors whom he accused of irresponsibly encouraging lawlessness among the students. He ordered the Guard helicopters to drop tear gas on the campus to disperse the crowd at the next on-campus demonstration.

The 70s

Guilty as Hell, free as a bird! America is a great country!
Bill Ayers

In the 1970s mass movements like the Vietnam War protests died down as the draft came to an end under President Nixon, but radical action and violence by small, committed groups intensified. The Weather Underground, led by William "Billy" Ayers and Bernardine Dohrn, plotted bombings of army bases, the Capitol building and the Pentagon, among others planned and executed, and spent several years as fugitives until emerging to be cleared on legal technicalities the charges against them (to "beat the rap").

In 1974 in Berkeley, a multiracial militant group calling itself the Symbionese Liberation Army (SLA) kidnapped 19-year-old Patty Hearst, a UC Berkeley student and granddaughter of the billionaire newspaper magnate William Randolph Hearst. The ransom they demanded was unusual: a food welfare program for the local poor. The militants confined Patty to a closet and raped and tormented her to the point of psychological exhaustion, wherein she agreed to "join" her captors, adopt the nom de guerre "Tanya X" and participate in their missions, including a bank robbery in which her image was captured on closed-circuit security cameras, machine gun in hand (loaded? — unknown). Half the gang died in a fiery shootout months later with police in Oakland, and "Tanya" spent a year and a half as a fugitive before being arrested in September 1975. She was convicted for her participation in the bank robbery, but later President Jimmy Carter commuted her sentence and Bill Clinton gave her a full pardon.

Other than that, it was quiet in Berkeley.

Many of the student movement leaders of the 60s transitioned from organizing street protests to establishment careers in politics, pushing relentlessly for left-wing causes like unionization, more social spending, higher taxes and universal healthcare. Jerry Brown—yes, the same as the one serving 2011-2019—eventually succeeded Ronald Reagan as Governor for two terms, 1975-1983, helped to fund the Black Panthers' social programs and granted collective bargaining rights to public employee unions[5].

Growing Up

I was very young during all of this, of course, having been born just after the election but before the inauguration of President John F. Kennedy. But these events and political currents established the social context in which I grew up.

Berkeley was progressive in many ways, not all of them corrupt. I attended primary and elementary schools that were racially integrated via busing, which had been duly legislated by the city council rather than ordered by the courts. While this did not lead to anything like utopian harmony, it gave us children the experience of engaging with people who were different from ourselves. In fifth grade I had two teachers in one class, in a team-teaching model. A couple of memories that stand out are the white teacher occasionally lecturing us in defense of President Nixon's much-maligned policies and decisions, while the black teacher had us singing Pete Seeger songs like "If I Had a Hammer," "Where Have All the Flowers Gone" and "We Shall Overcome" to his accompaniment on the auto-harp.

At Martin Luther King, Jr., Junior High School (renamed from James A. Garfield Junior High just four months after the civil rights leader's assassination) the faculty and administration, a plurality of whom were black, put a great deal of emphasis on learning the history of the civil rights movement of the 1950s and 60s, complete with the news footage of Sheriff Bull Connor's fire hoses mowing down non-violent demonstrators. These lessons were taught not just in classes but in large all-grade assemblies in the school auditorium, accentuating their importance. Our social consciousness was sincerely raised, but racial harmony did not necessarily always flow from this. In 8th grade, our sex education teacher opening answered the students' personal,

---

[5]   Edmund G. "Jerry" Brown, Jr., was the son of Edmund G. "Pat" Brown, who was also Governor of California, from 1959-1967, just prior to Ronald Reagan's term.

intimate questions about her own sex life and sexuality (just in case you thought that was something new).

At Berkeley High School, Leftism was the water we swam in, almost as unaware as fish are about the medium of their existence. My fellow students at BHS were either apolitical or Left, and I suspect that if you pressed one of the apolitically-appearing ones, you would probably get answers satisfactorily Leftist. I only recall knowing one student who actively (and cogently) dissented and engaged with Leftist students on substantive arguments from a conservative perspective, and even then only within a limited range of issues.

Berkeley High at that time was a large school of about 4,000 students, divided into two campuses: West Campus for ninth grade only, and the main campus adjacent to downtown for grades ten through twelve. My first six weeks of tenth grade in 1975 were delayed due to a teacher strike, courtesy of Governor Jerry Brown's expanding privileges for teachers' unions. When regular classes eventually resumed, one of the first lectures given to us by our history/social studies teacher was about the strike, with a decidedly biased, pro-union slant.

And so it went. While I was not particularly politically active, I internalized much of what I was immersed in. Not wanting to be judged a bad person, I adopted the values of the women's liberation movement, curbing any tendency I might have about being "sexist" or "chauvinist," with the exception of an unambiguously heterosexual orientation (well, I had to come out of the closet about that sooner or later, I suppose). In my social circle, chivalry, such as holding a door open for a girl, or carrying her books for her, was considered 'sexist' and discouraged (this indoctrination did not enhance my success with *real* women later in life!). It wasn't all that difficult for me to suppress aggressive macho tendencies. For example, I loved football, but being young for my grade and of slight build even for my age, the only conceivable position I might have played on the high school team would have been . . . the ball. So, becoming a "liberated man," i.e., an admissible wimp, wasn't too difficult for me.

Not that all life in Berkeley was political. I wasn't a red diaper baby like David Horowitz. We didn't attend socialist summer camps and learn to quote from the Little Red Book of Mao Zedong. Our parents could be classified, if we all must be, as members of the "hill liberal" establishment.

My childhood friends and I played pickup baseball, football and Kick-The-Can in front yards, backyards and in the narrow residential streets. When we were thirsty, we drank from the nearest neighbor's garden hose. With minimal adult supervision or schedule structure, after school or on weekends or any day of the week during the summer we rode our bikes with our dogs for miles and for hours through the residential streets and minor shopping areas, just returning home in time for dinner. I walked to school, frequently alone, half a mile uphill through several streets, since *kindergarten*. It was common for boys to deliver newspapers alone along two-mile routes in the pre-dawn darkness at age 11. If you were middle class or upper middle class, living in the foothills or the hills, it was in many ways an idyllic place to grow up, as innocent as Mayberry.

How innocent was it? To give a sense, when I was twelve or so, I organized a few of my nine- and ten-year-old friends into what I called an underground "army", declared myself to be its highest-ranking officer ("Sergeant") and led missions of domestic terrorism. We climbed trees at night at distances of 100 to 200 feet apart to relay signals to each other with cigarette lighters, and snuck out of our homes before dawn to place dog biscuits in all of our neighbor's morning newspapers. While I was never charged with a felony, much less convicted, somehow the parents on the block knew who had done it anyway.

My parents were not radical leftists, and by today's standards might even seem conservative. Their aspirations for themselves and their children were those of most well-educated middle-class (bourgeois) people: diligent study and hard work leading to gainful employment in a respectable profession. My father, Earl K. Hyde, was a PhD research scientist at the Lawrence Berkeley Laboratory (until 1971 the Lawrence *Radiation* Laboratory, before the "R" word became politically incorrect). The lab was the site of unclassified (read: not nuclear weapons) research. He rubbed elbows with Nobel laureates and later, as an administrator, senators and other high-ranking government officials. In 1964 he published, together with his colleagues Drs.

15

Isadore Perlman and Glenn T. Seaborg, a three-volume physics textbook titled "The Nuclear Properties of the Heavy Elements," which endured in active use by physics professors for decades. Seaborg was a Nobel laureate in chemistry and one of an elite club of scientists who have a chemical element named after him (106, Seaborgium). Seaborg had also been Chancellor of the University of California from 1959-1961 before leaving to head up the Atomic Energy Commission. He must have been grateful to have avoided the 'fun' his successor as Chancellor, Edward Strong, was subjected to.

Atypically, there was no television in our home until 1973, when I was twelve (I suspect that my parents finally gave in to the inevitable after years of fielding complaints from neighbors about little Howard constantly showing up asking to watch Superman). Eventually my parents bought a color set and became avid viewers of PBS (and BBC) programming like "Masterpiece Theatre," "Upstairs, Downstairs," ballet and opera (I watched *Gilligan's Island, Star Trek, The Six Million Dollar Man, James at 15[6]* and, also from the BBC, *Monty Python's Flying Circus*).

In other words, politically and culturally my parents were staunch establishment liberal Democrats, at a time when that meant John F. Kennedy, Adlai Stevenson, John Kenneth Galbraith, Franklin Roosevelt and Harry Truman. They believed in the primacy of government as the agent of fairness and of initiating and coordinating the highest priority projects of society, such as education, welfare and scientific research and in meeting the cost of such programs with the tax regime adequate to its flourishing. They were disdainful of businessmen, especially corporate executives, although they conscientiously invested in a conservative and diversified portfolio of stocks listed on the New York and Pacific stock exchanges, anchored in "blue chips" like IBM, AT&T, 3M, Pacific Gas & Electric (PG&E), GM and Ford. In addition to the aforementioned PBS programming, they were regular viewers of the weekly finance television program "Wall Street Week," hosted by Louis Rukeyser, about which more

---

[6]   *James at 15* survived for two seasons, the second one being titled *James at 16*. While never a huge hit and completely forgotten today, it was the series which depicted the angst of a teenage boy *like me at the time* more compellingly than any other show. The actor, Lance Kerwin, even looked a lot like me, in face and build.

   https://en.wikipedia.org/wiki/James_at_15. Google it and select the "Image" tab.

anon[7]. As nature lovers and amateur photographers, they were avid campers and wilderness backpackers. They subscribed to *The New Yorker* and *National Geographic* magazines. They were members of nature and environmental groups like the Audubon Society and the Sierra Club and had many close friends who were officers on the boards of directors of such groups. We never vacationed at resorts, least of all Disneyland, but mostly in campgrounds and on mountain and desert trails.

They were definitely not Hard-Left. My father expressed little sympathy for able-bodied young people smoking marijuana and panhandling on Telegraph Avenue and participating in disturbances, and my mother, speaking of the People's Park riot, said that "there were excesses on both sides." Their idea of the public (i.e., government-funded) education that they so staunchly supported was supposed to be one of high academic standards and focus on correct grammar, spelling, mathematics, classical literature, classical art and music and rigorous science—none of which our union-dominated public school systems are renowned for today. Social conservatives will appreciate that while my mother was not a Christian in the sense that evangelicals would understand the word (Unitarian from New Hampshire), she was shocked by the declining moral standards of dress among high school girls and college women, and even found Britany Spears' lyric scandalous (*"I'm not that innocent!"*). She didn't like Woody Allen; she considered him perverted. She didn't live long enough to see Miley Cyrus twerking at the MTV awards show, but her distress at the debasement of the culture put her nearly in the company of the religious Right.

One area in particular that my father differed with the accelerating leftward drift was in nuclear power. He staunchly supported the construction of nuclear power plants to displace coal, pointing out the manifest number of deaths in the coal industry versus the hypothetical (and in his estimation, low-risk) potential damage of nuclear. He had no patience for the popular superstition that nuclear power plants were like nuclear bombs, ready to detonate and vaporize a city at the first

---

7   "About which more anon" is a pompous and pretentious phrase meaning, "I'll tell you more about that later." But if it was good enough for Graham Chapman of Monty Python, then it's good enough for me. See "A Liar's Autobiography, Volume VI." I warned you I was a product of the 70s.

unanticipated vibration. And he rejected any and all comparisons to the Soviet Union and its dismal nuclear safety record, including, years later, Chernobyl[8], which he saw as the product of a second-rate team operating under Stalinist—which is to say, non-existent—regard for human life.

Nevertheless, they were definitely Democrats, favored high taxes, social programs and government patronage of the arts and sciences. They disdained Reagan and dismissed him as a B-movie actor, and enthusiastically supported every Democrat presidential campaign ticket: Humphrey-Muskie (1968; lost to Nixon), McGovern-Shriver (1972; lost to Nixon, who resigned before finishing his second term, making V.P. Gerald Ford President), Carter-Mondale (1976 and 1980; won the former, lost the latter to Reagan), Mondale-Ferraro (1984; lost), Dukakis-Benson (1988; lost to George H. W. Bush), etc. My dad's enthusiasm for Jerry Brown and Bill Clinton was lukewarm, but voting Republican would probably have been unthinkable.

So, since I'm writing this many years later from the perspective of an older, conservative libertarian constitutional Republican, how and why did my values change?

The short answer is that my values changed very little, apart from the natural evolution one experiences maturing from a boy to a young man to a family man. I still believe that poverty is in many ways an injustice requiring a remedy in society, that people should be judged not by the color of their skin but by the content of their character, that speech ought to be free, that the natural environment is valuable for its own sake, etc. But I have come to believe that businessmen, white men, rich men and Republicans are no more or less greedy or evil than anyone else categorically. And I believe that in order to secure the

---

[8]   From Wikipedia: "The Chernobyl disaster…was a catastrophic nuclear accident that occurred on 26 April 1986 at the Chernobyl Nuclear Power Plant in the town of Pripyat, in Ukraine (then officially the Ukrainian SSR), which was under the direct jurisdiction of the central authorities of the Soviet Union. An explosion and fire released large quantities of radioactive particles into the atmosphere, which spread over much of the western USSR and Europe…The battle to contain the contamination and avert a greater catastrophe ultimately involved over 500,000 workers and cost an estimated 18 billion rubles. During the accident itself, 31 people died, and long-term effects such as cancers are still being investigated."
      https://en.wikipedia.org/wiki/Chernobyl_disaster

blessings of liberty, good health, prosperity, opportunity and justice to the greatest number of people without respect to birth, ethnicity, sex, nationality, religion or any other qualifier, there has never been a more efficient, effective, just or virtuous system invented than Capitalism, properly understood. It is every alternative to Capitalism that I judge to be evil, by their fruits.

The Void

A funny thing happened on the way to my radical indoctrination in the social environment of Berkeley in the 1970s, and that is, the radicals forgot to explain themselves. They chanted slogans and repeated bromides, made accusations against "the system" and "the Establishment", proclaimed their righteous indignation over poverty, inequality, racism, war and injustice. But for the most part, being Marxists who had never bothered to take the time to actually read Marx (and certainly not any other economist before or since), they left a wide gaping intellectual and philosophical hole open for anyone with a sincere and honest desire to study, learn and understand, to step into. For all of the indoctrination, peer pressure and ideological propaganda that I was subjected to as a youth in Berkeley, there was very little substantive exposition of fundamental principles. There was a great deal of conceit, of presumption of superiority over our adversaries to our right, both morally and intellectually. But that conceit, in my experience at least, seems to have been so assumed as to require no demonstration, no proof; it was taken as axiomatic, tautological, obvious, unquestionable and unquestioned. We were intellectually and morally superior to the Right because the Right was inferior to us.

Even someone sympathetic to the causes fostered by the Left might be left in the end wondering, as I was, *So What?* That is, after free speech is achieved, after the society is racially integrated, discrimination against women and gays abolished, the war stopped, the rich taxed and the elections won, what are the guiding principles for how society should be organized? How does the production and distribution of goods, services, culture, science, technology, nature, health care, natural resources, environmental protection and justice work? In particular, what systemic conditions are the most favorable to enabling people to escape from poverty and achieve the American Dream, or at least some condition superior to wretched? In other words, what I was groping in the dark for at that time was, what are the lessons of economics? I had vague notions about how wasteful our society was, consuming multiples of the resources consumed by other countries and cultures, as the argument was framed. But apart from the New Deal and Great Society social programs, the latter of which were just getting under way at the time, there was no clear articulation beyond virtuous emotions and good intentions of why one system would work better than any other. The Leftist narrative, my schooling (in particular, the complete absence of any academic study of economics) and much else in my life was silent, leaving a vacuum.

Into that vacuum would eventually step Milton Friedman, Julian Simon, Adam Smith, John Locke, Charles Murray, Louis Rukeyser, Friedrich Hayek, George Gilder, Ludwig Von Mises, Ayn Rand, George Reisman, Steve Forbes, Thomas Sowell, David Horowitz and several members of the *Wall Street Journal* editorial board, among others. (Some Leftist readers might retort that if only I had seriously read Karl Marx, or at least John Maynard Keynes, before all of those right-wing reactionary scum, I might have stayed on the "true" path. But I had plenty of opportunity to read, evaluate and discard those as well.) The works and philosophies of these men and women would over time transform my world view because they explained better than the Left had the actual, real-world (as opposed to idealized) experiences of my own life, as well as those of others that I observed, and because they satisfied the requirements of academic rigor and intellectual honesty which had been ingrained in me as among the highest virtues even while I was still a liberal Leftist.

It only took about twelve years.

A Seed and a Departure

So how did my transformation come about? Well, I ran away to France on account of this Swiss girl.

Milton Friedman, "Free to Choose"

Actually, I'm getting ahead of myself. The earliest seed I remember being planted which would cause me to reconsider my inherited 'wisdom' was watching the 1980 PBS television series "Free to Choose,", authored and hosted by the dean of the Chicago School of Economics, Milton Friedman. PBS is not known for promoting conservative or right-wing programming, but Friedman's show got through on the strength of his Nobel Prize and congenial personality.

Dr. Friedman's series consisted of ten half-hour films of him lecturing to the camera from locations all over the world which served to illustrate his thesis, followed each by a half-hour discussion and debate session with leading intellectuals and statesmen of the day of the Left and the Right in the University of Chicago library.

In his films and companion book of the same title, Friedman makes a clear, bold and unapologetic case for free-market Capitalism. From the first episode he points out that the extraordinary development of the United States as an economic powerhouse and beacon of freedom to the world's poor (including his own immigrant parents), from the days of its founding through the era of massive immigration in the early twentieth century, was achieved under a regime of government policies of laissez-faire, of low taxes and nearly non-existent regulation of trade, labor, professional licensing or anything else. For example, he makes an earnest case that the sweatshop garment factories of New York, which he does not shrink from showing on film, far from being dens of exploitation, are fields of opportunity for those who work in them, however many regulations and (non-existent) union rules they may violate. He says, "Their life may seem pretty tough compared to our own. But that's only because our parents or grandparents went through that stage for us. We've been able to start at a higher point."

Friedman interviews several adult American children and grandchildren of immigrants in their homes, exhibiting the level of prosperity that these Americans had achieved which was unimaginable to their impoverished ancestors. He asserts that this prosperity is the result of free-market Capitalism and opportunity.

Friedman takes his audience to Hong Kong, "a place where there is an almost laboratory experiment in what happens when government is limited to its proper function and leaves people free to pursue their own objectives. . . If you want to see how the free market really works, this is the place to come," he said. He shows that the conditions of the working class people there, while poor by Western middle class standards, were the best and most attractive in all of Asia, and resulted in a phenomenon unknown in most of the world: upward mobility. Real (inflation-adjusted) wages increased 400 percent in the 30-plus years since the end of World War II. People from the People's Republic of (communist) China risked their lives for the opportunity to be "exploited" under the free-market system of Hong Kong, which at that time was still a British colonial protectorate (hugely politically incorrect). Hong Kong is tiny next to the PRC and has no natural resources beyond its harbor, but it achieved the status of a world economic powerhouse via the lightest taxation, tariff and regulation regime in the world. Industries in Hong Kong advanced up the ladder from assembling cheap plastic toys to manufacturing sophisticated electronic microchips and beyond.

Just to be sure there is no doubt, he continues narrating a scene of Hong Kong's skyline: "This miracle hasn't been achieved by government action, by someone sitting in one of those tall buildings telling people what to do; it's been achieved by *allowing the market to work*" (my emphasis).

From Hong Kong he segues to Scotland for an exposition on Adam Smith and "The Wealth of Nations"[9], published in the same year as the American Declaration of Independence, 1776. He uses the University of Glasgow, where Smith taught moral philosophy in the eighteenth century, as the backdrop for what is perhaps his most memorable demonstration, at once dramatic and utterly mundane. He holds up a common yellow pencil and explains how it required thousands of people from all around the world cooperating to manufacture it and put it into his/our hands. "There's not a single person in the world who could make this pencil," he declares[10]. To paraphrase: the lead (graphite) probably comes from South American mines. The wood may be from a tree in Washington State. To cut down the tree required steel. To make steel required iron ore. The rubber for the eraser is probably from Malaysia, but rubber is not native to Malaysia; it was imported there from South America. The brass ferule that holds the eraser in place, the paint, and all of its chemical components, the glue . . . well, hopefully you get the point. And all of this cooperation, cultivation, harvesting, processing, manufacturing, transportation and marketing delivers this pencil into your hands for a trifling price without any government bureau dictating orders or coordinating economic activity. The information transmitted by the price system accomplishes all of that, even though it required the cooperation of thousands of people who don't all speak the same language, who practice different religions and who might even hate each other personally if they ever met. Free markets not only promote prosperity and efficiency; they promote harmony and peace more effectively than government-directed "peace missions."

He goes on:

> Those of us who have been so fortunate as to have been born in a free society tend to take freedom for granted, to regard it as the natural state of mankind. It is not. . . The [British colonial] government of Hong Kong . . . has ensured

---

[9] The complete title is "An Inquiry into the Nature and Causes of The Wealth of Nations." While this is Smith's most famous work, his 1759 book, "The Theory of Moral Sentiments," is also highly worthwhile. From Chapter 1: Of Sympathy: "How selfish soever man may be supposed, there are evidently some principles in his nature, which interest him in the fortune of others, and render their happiness necessary to him, though he derives nothing from it except the pleasure of seeing it."

[10] In the companion book, Friedman gives credit to Leonard E. Read, who wrote a children's picture-book story titled, "I, Pencil: My Family Tree as Told to Leonard E. Read."

that laws are enforced and contracts honored. It has provided the conditions in which a free market can work . . . It has NOT tried to direct the economic activities of the colony . . . Prices are the key. The prices people are willing to pay for products determine what's produced. The prices that have to be paid for raw materials, for the wages of labor and so on, determine the cheapest way to produce these things. And in addition, these selfsame prices—the wages of labor, the interest on capital and so on—determines how much each person has [possesses] to spend on the market. It's tempting to try to separate this final function of prices from the other two, to think that somehow or another you can use prices to transmit the information about what should be produced and how it should be produced without using those prices to determine how much each person gets. Indeed, government activity over the past few decades has been devoted to little else. But that's a very serious mistake. If what people get is not going to be determined on what they produce, on how they produce it, on how successfully they work, what incentive is there for them to act in accordance with the information that's transmitted? There's only one alternative: force—some people telling other people what to do... The fundamental principle of the free society is voluntary cooperation.

I hadn't heard economics explained anything like that way before.

Friedman also points out that the great scientific and philanthropic achievements of Western civilization were not achieved by governments but by people deeply interested in a particular subject or mission, free to pursue that interest or mission without forcible interference. Years before I would read about the failures of the welfare state in Charles Murray's "Losing Ground," Friedman challenged the premises on which that state was founded.

One of the people who frequently appeared in the library discussion scenes was a (relatively) young, black professor, a protégé of Friedman, in a nice suit and tie and with a modest 70s afro "natural" hairstyle. I took almost no notice of him at the time, but a dozen years later I would begin to read his work, and he would eventually become my most-read and most-recommended author. His book with the understated title "Basic Economics" tops the list on the bibliography page of my website www.CitizenEcon.com. His name was (and still is!) Thomas Sowell.

It is interesting to contemplate that for many years Friedman insisted upon calling himself a "liberal," which he meant in the classical sense that the word was known in the nineteenth century, before progressives and Leftists co-opted it and turned it essentially into its opposite. A liberal, in Friedman's view, was a person who favored individual liberty, limited government, free markets and free trade—the heirs of Adam Smith and the classical economists, excluding Marx. Some of his writing can be either quaint or confusing to the post-1990s reader by the way he uses the word[11].

Friedman could also profess to be non-partisan, in the sense of valuing scientific truth over petty political bickering. While this is a noble sentiment, the Democratic Party has so thoroughly rejected his principles and philosophy since that time that there can be no more pretense of compatibility.

One of the remarkable things about the series to me was that it was the first time I had been exposed to any serious intellectual exposition of economics at all. I was nineteen years old and a freshman in college, having taken two years off after high school to work in gas stations and McDonald's restaurants while pursuing my dreams of glory playing trumpet in the top-40/funk/soul band 'Travelers 'N Time', or 'TNT', and for all the political upheavals of my home town and nation during my youth, nobody had ever taught me any actual principles of economics, whether free-market, Keynesian or Marxist. The only thing I can remember coming close from Berkeley High School was a single lecture by my social studies teacher that went something like this: "Well, so imagine there's this factory that makes, say, dustpans. And eventually it makes so many dustpans that people don't buy as many of them as they used to, because they have enough already [echoes of Marx's "anarchy of production"—wonder where she learned it]. Then

---

11   A similar and perhaps more severe confusion and non-equivalence is encountered in the Spanish language, where the Castilian palabra "liberal" (accent on the final syllable) still retains much of its nineteenth century meaning, while "conservador" (ditto accent) implies a social philosophy dominated by the Catholic church hierarchy or the royal court of Spain.

the factory has to lay off workers because it doesn't have enough money from dustpan sales to pay them. And then the workers, as consumers, because they have no money to buy dustpans, stop buying them themselves even more, so the factory has to lay off even more workers, and so on, in a vicious downward spiral."

That's it! The sum total of my economic education through high school! Any wonder why some people call it the "dismal science"? Hardly a foundation for an adult citizen-voter taking his civic responsibility for weighing the relative merits of proposed tax, regulatory, trade, environmental and immigration policies.

And the thing is, I wanted to know. I *needed* to know. Apart from the self-interest of hoping to survive in a complex world, for which economics might provide some insight, I was genuinely concerned with the plight of people less fortunate than myself and I wanted to be part of the solution. I was an earnest and sincere liberal, ready to dedicate myself to liberal virtues and causes. Yet no one had taught me the most basic concepts of the discipline that was key to it all.

Nor would they, even over the course of ten more years, at five different institutions of higher learning. It would not be until I enrolled in a part-time MBA program at the age of thirty-one that I finally was required to take a course in economics, and even then, the approach to the discipline was of limited (and in some aspects, negative) value.

Leaving Berkeley

After two years past high school in which I dedicated myself nearly full-time to my band, I belatedly started college as a Music major at California State University, Hayward (now Cal State East Bay), close enough to Berkeley to commute to class. It was a good experience and I soon discovered, contrary to my poor performance in high school, that I could write well and get A's in English if I studied hard and applied myself. That was a boost to my confidence that has had an enduring impact on the rest of my life.

After one year, however, I felt a new pang of yearning for adventure. I received an air-mail letter (keep in mind that this is *way* before texting, Facebook and Skype—before anyone besides a few confirmed geeks owned a personal computer—and communicating across a continent and an ocean was an expensive proposition) from a girl in Switzerland whom I had met at my own home in Berkeley when her father, a colleague of my father's, had brought his family with him on a trip to the United States. What follows is a bit incongruous, but bear with me: Kathy and I became pen pals, and this correspondence inspired me to start thinking about a much larger world than the one I knew intimately. Before long I had the brilliant idea of dusting off the C-minuses that I had earned in French class in High School, study in earnest and travel to France for an extended period. In my second year at Hayward, I dedicated at least as much attention to French as to Music, and applied for the Cal State international program in France, which was to be a complete academic Junior year in Aix-en-Provence, a quaint old university town in the south, near Marseilles. In the fall of 1982, I packed my bags and with about fifty other students from all over California, made the journey across the country and the Atlantic Ocean.

What I had no way of knowing at the time was that I was leaving for good; while I would visit once or twice per year, apart from a couple of months in the summer of 1987, I would never live permanently in Berkeley, or the Bay Area, again[12].

---

12   During 1997-98, I commuted weekly from Granada Hills (Los Angeles), 350 miles to Redwood Shores (Silicon Valley) to work for Oracle Corporation. That's as close to Berkeley (20 miles away) as I got; moving to the Bay Area permanently didn't work out, in part due to the astronomical cost of housing there, and my next assignment required flying weekly between L.A. and Detroit (which I came to call 'America's rotting corpse of a city'). The stress of *that* assignment and travel, combined with other factors, known and unknown, cost me a third of the field of vision in my left eye, permanently, to ischemic optic neuropathy. But I digress.

La Belle France

Le Bohemien

From the late fall of 1982 to the summer of 1986, I lived the life of a bohemian artist musician and marginally legal immigrant in Paris, France. After 3 months in the Cal State international program in Aix-en-Provence, feeling overwhelmed by the academic load which competed adversely with my ambitions of pursuing my career in music, I dropped out and moved—alone—to Paris, where I personally knew a grand total of three people, all of whom I had met during the previous summer in California. My friend Jean-Pierre, also a trumpet player who had travelled to the U.S. for a master class with my teacher Claude Gordon, introduced me to a rehearsal jazz band, and from there I slowly grew my network of colleagues and referrals.

I played trumpet in jazz and pop bands, with the occasional classical or opera gig (Mozart's *Marriage of Figaro* in particular) thrown in. My heroes, whom I did my best to emulate at the time, were the trumpet players of and/or derived from the bebop era: Dizzy Gillespie, Woody Shaw, Freddie Hubbard, Miles Davis, Maynard Ferguson and Clifford Brown. With the exception of Brown, who had died at age 25 in 1956, I was able eventually to see all of the above live in concerts. The French classical virtuoso trumpeter Maurice André was also an idol whom I had the privilege of meeting, in his dressing room, on the occasion of one of his performances. My contemporaries on the world stage were the (then) young prodigies Wynton Marsalis and Terrence Blanchard, members and later alumni of the incomparable unofficial graduate school of jazz known as *Art Blakey and the Jazz Messengers*, led by the eponymous drummer. Blanchard would go on to write the musical scores for Spike Lee's movies, which include the best cinematic depiction of an actor (Denzel Washington) faking playing trumpet ever made, *Mo' Better Blues*. The reason they are world-famous and you've never heard of me is simple: compared to them, I suck. Although we were roughly the same age, I was just getting started studying the discipline in my late teens and early twenties, whereas they had been born into the culture (New Orleans) and had put in their proverbial

10,000 hours of practice before the age of eighteen, or earlier. Inexplicably, my white privilege failed to pave for me a royal road to success in that field.

In order to practice my loud instrument several hours a day in a crowded city (and spare my apartment neighbors), I scouted out several outdoor locations near or under the *Périphérique*, the freeway that surrounds the city. The white noise of the traffic drowned out my sound without disturbing my practice. I was only detained by police once (twice in Topeka, Kansas within a 12-hour period on a trip in 1985, but that's a different story…).

Sometimes it could be cold playing trumpet outdoors during the winter, and gloves and a fake-fur Russian-style hat were necessary among other layers. As a matter of fact, the winters of 1983 and '84 were particularly chilly. One time I was wandering near the canals at the north end of the city, and stopping half way across a bridge, I picked up a stone about the size of a horse's head and dropped it onto the canal. It bounced. Minus 15.

Jewish weddings and bar mitzvahs were my most lucrative and reliable sources of cash income. There were disastrous gigs that I'd rather not talk about, and peak experiences like the recording studio date where I nailed every note, sight unseen, of a sophisticated lead line on the first take, with engineers and producers watching the clock (no pressure!). I think the compliment I had received from my trombone player friend Jean-Claude, "Je ne suis pas super-lecteur comme toi" (I am not a super sight-reader *like you*), had given me the confidence to execute. Words are insufficient to describe highs like that; it's the feeling one must get after rescuing a baby from a burning building without a moment's warning (I know, that's happened to you many times).

A high point of my musical career in Paris was recording three albums over three years, and performing concerts all over France, with the twenty-piece jazz orchestra Bekumernis, led by composer Luc le Masne (pronounced "le Mann"). One such concert took place in a 2,000-year-old Roman amphitheater in Nîmes, a concert headlined by Miles Davis.

Politics in France are more fragmented than in the United States, with four or five viable parties contending for hegemony, but at the time it was dominated by the PS—*le Parti Socialiste*—under President François Mitterand (1981-1995). While I could never comprehend the politics and party machinations, my semi-permanent residence gave me an up-close experience of what advanced socialist economics was really like.

Taking in French life as a resident, as opposed to as a tourist, I became acutely aware that the standard of living there was about one-third to one-half less than that of the United States. That is, persons of comparable professions, whether doctors, lawyers or brick-layers, earned wages and salaries permitting them to enjoy a material standard of living substantially less comfortable in France that that of the corresponding cohort in the United States, although collectively they owned centuries-old monuments, culture, art and architecture that were priceless. There were considerable restrictions on French citizens as to what they could do with their own wealth and possessions, such as strict limits on how much cash they could take with them out of the country, even just for a vacation. Taxes and *les charges sociaux* (social welfare/security taxes) took away easily 55% percent of the most modest salary before it was ever seen by the worker. As for students, let's just say that the university restrooms were not provisioned with toilet paper. What I saw actually made me think of what I had heard about life in the Soviet Union, although that was in reality far worse.

I remember once sitting in a Paris Métro subway train car when an elderly French gentleman struck up conversation with me. When he realized that I was American and that I understood French, his face lit up and he began praising and thanking America from the depths of his half-broken soul. *"C'etait grâce à eux! C'etait grâce à eux qu-on a gagné la guerre!"* ("It was thanks to them [the Americans] that we won the war!") The war was already forty years in the past, but time had not diminished his passionate gratitude for what America had done for him and his country, and I was the unwitting (and undeserving) recipient of his praise.

Still, I shunned the conservative or right-wing newspapers for those of the Left, the Hard-Left and the radical extreme Left. I read the weekly *Nouvel Observateur* (center Left), the daily *Libération* (the Hard-

Left legacy paper of the *soixante-huitards*, the students who had nearly burned Paris to the ground in 1968) and the *hebdomadaire* (weekly) rag of the *Fédération Anarchiste*, which as I purchased from activist street vendors outside one of the central train stations. In one adventurous (or idiotic, take your pick) moment, I even paid for a personal ad in *Libération* which read something like "Young American Single White Male Seeks Young Russian Single White Female". The editors thought this so extraordinary that they blew it up in the center of the personal ads page (didn't get any replies though, and, maybe just as well).

My personal friends were mostly on the Left and despised Ronald Reagan in particular; they were convinced he was going to provoke a nuclear war with the Soviet Union, then under Yuri Andropov, with Western Europe as the theatre. One notable exception was a refugee from Iran who had a fatwa on his head, courtesy of the same Mullahs who would in 1989 condemn Salman Rushdie, author of "The Satanic Verses". *He* was an unabashed fan of Ronald Reagan. He knew I was a liberal Leftist, but patiently warned me how the forces of tyranny would use democratic freedoms to undermine both democracy and freedom, and how in the Soviet Union there were mental hospitals whose true purpose was to render people insane through mental and other torture.

Social and political cartoons for adults are much more a way of life in France than they are in the U.S., and my favorite cartoonist was the feminist/post-feminist Claire Bretecher, whose strips appeared (as she quipped, "for as long as God permits") in the *Nouvel Obs*. There were plenty of provocative, vulgar, outrageous, smutty and yet apparently perfectly socially acceptable titles to choose from, but I steered clear of the grittiest ones. Charlie Hebdo did not yet exist.

In my second year in Paris, I lived in an eighth-floor garret *chambre de bonne*—maid's room—that had only cold water and an uninsulated Turkish toilet (basically a hole in the floor with footholds, also cold water only) down the hall which I shared with the occupants of two or three other such rooms. One neighbor was a very black, 6-foot-2-inch student of theatre arts from Gabon, Africa, and another was a much smaller, female architecture student from Romania. Bathing consisted of dumping an ice-cold bucket of water over my head while standing over the drain, lathering up while the bucket refilled, and then one more bucketful to rinse. My friend from Gabon had an electric probe he would lend me to heat the water, but he wasn't always available at convenient times, so showering in Paris's sub-freezing winter was a bracing adventure. When I fell ill, again my kind Gabonese friend ministered to me.

My other friend, the architecture student from Romania, once gave me a very simple lesson in economics and socialism. "Where I come from," she said, "I may have money in my pocket. But the stores are empty; there is nothing to buy."

That *chambre de bonne* was in the seventh *arrondissement*, or quarter, near the *Ecole Militaire* (military college) and walking distance to the *Tour Eiffel* (and the American College—later University—in Paris, where I enrolled for one semester in 1983). Not having *eau chaud* (hot water), a *frigo* (fridge) or a *cuisine* (kitchen) got old, so after a year there, I set out to find something better.

Le Contrôle de Loyers et le Chômage

That's when the full effect of Paris's rent control laws hit me hardest. There was no internet, no Facebook and no Craigslist in those days; if you didn't know somebody who knew somebody (and who would I know?) you had to find an ad in the printed newspaper, sold in kiosks around the city. And it seemed as if you needed to get to the kiosk one hour *before* the paper was printed in order to be the first person calling to answer an ad. The majority of the calls I made answering apartment rental ads were answered *"loué!"* (already rented to someone else). Prospective tenants were beggars.

I showed up for an appointment to see a flat in a remote northern part of the city, a very drab, run-down, grey, sooty neighborhood inhabited primarily by north African immigrants. When I arrived, I found I was approximately the twenty-fourth person standing in line on the creaky, narrow spiral staircase, waiting for the landlord's representative to show up. When she finally did, an hour late, which is to say on time by French standards, after a perfunctory showing of a flat most Americans would consider unfit for human habitation, she asked those who were interested to follow her on foot several blocks to the office where she would receive people's deposits of applications, credit histories, bank accounts, social security numbers, residence permits, military discharge papers and first-born children. A couple of the applicants patiently asked why they couldn't simply give those things to her right there instead of following her several blocks. The atmosphere got to be a bit tense. Her answer was an attempt to feign good manners, while implicitly revealing that doing things her way would reduce the list to a more manageable number. With twenty-four beggars, why not wear them down by whatever means necessary?

That was my lucky day. I lived happily ever after for two years in that studio, or at least as happily as one who could read between the lines as to the chances of finding anything better within six months could be. As I said, the *quartier* was not particularly attractive. There were some seedy, young drug-addict types in the neighborhood, at least one of whom burglarized my flat, but the older Tunisian grocers were friendly, they stocked my favorite Pelforth beer and Beaujolais nouveau (red wine), and I never saw burka-clad women or a public Islamic prayer takeover of any street.

The social safety net is billed as far more secure in France (and Germany, and most other European nations) than in the United States, with strong protections for employees against layoffs or firing, and generous *chômage* (unemployment) benefits. Yet in spite of this (actually, as I would come to understand only later, *because* of this), the unemployment rate was chronically twice as high as in the United States and there were also elevated levels of homelessness, public drunkenness and social despair (highly visible in the Metro subway stations that constitute the primary transportation arteries of the city). Labor markets are rigid and inflexible in Europe. If you've got a good accredited career job in Europe, you've got it made; if you lose it, or if your job function becomes obsolete in spite of union featherbedding rules, you are worse than screwed. In the 30 years since returning to the United States from Europe, my career has seen many ups and downs, and downs, and downs, including attending many support groups for unemployed people, but I have very rarely encountered the kind of desperation I saw in the eyes of middle-aged European professionals whose careers had derailed. They had nowhere to go, in a way few Americans can comprehend.

Touche Pas à Mon Pote

Speaking of Islam in France, immigration from former French-colony Muslim countries, especially Tunisia and Morocco, was already a sore point of contention in French politics in the 1980s. The Israeli-Palestinian conflict spilled into Paris in the form of terrorist bombing attacks once or twice a year. And the transformation of French society due to Muslim immigration was causing alarm to the conservative and traditional French community, especially the *Front National* party of Jean-Marie Le Pen, considered by its adversaries as the French equivalent of the Nazis. The Left and liberal press and parties took a pro-immigrant and, in their definition, anti-racism stance.

At that time there was a popular movement intended to diffuse tension between French and post-colonial immigrants, led by the organization *S.O.S. Racisme*. This organization, known for its slogan *Touche pas à mon Pote* ("Hands off my buddy"), highlighted news stories about immigrants being abused and assaulted by reactionary French thugs, and urging racial tolerance. Its figurehead leader was the mononymous celebrity comedian Coluche, a French version of John Belushi: Italian ancestry, overweight, obnoxious, foul-mouthed but ultimately loveable, personal friend of the *Président de la République*. Ethnic humor at the expense of anyone—French, Belgian, Arab or Jew, black or white—was fair game without losing his politically correct credentials. A few of his tamest samples:

> American President visiting an Indian reservation: "My friends the Sioux!"
>
> Sioux tribe in unison: "Humpha!"
>
> President: "I am very happy to be here among you!"
>
> Sioux tribe: "Humpha! Humpha!"
>
> The president was very pleased with the positive reception he was getting. Later, however, when walking back toward his limousine, an aide cautioned him, "Watch out, Mr. President, you're about to step in the humpha!"

Or:

> A Frenchman was driving in the Belgian countryside when he ran over a chicken in the road. Full of remorse, he presented the corpse at the nearby farmhouse. He said to the farmer, "Is this yours?"

The Belgian farmer replied, "No, we don't make flat chickens."

Or, simply, "Sometimes the joke is funnier when it's about a Jew. Especially if you're . . . not a Jew."

Coluche's signature opening for a joke was "C'est l'histoire d'un mec...", ("It's about a guy..."), as famous and effective in France as Rodney Dangerfield's signature "I don't get no respect!" or Ray J. Johnson, Jr.'s "You doesn't hasta call it [fill in the blank]."

At the time I left France for good, just after Bastille Day 1986, the S.O.S. Racisme / *Touche pas à mon Pote* movement was ascendant in public opinion, but the amiable Coluche who had given the organization its warm-and-fuzzy feel had died in a motorcycle cruising accident just the month before. The organization still exists in 2016, but a lot has transpired in the interim, including 9/11, an increasingly aggressive Islamist and anti-European / Christian / Judaism political movement (which pre-dates 9/11), the Charlie Hebdo editor murders of January 7, 2015 and the Islamic terrorist attack of November 13, 2015 that left 130 dead in Paris. The ideals of *S.O.S. Racisme* are due for more critical scrutiny than in those more naive days.

Coming Home (Almost)

Move In Today!

My Paris apartment-hunting story contrasts sharply with my experience after returning to the U.S., this time Los Angeles, in the fall of 1986. I nearly had a heart attack and drove off the road upon seeing all of the "Apartment for Rent" signs on the wide boulevards. "Now Renting!" "Move in Today!" "First Month Free!" I thought, you've got to be kidding! How can they do that? Shouldn't I pull over right now and run in before the mob of desperate prospective renters shows up? Such a scene was unheard of, or unseen-of, in Paris. I felt like Robin Williams' Russian immigrant in the American grocery store, shopping for coffee, in *Moscow on the Hudson*, overcome by the abundance.

The explanation, of course, is that whatever rent control laws exist in Los Angeles are about a hundred tons lighter that they are in Paris, or for that matter, New York. For as I would understand only years later from economics in general and Thomas Sowell in particular, rent control laws don't control rent any more than public interest law firms necessarily serve the public interest or antiwar movements necessarily prevent war. So-called rent control laws make it illegal for consenting adults to do whatever they want in their bedroom, like let one person sleep in it while the other one (the one who sacrificed his or her hard-earned cash to build or buy the place) collects a check as compensation, unless the terms conform with what the government says they should be. Mutually-beneficial, voluntary exchange is by degrees outlawed.

Rent control doesn't make rent cheap; it gives landlord the incentive to dial down the quality of the housing to match the market price that would prevail at that level of quality, by such means as deferred or neglected maintenance, low-quality materials etc. It otherwise makes rent unprofitable to the landlord, and when something is less profitable, it is less attractive to be supplied, and accordingly, less of it *is* supplied. Ergo, less construction of new housing which would fall under the law; shortages. Ergo, twenty-four people waiting in line two hours, begging to see a crummy unit in a slummy part of town. There were thousands of vacant rental units in Paris at the time I had been begging for the opportunity to rent one, but to offer one for rent under the regime was a money-losing sacrifice. Likewise, Thomas Sowell has documented that there is more than enough vacant housing in New York to accommodate all of the homeless people who are sleeping on grates outdoors in the winter time.

Even so, in the late 1980s I was still very much a liberal Leftist. I donated—my only donations to any cause—to the ACLU. My favorite radio program was 'Baldy and Scout', a call-in show hosted by a couple (literally, a couple) of amateur radical Leftist political satirists, on Far-Left Pacifica Radio KPFK 90.7 FM (daughter station to Pacifica's Berkeley flagship KPFA 94.1), which also carried unabashed pronouncements from the CPUSA, the Communist Party USA. The show had its regular callers, among them a man who identified himself only as "Commander—Zeeeero!", who engaged the hosts with light banter and occasional serious discussion of real issues such as traffic congestion and the need for better public transportation. One day when he called in he was decidedly less jovial than usual and related the source of his distress: another relative newcomer on the airwaves named Rush Limbaugh. That was the first time I had ever heard of Rush and had no idea at the time of the significance.

The Ultimate Resource

There is only so much oil in the ground
Sooner or later there won't be much around
Tell that to your kids while you're driving 'round downtown
That there's only so much oil in the ground

We can't cut loose
Without that juice
Can't cut loose
Without that juice
If we keep on like we're doing
Things for sure will not be cool
It's a fact we just ain't got sufficient fuel
The Tower of Power[13]

Milton Friedman's "Free to Choose" had planted a seed in my subconscious but had not yet borne fruit. My personal experience in France had opened my eyes but not compelled me to take a firm stand for incompletely understood principles. The author and work which finally forced me to submit my beliefs to a thorough and uncompromising review was Julian Simon and his book "The Ultimate Resource."

As a liberal I had been taught from a young age the values and virtues of the environment, ecology and conservation. I already mentioned my parent's involvement with organizations like the Sierra Club and the fact that most of our vacations were outdoors, in campgrounds and on wilderness trails. Above all, I accepted as gospel the received wisdom that natural resources were finite and, at our ever-accelerating "unsustainable" rate of consumption they were due to be exhausted within a generation. Moreover, out-of-control industrial development threatened to choke us all with toxic air, water and noise, especially if the as-yet underdeveloped world followed the capitalist

---

13   Tower of Power is a multiracial techno-funk/soul group with an intensely loyal following in Oakland and the Bay Area. The devotion of its small fan base has enabled it to survive, albeit at times on prison rations, for nearly fifty years (see Fortieth Anniversary concert CD/DVD). Each of its original members were as gods to the corresponding instrumentalists in my band Travelers 'N Time, and we considered it one of the highest honors of our career when we were able to play second warm-up band to them in Sacramento in 1979.

West's lead, multiplying destruction by an order of magnitude. I had personally experienced with heightened consciousness the double-dip recessions of the 1970s when we had to wait in hours-long lines to purchase gasoline, and even then, were restricted to doing so on certain days of the week based on whether our license plate ended with an even or odd digit. My first experience of losing a job came as a result of the spike in oil prices of 1978 that made it uneconomical for my employer to hire full-service gasoline station attendants. The Tower of Power song rang in my head, and its message rang even in the heads of millions who had never heard it, as I contemplated the apocalypse of imminent natural resource exhaustion.

Imagine then my shock—nay, my outrage—when a book with the following subtext on its front cover landed on my required reading list for a course in environmental geography at the University of Southern California (USC) in 1989: "Natural resources . . . pollution . . . world's food supply . . . pressures of population growth . . . Every trend in material human welfare has been improving—and promises to do so, indefinitely (With an Appreciation by Milton Friedman)."

I called my father told him of this shocking development. "How can a professor make such a book required reading for a course?" I asked. His reply, typical of my dad, ever the scientist, was, "Maybe he's trying to make you think."

I accepted the challenge, read the book, and found my thin intellectual defenses (superficial prejudices) faltering. Simon debunked not just a few contemporary fads about running out of oil, but over two hundred years of environmental scares—some of them innocent, some malicious, but all of them erroneous—that Western civilization was due for catastrophic calamities, famines, plagues and death, as an inevitable outcome of population growth and resource over-consumption. These theories went back at least to Thomas Malthus in the early nineteenth century, who forecast famine in the next generation due to inexorable force of population growing faster than the food supply. But Malthus' famine never materialized. Throughout the Western world, in the absence of wars, where the conditions of liberty and free markets prevailed, living standards *rose* consistently even as population grew and life expectancy increased. The scarcity of natural resources, as expressed by market prices, fell, dramatically and

40

consistently. Great Britain, then thought to be already over maximum capacity at seven million people, now supports over fifty million at a much higher standard of living.

But how could this be so, since we all "know" that we're consuming everything faster than nature can possibly replenish it? Simon's answer was to demonstrate a very simple proposition: that in a free-market economy, the average person is able to produce more than he or she consumes, and that it is human ingenuity above all that makes valuable resources out of the Earth's dirt, rocks and gunk.

To illustrate the mechanism, Simon presents the cycle of entrepreneurship. I recap this lesson in my 2013 column, "The Entrepreneurial Cycle: From Scarcity to Abundance," reprinted later in this book. For now, suffice it to say that it is precisely the appearance of shortages or other potential problems which motivate people to try to solve them, and human ingenuity for creative problem-solving, if it is not crushed by government tyranny, has always been up to the challenge. In a trifling example, Simon even illustrates how this mechanism operates at a university facing a shortage of parking spaces for professors. His title expressed his thesis concisely—that in the final analysis, it is human beings, living in liberty under the rule of law and with private property rights, that trump and precede any and every other thing we call "resources."

Simon was especially critical of Paul Ehrlich, who, since the 1960s, had been making dire predictions about natural resource exhaustion and imminent famine. Simon placed a highly-publicized bet with Ehrlich that, consistent with Simon's theory and contrary to Ehrlich's, a basket of commodities of Ehrlich's choosing would be lower in price (and hence objectively more abundant) in 1990 than in 1980, the year of the bet. Ehrlich accepted the wager and lost. Ehrlich partisans contended later that if the period had been extended to thirty years, ending in 2010, Ehrlich would have won. But that, even if true, begs the question what philosophy of governance prevailed during the 80s versus what prevailed since (hint: Ronald Reagan was President from 1981 to 1989).

Yes, there's only so much oil in the earth
It's a fact of life, for what it's worth
Something every little girl and boy should know from birth
That there's only so much oil in the earth

There's no excuse for our abuse
No excuse for our abuse
We just assume that what we use
Will not exceed the oil supply
But soon enough the world will watch the wells run dry.

That was in 1975 (the song, anyway), and the wells still haven't run dry, despite the consumption of forty years, nor are they likely to in four hundred years. We are getting so much oil out of the ground now that workers are being laid off and companies going bankrupt from Texas to Saudi Arabia because the glut-induced low price per barrel (coupled with the high government-imposed tax wedge that puts the brakes on the demand side of the equation) is insufficient to permit them to recoup their costs. This in spite of the Democrats' deliberate efforts to suppress petroleum production by denying drilling and pipeline permits and imposing carbon taxes and climate change regulations.

Tower of Power performed that song, without irony, at their fortieth anniversary concert in 2008 and again as recently as January 2016 in Agoura Hills, California (I was there). If some 1970s funk revival band can sing that again for us in 2055 and point to a 100-ounces-of-gold-per-gallon price of gasoline as proof of a prophecy finally come true, it will be because governments finally succeeded in suppressing liberty and scientific and technological innovation, not because of any absolute physical exhaustion of resources.

Simon's influence poured the foundation for a pro-free-market, pro-capitalist philosophy on my part. But abandoning years of indoctrination, even if it merely took the form of the assumed common "values" of the culture into which I was born (what Andrew Breitbart called the "default factory setting") doesn't just happen overnight. I needed more experience, especially of adult responsibility, and I needed additional, systematic, academic instruction.

The Daughter of a Shahid

Ex-spouses have a habit of getting airbrushed out of memoirs, but I would be remiss if I didn't give credit to a person who had a significant influence upon my intellectual evolution. Her name was Nahid Hafez and she was a non-practicing Muslim immigrant from Egypt. At a time (the late 1980s) when I was still a liberal Leftist, she was a staunch Republican (how we got past our first date is something of a mystery).

Nahid and I met when I was still an over-aged undergraduate, in my late twenties. She urged me in my college planning to take a course in economics. I didn't see the point, and *it wasn't a graduation requirement*, so I let it go.

In our political discussions that inevitably degenerated into arguments, I lost most of the time. Regarding poverty, she had seen, up-close on a daily basis in Egypt, poverty that made American poor look like the Rich and Famous by comparison, so my liberal bleeding heart for the plight of welfare recipients in America didn't impress her. On socialism, she had experienced firsthand the decline and stagnation that had followed the 1952 overthrow of King Faruk and the implementation of socialism under president Gammal Abdul Nasser. Years later, Thomas Sowell would quote her own autobiographical book in one of his revised editions of "Basic Economics," from her firsthand experience with rent control in Egypt.

Speaking of years later, on September 11, 2001, we had just returned home to Los Angeles from a trip to Egypt and France together. As she saw the second plane hit the North Tower, she said, "This is Islam." For her, the assault was personal; the demons of her childhood had followed her to the land where she had thought she would never have to confront them again. It was a psychological blow that would push her full-circle from her origins. During the 1950s her father, Colonel Mustafa Hafez, had been commissioned by President Nasser to lead commando raids into Israel from Gaza. When the Israeli Mossad assassinated him (sparing the family, which included five children, even though they had the opportunity), she and her siblings became pawns in the Arab-Israeli Jihad revenge cycle. "Which one of you children will avenge your father the shahid (martyr)?", they were asked.

As an innocent child in 1956, she had had no answer. But after 9/11, in complete defiance of her assigned social role, she publicly renounced Islam and Jihad and proclaimed her support for the United States and even Israel, naming her new website ArabsForIsrael.com. The humble mother of three who worked as a claims representative for an insurance company became Nonie Darwish, public speaker and author of "Now They Call Me Infidel: Why I Renounced Jihad for America, Israel and the War on Terror" (published in 2006 by Sentinel), "Cruel and Usual Punishment: The Terrifying Global Implications of Islamic Law" (2009 by Thomas Nelson), and "The Devil We Don't Know: The Dark Side of Revolutions in the Middle East" (2012 by Wiley).

In the late 1980s, before we were married, Nahid introduced me to the Rush Limbaugh radio show. At first I (like any self-respecting liberal) was horrified, but over time, similarly to Andrew Breitbart's accounts, Rush's logic, facts and even outrageous satire began to penetrate through my deeply held but poorly defended beliefs. By the mid-90s I would tape-record all three hours of his show daily so as not to miss any of it if I could help it.

It was from Rush that I learned (this time definitively) about economists Thomas Sowell of the Hoover Institution and Walter Williams of George Mason University, among others, and began reading their works, eventually devouring at least twenty of Sowell's forty-plus books. Their disciplined expositions of economics, history and philosophy combined with dry, intelligent humor, provided the serious academic backing to Rush's populist rants and spoofs.

A High-Tech Lynching

The point of no return came for me in 1991, as it did coincidentally for Andrew Breitbart, with the Supreme Court Justice Clarence Thomas Senate confirmation hearings. (As it happens, it also occurred with less than a week to go before my wedding date with Nahid— God's way of blessing my marriage to a staunch Republican, I suppose).

President George H. W. Bush had nominated a black man to the Supreme Court. But because Thomas was not a liberal, as blacks are expected to be, was not a cheerleader for Affirmative Action, and in particular was not a staunch supporter of abortion, he had to be "Borked"—attacked so savagely that the American people would believe he was Evil Incarnate, as they had done successfully a few years earlier to Ronald Reagan's ill-fated nominee, Robert Bork. And so they put up Anita Hill, a longtime career associate and subordinate of Thomas, to level classic accusations of sexual misconduct against him.

'Borking' Bork, a white conservative, was one thing, but now we had the cognitive dissonance-inducing spectacle of old, white, privileged Senators, including the former Ku Klux Klan wizard Robert Byrd, blocking the gate to a highly qualified, educated, accomplished, almost iconic up-from-poverty black American, slamming the door from the Left. Nothing in my prior experience had prepared me for such a spectacle. And as several women and blacks testified in Thomas' defense, a complete reassessment of my understanding of the world was required.

Above all, the testimony of three very articulate and well-dressed professional black men, John Doggett, Stanley Grayson and Carlton Stewart, shattered my image of what blacks could or should be. While I don't recall any of them saying explicitly, "I am a conservative and/or a Republican," implicitly they were defending a conservative black man, at significant cost to themselves, against a politically motivated assault from the Left.

Doggett was a former Yale Law School fellow of Thomas and President of International Management Consulting Group. Stewart was a graduate of the University of Georgia Law School, who had been Special Assistant to Clarence Thomas at the Equal Employment Opportunity Commission, or EEOC. Grayson was an attorney at Goldman Sachs. A few excerpts of their testimony follow.

Stanley Grayson:
> During the weekend of August 10, 1991, while at the hotel and conference headquarters for the American Bar Association's convention in Atlanta, Georgia, I was introduced to Professor Anita Hill by Mr. Carlton Stewart. At this meeting,

45

Ms. Hill, Mr. Stewart and I sat and conversed for at least thirty minutes. During the course of our conversation, in the presence of Mr. Stewart, Ms. Hill expressed her pleasure with Judge Thomas's nomination, and stated that he deserved it. During this time Ms. Hill made no mention of any sexual harassment by Judge Thomas, nor did she in any way indicate anything that might call into question the character or fitness of Judge Thomas for the U.S. Supreme Court. To the contrary, she seemed to take great pride in the fact that she had been a member of Judge Thomas' staff at the Equal Employment Opportunity Commission.

Carlton Stewart:

In August 1991, I ran into Ms. Anita Hill at the American Bar Association convention in Atlanta, Georgia, whereupon she stated, in the presence of Stanley Grayson, how great Clarence's nomination was and how much he deserved it. We went on to discuss Judge Clarence Thomas at our tenure at EEOC for an additional thirty or so minutes. There was no mention of sexual harassment or anything negative about Judge Thomas stated during that time.

[Later:] Clarence Thomas is a sitting federal judge. This process has treated him, in the last several days, like he is a foreman in a manufacturing plant. We are dealing with claims that are . . . that's a nullity at law. Allegations come in ten years, eight years, whatever, way beyond the statute of limitations, and I think we need to keep these things in focus and in vogue when we are trying to make a decision about who is telling what. We have two witnesses today for Miss Hill, who were told two different things. Two were told that she was being sexually harassed by her superior and two were told by her boss. We still don't know who they are. There were giant leaps in logic to conclude that it was Clarence Thomas, but that is clearly not the case. Many were asked the question of why we are here. We are here because of a leak, not because of allegations, but because of the leak. This is publicized because of a leak by the committee—somebody on the committee. Clarence should not be the person who receives the brunt of this. The very same rights they accuse him of being against, they took from him by leaking this information.

But the most mind-blowing to me at the time, was this testimony by John Doggett:

> At this time, I was a Democrat [implying that he no longer was]. At this time, I really had some reservations about whether or not the Reagan revolution was good for this country. At this time, I was being hammered by Reaganites, because of my attitudes, and when I found out that somebody who had been a classmate of mine, who I had assisted at Yale Law School, was now in the position of being one of the top-ranking blacks in the Reagan administration, I wanted to go talk to this man and find out what was going on because I knew he would tell me the truth. One of the things that Clarence Thomas told me that really stuck in my mind, and one of the reasons I said, "I've got to get this information to this committee and let them decide whether or not it is valuable," is that he said, "John, they call me an Uncle Tom. They are at my back. They're looking for anything they can use to take me out." He was quite aware of the scrutiny that he was under and the fact that his positions were very unpopular[14].

Prior to this moment, it would have been inconceivable to me that self-respecting black men could say such things, even to express the *possibility* that Reagan was anything other than a blood-soaked vampire. In my mind, blacks were wedded to the civil rights movement, which was liberal and wedded to the Democratic Party. Anything which was not liberal or Democratic had to be anti-civil rights and anti-black. But that clearly wasn't the case; it was merely a case of my successful brainwashing by the Left.

I had no more reason to cling to my liberal, Leftist "default factory setting" for fear of becoming a Nazi or a Klansman, as Leftists had successfully instilled in me that must lie on the other side. I was finally completely free to challenge any and all previously understood notions, cherished beliefs or sacred cows in the light of facts, logic, intellectual honesty and unconstrained debate. From that moment forward I

---

14   Watch the video at: http://www.c-span.org/video/?22288-1/thomas-second-hearing-day-3-part-5

enthusiastically pursued anything that might contribute to my understanding of politics, society and economics, with nothing ruled taboo a priori.

I cannot leave this topic without noting some of the more farcical aspects of the hearing spectacle, during the same segment. Apparently Doggett had had a minor "he said, she said" history of his own with Anita Hill, in which her story was that he had led her on then let her down, while his side was that he had done everything possible from the beginning to make it clear that the only relationship he was interested in was professional. This led to a line of questioning and discussion (keep in mind that this is a United States Senate confirmation hearing for a Supreme Court Justice!) that strayed into the murky waters of the singles dating scene in the brutally competitive Washington, D.C. professional society.

Here is then-Senator Joe Biden, younger and more the respected parliamentarian than he is known as the lame duck Vice President, speaking slowly and dramatically:

Mr. Doggett, I don't doubt what you said, but I kind of find it equally bizarre that you would be so shocked. Maybe it has never happened to you. I know a lot of men who call a woman and ask her out or ask to meet . . . Ask to have dinner. Say "let's get together for dinner," but afraid to say fully "let's go out together for dinner. Let's get together. We live in the neighborhood; let's go to dinner." And that the person calls back or you call again and speak to her again and the date is set. And then for whatever reason she doesn't show up. You are still interested. You call back. You say, "How come you weren't there?" You say, "Well, I thought that you were going to call." And you thought I was going to call, etc. And it goes back and forth. Then there is a pregnant pause and you hang up. Maybe I am just accustomed to being turned down more than you were, when I was younger [Doggett listening patiently]. But some men sit and say, "Gee, I wonder whether she's just bashful; that was the reason for the pregnant pause. I wonder if she really wants me to call her back. She didn't say, 'don't call me again.' She didn't say, 'I don't want to hear from you again.' Maybe." And when you see her a little while later at a party and she is leaving town. And you walked up to her and you say, you know, "Can I talk to you?" And she says, "Yes."

And you walk over to the corner of the party and say, "You know, you really shouldn't let guys down like that. You led me to believe that you wanted to go out with me. You shouldn't do that to women or to men." And if she turned around and said, "You're *fantasizing*! How could you ever think that?"

This line of questioning and discussion went on for several minutes. Golly-gee willickers, Uncle Joe! Is this really what goes on in the World's Most Deliberative Body? It does illustrate that male-female interaction, especially among adult singles, is a frequently awkward game where misunderstandings are legion, and maybe, just maybe, we should accept it as a fact of life and stop looking for the slightest provocation to be outrageously offended.

But the thing that is most entertaining about this exchange is the unspoken subtext, what everyone in the room then, or watching then or later, is thinking and knows: that Doggett is the most handsome man and desirable catch in the room, and any single woman (or single gay man) would be willing to humiliate herself (or himself) for the opportunity to go out to dinner with him.

A Formal Introduction

In 1992, while working full-time, I enrolled in the weekend MBA program at Woodbury University in Burbank, California. I was finally required to take a formal course in economics, "micro" and "macro" combined into one term. While it would be both my first and last formal course in the discipline, it was for me—to mangle a metaphor—the spark that launched a thousand ships[15].

From *culture* we get values. Our values inform our goals. *Politics* teaches us how to accomplish our social goals through the means of organization, non-violent cooperation or violent coercion, devious dirty tricks or democratic processes and parliamentary procedures.

---

15   Besides the course, I am very grateful to my friend and neighbor Robert Harding, who coached and tutored me through that watershed phase of my life. Bob was a retired navy officer who had just recently earned his PhD in Economics from UCLA at the age of forty (-ish) and philosophically was a Friedmanian monetarist.

Economics informs us whether the policies that we advocate and implement are likely to achieve their ostensible goals. It was economics that taught me that the means I favored as a liberal Leftist were counterproductive to achieving the very ends that my values sought. And that, in turn, changed my beliefs about the best means to those ends.

And so, with those beliefs fully transformed, I was ready to assume a new and surprising philosophical and political identity. In 1988 I had voted for Michael Dukakis. In 1992 I voted for George Herbert Walker Bush (I lost both times; in fact, I have only "won" two of the nine presidential elections of my adult life). Life would never be quite the same, but my journey was far from over. In fact, it had just begun.

A Conservative Libertarian Blog and a Republican Club

In the next chapter, I will detail the leading influences and works which fleshed out my intellectual journey in classical political economy which gave me the foundation to become a published columnist, author and speaker. Before I go into those details, I will skip ahead here a couple of decades to describe a few significant outcomes of my self-directed course of study.

In 2006 I began writing for the public on my own blog. Created as HowardHyde.blogspot.com, since my mission as I saw it was a vigorous defense of capitalism, I soon acquired and mapped the domain HHCapitalism.com to the site. More recently I made it over as CitizenEcon.com, intended as a one-stop shop for a citizen's course in economics and repository showcase of my works and appearances published elsewhere.

I wasn't eager to turn my philosophical transformation into an overtly partisan mission. I wanted to be like Milton Friedman: academic, transcendent, and not wedded to any specific party platform. But after Barack Obama was elected and the prospect was raised of socialized medicine being passed where it had failed in 1994, my sense of alarm propelled me onto the streets outside of my congressman's townhall meeting, handing out the pamphlet that I wrote, "121

Reasons to Reject Obama-Reid-PelosiCare." I felt the need to get out of my armchair and get involved, and the Republican Party, with all of its warts, became the appropriate vehicle for that involvement with increasing frequency. I was recruited to the campaign of 2010 congressional candidate Navraj Singh, becoming his Webmaster and Chief Policy Analyst, writing most of his platform and posting regularly on his campaign blog.

I also began to submit my articles for publication at FrontPageMag.com, AmericanThinker.com and other venues, and over the following months and years my reject ratio improved.

In February 2013, I published a short (12,000-word) book, *Pull the Plug on Obamacare: A Citizen Pamphlet*, and sold it on Amazon.com. One doctor discovered it and ordered 600 copies to give to his patients, and made me sign every one. In 2013 and 2014 I attended the Conservative Political Action Conference (CPAC) in Washington D.C. and handed copies of my book personally to Allen West, Ann Coulter, Rick Perry, John Alison (President of the Cato Institute), Ben Carson, Ted Cruz and others. (Cruz has yet to credit me with inspiring his 2013 Obamacare filibuster.) Part III of this book contains more of my analyses of this subject.

In the fall of 2013, I was elected president of the Southern California Republican Women and Men, an independent club founded in 1935, affectionately known by its vocalized acronym "SCReW'eM!" I had attended meetings of this club on and off for perhaps a decade and a half, and had long regarded it as my preferred Republican organization for its very intellectually engaging and dynamic discussion and debate forum, pioneered twenty years earlier by past president Tom Hanson. I had made my first public speech to any Republican group at SCRWM in 2010, a speech accompanied by photos and slides titled "Confessions of an Ex-Liberal Socialist Progressive Democrat from Berkeley"; the precursor to this book.

I don't quite remember how it happened, but my name got advanced, and I must not have objected vigorously enough, although I do remember saying, "Only if you, you, you and you be my executive board," and—long story short—it came to pass. A few of the chapters in the later parts of this book are derived from speeches and/or articles composed originally for the club.

If only my Berkeley High School friends could see me now (oops, someone just informed me of the invention of the Internet and Facebook).

The Curriculum

This chapter is among the most academic treatments in the book, something of an annotated bibliography placed in the body in semi-narrative form instead of a sterile listing in an appendix, and may be skipped by those ~~lazy, feckless brain-dead slackers~~ who find such discussions too tiresome. Yet it is my hope that intellectually curious compatriots and young people will have the courage to stick it out, to get the full sweep of the discipline and of my intellectual journey, the better to comprehend what follows and to arm themselves for intellectual combat, even if that combat is against conservatives. It sets the stage for the re-evaluation and re-interpretation of the events of the 60s in Berkeley and the rest of the world in the chapter "Berkeley Redux," as well as everything else that follows. For serious scholars, it is mandatory.

Keep in mind: I had a long and indulged on-and-off-and-on-again undergraduate career spanning ten years (twelve if you count the two years I took off after high school to work at gas stations and McDonald's and play trumpet in my band) at five different institutions, earning perhaps twice the total credits normally required for a B.A. degree, yet *I never learned any of this stuff*. The majority of the material that I have considered essential to my intellectual development in my adult life came from authors who were never assigned in college.

For example, my freshman geography textbook probably had one hundred authors and editors, as well as hundreds of charts, graphs and photographs; yet in terms of substantive content, practical insight and inspiration, it paled next to the work on the significance and interplay of geography, culture, migrations and conquests by a single author: Thomas Sowell[16].

Neither do most economics majors learn most of what I present here, a fact I find astonishing, if not outrageous. I have more to say about this in my 2013 speech to the annual meeting of the Association

---

[16] On this subject, see Sowell's book 'Wealth, Poverty and Politics: An International Perspective'. Also, 'Migrations and Cultures', 'Conquest and Cultures' and 'Race and Culture'. But I'm getting ahead of myself...

of American Physicians and Surgeons ("The Tea Party for Doctors") in Part II.

My only regret is that I lack the time to expand each of the articles in this chapter by a factor of ten (maybe in the Second Edition). These are teasers.

Econ 101, 102, 103 . . .

Economics as it is taught in universities today, like all disciplines, is the culmination of decades and centuries, if not millennia, of evolution, both of scientific/academic debate and petty-political gamesmanship. The methods and tools of the practitioners, indeed the very concept of what the discipline is about, evolved over time, and what people mean by "economics" may be very different from one era to the next or even among different groups of people within the same era. And so, the contemporary technical/mathematical approach to economics, with its equations and amazing graphs that seem to pack such awesome explanatory power into small packages, would, within a few years of my formal university course, give way in my mind to what I saw as the bigger picture, or more meaningful to the non-professional economist citizen. That picture emerged to me as I immersed myself, through independent reading of the history, philosophy and development of the discipline over the last 250 years.

First I read Adam Smith, considered the founding father of modern economics. His magnum opus, "The Wealth of Nations" (1776) is over a thousand pages long; I read it cover-to-cover. Call me a geek, but to me it was like reading Shakespeare, a spiritual rapture. Then, I dove into a survey of all the great economic thinkers since Smith to the present day.

During the 1990s, while in "real life" I launched my bill-paying day job in information technology, the audio series *"Great Economic Thinkers"* and *"Giants of Political Thought"*, by Knowledge Products Audio Books, a division of Carmichael & Carmichael Inc., became the core curriculum of my self-directed study. Consider this section an unpaid endorsement (unless you're an executive at C&C, in which case, start cutting some checks).

The Knowledge Products audio titles are not just classic books read verbatim, as some of their titles suggest; they are minor radio-theatre-like productions, with storytelling and professional actors' voice characterizations of historical figures. The production values are a bit hokey by 21st-century standards, but still very educational and highly recommended to both the lay reader and the serious student. Best of all, the economics series in particular is narrated by the popularizer of free-market capitalist principles and thirty-two-year host of the PBS series, "Wall Street Week with Louis Rukeyser".

"Great Economic Thinkers"

Originally published in 1988, these are still available, also as a complete boxed set. The titles which had the most influence on me are listed here, in rough historical chronological order, with a few comments as to their content and personal significance.

- **The Classical Economists** (Adam Smith, David Ricardo, Thomas Malthus; see also "The Wealth of Nations: Parts I and II," below)
  Smith opens his "Wealth of Nations" with a dramatic case study that illustrates the power of the division of labor: in the "trifling" manufacture of pins, one worker working alone might strain to produce a single pin in a day, yet a team of specialists, each being dedicated to one simple operation in the overall process of manufacture, could produce as many as 240 pins *per worker* per day. From there he discusses the nature of prices and supply and demand—with the emphasis on *effectual* demand as opposed to mere impotent wishes ("A poor man may be said to have a demand for a coach-and-six [horses], but . . .").
  But Smith's most important contribution, indeed the theme implicit in his title, is to the debate over free versus restricted international trade, coming down on the side of the former. His book stands as a repudiation of beggar-thy-neighbor

mercantilism (protectionism), counseled by many merchants of the day to protect their own special interests and presumably those of the sovereign or king, by ensuring that more gold returned to the country than left it. Smith argued that real wealth does not consist in gold but in the things that gold can buy, and if one country can produce some items more cheaply than another and vice versa, then both countries would be better off if they were to specialize in what each one produced most cheaply and exchange their surpluses with each other. Steven Covey would call this "win-win." The free-trade concepts of *comparative advantage*, *absolute advantage* and *economies of scale* have their roots in Smith's exposition.

- **Das Kapital** (Karl Marx)
  Does this need introduction? Shouldn't we avoid this like the plague?

  Well, actually, this audio title and the original book should be read again and again, both to "know one's enemy" and to delight in the surprises. Some of Marx's work is actually quite rigorous and scientific; it is only when he deliberately steers political and polemical that he goes off in the deep end. One of my favorite personal insights into our modern economic malaise is, "Where are all of the good Marxists when you need them?" That is, whatever happened to the notion that the worker should receive the full value of his/her labor? It is all the layers of bureaucracy, taxes, regulations, government-coerced third-party agency/middleman fees, legal liability, instability and other costs and risks *created by the effect the Left's policies* which have driven a Grand Canyon-sized wedge between what it costs the employer to engage an employee and what that employee ever sees in his/her own pocket. What favor have the Marxists done to the workers if it costs $100,000 to hire one employee at a salary of $50,000, of which the latter will see $40,000 if lucky? Or if it costs $250,000 to hire one at a $100,000 salary, of which the employee is unlikely to see more than $60,000? The employer is willing and able to give up $250,000 in exchange for the worker's labor, yet the worker only sees $60,000; is that labor justice? Do we blame Marx, or do we exhume his body and hook it up to Dr. F's electrodes so that he may rebuke his idiot disciples?

More recently, I discovered a very illuminating essay on the personal life of Karl Marx in "The Thomas Sowell Reader," which I also heartily recommend. In short, Marx was a child of bourgeois privilege, a living contradiction to his own theories of class consciousness, who squandered multiple family fortunes in pursuit of his dubious championing of the poor proletariat.

- **Early Austrian Economics** (Carl Menger, Eugen von Bohm-Bawerk)

    Carl Menger achieved a breakthrough with his theories of marginal utility, which solved critical theoretical problems that had eluded Adam Smith and misled Karl Marx. For example, Smith had struggled to explain why diamonds should be more valuable than water, since water is about the most useful thing in the world. He posited a (bipolar) theory of value-in-use versus value-in-exchange that wasn't very satisfactory. Marx propounded an elaborate and tortured *labor theory of value*. It was Menger's insight that the question was wrong; diamonds are *not* categorically and in all instances "more valuable" than water. What mattered was not comparing whole classes of one thing to whole classes of others, but specific quantities in the hands of specific people at specific times and places and under specific circumstances. A lost man dying of thirst in the Sahara Desert would be willing to give up any number of diamonds in exchange for one cup of water, but a drowning man would give up diamonds to have the water taken away. It all depends on the specific context. What counts is not all the water or all the diamonds, but the *next* diamond and the *next* incremental quantity of water, in the context of what quantity one already has.

    "Some more Godiva fudge ice cream?"
    "No, thanks, I'm full."

    If Menger had come before Marx, perhaps the world might have been spared innumerable catastrophes. See Menger's "Principles of Economics," not to be confused with Alfred Marshall's book of the same title.

- **The Austrian Case for the Free Market Process**
  Ludwig von Mises and Friedrich Hayek pervade the essays in the later parts of this book. See "Human Action" later in this chapter.

- **Frank Knight and the Chicago School**
  Precursor to Milton Friedman.

- **Joseph Schumpeter and Dynamic Economic Change: Capitalism as "Creative Destruction"**
  Economies do not advance only by incremental improvement, but by disruptive events—creative innovation which renders older technologies, ways of doing things and—crucially—*privileges*, obsolete (think automobile versus horse-and-buggy as a society's dominant mode of transportation; online shopping vs. brick-and-mortar, email vs. the traditional postal service, Uber vs. traditional taxis etc.). It is the politician's natural inclination to restrain progress and innovation in defense of the entrenched vested interests that fund his or her election campaigns; but doing so is fool's errand for the well-being of society as a whole.

- **The Keynesian Revolution** (John Maynard Keynes) Keynes is (lamentably, in my humble opinion) perhaps the single most influential economist of the twentieth and twenty-first centuries. His theories have been used to justify massive government spending and deficits as somehow beneficial to the economy; the policies and powers of the Federal Reserve system and Fannie Mae and Freddie Mac; innumerable "stimulus" packages; and TARP, the Troubled Asset Relief Program, a.k.a. the $800 billion bailout of the big banks and General Motors of 2008.
  The sub-discipline of macroeconomics grew out of Keynesian theory. It treats economic activity in terms of aggregates—large numbers of people, industries, sectors and transactions as collective masses where the individual circumstances of human preferences and voluntary cooperation and exchanges, let alone human ingenuity, innovation, disruption or

entrepreneurial risk-taking, are completely washed out of the amalgamated equations.

When I took that course at Woodbury U., I went along with the spoon-fed conclusions like. "The government should deficit-spend during recessions and save during boom times," enough to get my grade. But I was always suspicious of the macroeconomic formulations. In the back of my mind, I had questions. The government should deficit-spend *on what?* Toilet paper? Dog food? What if the people already have enough toilet paper or dog food? Doesn't it matter *what* the money gets spent on? And if money spent by the government has a multiplier effect, as it is re-spent and re-spent successively, doesn't money spent by private individuals and businesses (before it is taxed away) have the same multiplier effect? Why should it become pixie dust when the government is doing it? Saying what the government should do is not the same as describing what it is most likely to do, given the *incentives and constraints* (thank you Thomas Sowell) faced by the politicians who populate it.

These questions and more raised by Keynesian theories will be an integral part of essays later in this book.

- **Alfred Marshall & Neoclassicism: Economics Becomes a Science**
  Marshall's textbook, "Principles of Economics" (not to be confused with Carl Menger's book of the same title, originally published in German) dominated university curricula through eight editions from 1890 through 1920. For good and for ill, it took economics in the direction of a rigorous academic science and profession, and further away from the layperson citizen's philosophical understanding.

- **Struggle over the Keynesian Heritage**
  The controversy, unresolved issues and paradoxes left in the legacy that Keynes left behind. Keynes wasn't a "Keynesian," just as Marx may not have been a "Marxist."

- **Monetarism and Supply Side Economics** (Milton Friedman, Robert Mundell)

See my extended exposition of Friedman's "Free to Choose" television series and book, earlier in this book. I tread only lightly on the specifics of monetarism. In brief, there is a debate as to whether and by what rate the government or central bank (the Federal Reserve Bank, or "Fed") should inflate the money supply in correspondence with economic growth. This debate matters because one of the claims of the monetarists like Friedman is that the Great Depression of the 1930s would have been greatly alleviated if the government had expanded the money supply instead of permitting it to contract. My own opinion: Would it be such a terrible thing if you could buy a cup of coffee for 15¢?[17] Pennies were useful in my youth.

"Giants of Political Thought"

This was a separate series of audiobooks by Knowledge Products which figured prominently in my self-directed curriculum:

- **Two Treatises of Government** (John Locke)
  Locke had a major influence on the founders of the United States. He was a revolutionary who lived and wrote about a hundred years earlier, during the English Revolution of the 1680s. What impressed me most about his work was the systematic philosophical and theological foundation and justification for the institution of private property. In brief, somewhere between plucking, cutting, boiling, biting chewing, swallowing and digesting, an apple must at some point become the private property of the consumer; and what is taken out of Nature in common becomes private property once the individual has mixed his labor with it in some way. Learning how language has evolved in the past 300-plus years adds enrichment. For example, today we would say, "That land is my property." In the seventeenth century the same concept would be expressed as, "I have a property in that land." It was Locke who coined the phrase "life, liberty and

[17]   Pennies were in common use in the sixties and seventies. Today they are so worthless that I couldn't even find the cents symbol ('¢') on the computer keyboard; I had to dig for it under Start => All Programs => Accessories => System Tools => Character Map. The symbol was standard on typewriter keyboards for over a century. See Murray Rothbard: "What has the Government Done to our Money?"

property," which was adapted by Thomas Jefferson in the Declaration of Independence as "life, liberty and the pursuit of happiness." That modification may be the earliest recorded instance of political correctness trumping a simple, unambiguous and fundamental concept.

- **The Wealth of Nations: Parts I and II** (Adam Smith)
  Adam Smith in depth; see "The Classical Economists" above.

- **The Federalist Papers** (Alexander Hamilton, James Madison, John Jay)
  Alexander Hamilton, James Madison, and John Jay published dozens of anonymous essays in 1787 to persuade public opinion in favor of adopting the Constitution, then only being drafted at the convention in Philadelphia. The Federalist Papers are those essays collected into a single volume.

- **Democracy in America** (Alexis de Tocqueville)
  In the 1830s, a French aristocrat toured the United States and wrote about the astonishing (entirely foreign to a European) independent, entrepreneurial and civic-minded spirit of free Americans, and the sloth and degradation of both slaves and masters that he witnessed in the southern states.

More Giants

Beyond that "core curriculum," here are the key thinkers and works that had great influence on my evolution.

- **Charles Murray: "Losing Ground" (1980)**
  Published in 1980, the most significant indictment of Lyndon Baines Johnson's Great Society programs launched fifteen years earlier, in 1965. The conditions which those social programs were intended to improve had all gotten worse, at an economic cost of billions of dollars.

- **Robert Bartley: "The Seven Fat Years: And How to Do It Again" (1992)**

Reflections on the successes of the economic policies (tax cuts, reduced regulation) of the Reagan administration (1981-1989) and astonishment that the electorate and Reagan's successor, George Herbert Walker Bush, were actively undoing Reagan's achievements, as if there was only so much prosperity and happiness that they could tolerate.

- **Jude Wanniski: "The Way the World Works" (1978)**

Wanniski was a member of the Wall Street Journal editorial board in the 1970s. In this free-market treatise, the most indispensable part that stood out to me was the in-depth analysis of the Great Crash of October 1929 and the ensuing Great Depression, focusing in particular on the anti-free trade, protectionist Smoot-Hartley Tariff. Wanniski defends his thesis by connecting the dots between the stock market and political news, day-by-day and even hour-by-hour during that critical period.

- **George Gilder: From "Wealth and Poverty" (1981) to "Knowledge and Power" (2013)**

In "Wealth and Poverty," Gilder takes up the questions that had been the central theme of Adam Smith's work: the nature of wealth, what it really is and what it consists in. Gilder argues that mere riches, like lots of money or, in the case of some nations, oil or other natural resources, does not constitute real wealth. By this measure, even the Saudis are not truly wealthy. Certainly, the average Nigerian or Venezuelan is not. Rather, wealth consists in all the things, tangible, intangible and *moral*, which make the production of riches consistent and dependable over the long term: knowledge, ingenuity, creativity, science, faith, discipline, thrift, family, self-control, freedom, private property rights and the respect for the reciprocal rights of others.

He further argues that Capitalism, far from being a system of greedy exploitation of the poor by the rich, begins and ends with giving, the competition between friendly rivals to see who can offer the best gift.

In "Knowledge and Power," Gilder argues that Capitalism is not primarily a mechanical system of carrots and sticks, of punishments and rewards, but of information. Economics is about delivering the most highly valued products and services to each individual at the lowest possible cost. There is so much information in this system, and so rapidly and continuously changing, that no computer, let alone government, is capable of comprehending it all, in order to coordinate all of the activities most effectively. Rather, what is needed in order to optimize the effectiveness of an economy is a clear and quiet channel through which information (mostly encapsulated in market prices) may flow. This is the only way that the people who have the most relevant, detailed and up-to-date knowledge may take the best action possible.

Unfortunately, most of what government regulations accomplish is to suppress, distort and destroy information, making it impossible for people who otherwise would be able to make the right decisions based on the realities of the relative scarcities and abundances in the economy. Regulation and bureaucracy substitutes power in the place of competence, putting authority to act and to coerce others into the hands of persons having the least amount of, least relevant, and/or least current knowledge. This can and does only result in general impoverishment, recession and depression.

Government interference in markets is analogous to static interference on a communications channel, like noise on a phone line, making it difficult by degrees for the message to be transmitted, received and understood, up to and including the complete eclipse of information.

As this book goes to press, Gilder has just released his latest: "The Scandal of Money: Why Wall Street Recovers but the Economy Never Does."

- **Friedrich Hayek: "The Road to Serfdom" (1944)**

"The road to Hell is paved with good intentions" (Various attributions).

Hayek published this work toward the end of World War II to warn a democratic West that he perceived to be winning the war but losing the argument, seduced by the sweet promises of socialism. He dedicated it "To the Socialists of All Parties," driving home the point that "right" or "conservative" politicians were not immune to the infection.

One dominant theme is that socialism must inevitably lead to despotism because, unlike freedom, it creates centers of power which are irresistible temptations for the most brutal and ruthless among political leaders. It engenders an environment in which only the most barbarous and cruel dictator may survive, thus maximizing the probability of violent conflict and repression.

History has borne out Hayek's warning. The countries most fanatically committed to socialism have become the most repressive, while freer nations have suffered in proportion, as they have made concessions to collectivism.

Hayek was awarded the Nobel Memorial Prize for Economic Science in 1974.

- **Ludwig von Mises: "Human Action" (1949) and "Economic Policy: Thoughts for Today and for Tomorrow" (1959)**

Von Mises was born in 1881 and expired 92 years later, in 1973. He wrote a devastating critique of socialist theory in 1922 (completely counter to fashionable intellectual trends at the time), which Hayek credits for his own conversion to the free-market philosophy. Mises fled the Nazis in the late 1930s, first to Switzerland, then to the United States. There, he published his magnum opus, "Human Action," in 1949.

If 900 pages of academic prose so impenetrable that it might as well yet be *Deutsch auf der Wienersprachenakademie* isn't quite your thing, then see the 100-page plain-language "Economic Policy: Thoughts for Today and for Tomorrow." This is a transcript of a half-dozen lectures that he gave in Argentina in 1959, in which he lays out essential principles of economics and public policy in a superbly comprehensible and compact manner. Considering what has happened to Argentina in the intervening years, one has to lament, if only someone with power had taken him seriously, how much suffering could have been avoided.

Here is one of his arguments from that book on the futility of government-imposed price controls, cut down to its skeleton:

> The government declares a maximum price for milk...But what happens? On the one hand, the lower price of milk increases the demand for milk; people who could not afford to buy milk at a higher price are now able to buy it at the lower price which the government has decreed. And on the other hand...the private producer cannot take losses in the long run. And as he cannot take losses in milk, he restricts the production of milk for the market...Thus the government's interference with the price of milk will result in less milk that there was before, and at the same time there will be a greater demand...The government at the same time starts controlling not only milk, but also eggs, meat, and other necessities. And every time the government gets the same result, everywhere the consequence is the same...Once the government fixes a maximum price for consumer goods, it has to go farther back to producer's goods, and limit the prices of the producer's goods required for the production of the price-controlled consumer goods...And as the government goes farther and farther, it will finally arrive at a point where all prices, all wage rates, all interest rates, in short everything in the whole economic system, is determined by the government. And this, clearly, is socialism[18].

Keynes once said that men who shun theory and consider themselves "practical" men are more likely the unconscious slaves of some defunct economist. Nothing has happened in economics

18   From the 3rd Lecture, Interventionism, of Economic Policy: Thoughts for Today and for Tomorrow, published variously by Regnery and the Ludwig von Mises Institute (www.mises.org).

in the late twentieth and early twenty-first centuries that hasn't been influenced to some degree by Mises. Read 'Economic Policy', then bite the bullet and read 'Human Action'.

- **Murray Rothbard: "Man, Economy and State" (1962) and "America's Great Depression" (1963)**

I flag this scholar and theorist with the strongest caveat and caution of the bunch. Rothbard has some very original rigorous and even indispensable analyses, working out the details and implications of von Mises' "Human Action" in the above-named treatise. But he eventually goes over a cliff from whence he is unrecoverable. It is one thing to assert that government is not necessary even for such services considered as basic as police and defensive armed forces; it is another to revile anyone and everyone who doesn't immediately jump onboard to that point of view. It is worse still to focus one's activism as a libertarian economist on hollowing out the existing government from its core rather than reining in the elements that have strayed farthest from the core. Militant libertarians like Rothbard end up contradicting everything they start out ostensibly standing for.

In particular, Rothbard's bitter diatribe against Ronald Reagan in 1989 convinced me that his brand of absolute purism had no practical value.

With those caveats out of the way, Rothbard's analysis in "America's Great Depression" (First Edition 1963; Fifth Edition 2000) is indispensable, not just from a historical perspective but in explaining the more general "Austrian" (derived from Mises, Hayek, Menger, et al.) theory of how market booms and crashes come about. See his chapter, "How the Business Cycle Happens"; reading this in early 2007, it was easy to recognize the signs of the gathering storm that would break later that year.

I am sympathetic to Rothbard's "The Case Against the Fed." Rothbard is the inspiration for Ron Paul and Lew Rockwell (of LewRockwell.com) and still exerts influence at Mises.org. See "Libertarianism and Republicans" in Part IV for my more detailed criticism.

- **Ayn Rand: "Atlas Shrugged" (1957), "The Fountainhead" (1943), "The New Left: The Anti-Industrial Revolution" (1971), which includes "The Cashing-In: The Student "Rebellion" (1965)**

Rand was born Alisa Rosenbaum in Russia in 1905 and immigrated to the United States in 1926. Her critiques of socialism, collectivism and economic ignorance are devastating. In her epic fiction, she speaks through her characters to debunk Marxist notions and half-baked ideas about how the world works, or should work. Even a subject as dry as the nature of money, something which pedantic economics professors have bored untold generations of students to death pontificating over, she brings to extraordinary vitality in "Francisco's Money Speech" in "Atlas Shrugged"; she tips over sacred cows by arguing, with trenchant logic, that money is the root of all Good. As an ally of pro-capitalist, pro-free-market Americans, she is without peer.

Rand's work has its flaws, and her appeal to American conservatives will always be limited, in a society founded on Judeo-Christian traditions, by her militant atheism. But religious conservatives should not write her off; her arguments are conducive to the kind of society in which religious liberty will have its greatest opportunity to flourish.

Rand's extended essay analyzing and criticizing the Berkeley Free Speech Movement of 1964-65 will be quoted at length at the end of the chapter "Berkeley Redux."

- **George Reisman: "Capitalism" (1996)**

Reisman was a disciple of Ludwig von Mises and Ayn Rand and taught at Pepperdine University in Malibu, California, before retiring sometime in the 2000s; his blog (http://georgereismansblog.blogspot.com) is active in 2016.

His book title is short because after the million words that he packs into what I call his "suitcase bomb," there was almost nothing left. It is 2,000 large-format, small-type pages, weighing several pounds, with two columns of text per page, and worth every paragraph for its systematic exposition and analysis of what capitalism is and how it works, and why socialism doesn't. Reisman's influence on me is perhaps most pronounced in my essays on employment, "Where Do Jobs Come From?" and "Why does the Pay Suck?" in Part II.

- **Ronald Coase: "The Firm, the Market and the Law" (1990) and "Essays on Economics and Economists" (1994)**

Coase is an economist's economist, writing more for his colleagues than the general public; hence, he is less well-known, but no less valuable. Among the questions he grapples with are, why do firms, including corporations, even exist? That is, why can't every worker or professional operate as a free agent, reciprocally contracting with other workers on a day-by-day or month-by-month basis, with their activities coordinated by the price system? After all, there are inefficiencies inherent in large organizations where market prices for the services that different departments render to each other are absent. What are the natural boundaries or balances between organizations operating as a single entity with contrived internal cost accounting, versus projects undertaken by multiple entities coordinated by true market prices? This has profound implications for mergers, acquisitions and conglomeration versus splitting firms into multiple entities, and for the tendency of government regulation to skew that balance away from where it would naturally occur in a free market (usually favoring larger, more conglomerated, inefficient behemoth corporations).

Another interesting line of inquiry: What is the true nature of natural monopoly, where the government is required to step in? It is commonly believed that the services of a lighthouse, for example, must necessarily be provided by government; yet lighthouses were privately owned and operated in England for 400 years.

Coase hypothesized that any economic or even social problem could be solved by the judicious assignment of property rights. For example, if two neighbors live close to each other and one wants peace and quiet while the other wants to play loud music, then the market can resolve the dispute even if the assignment of rights is arbitrary. If the noisy neighbor is assigned the right to play loud music, then the one who wants quiet can offer something in exchange for silence, either in the absolute or at certain times of day, including paying him to make noise somewhere else. If the quiet neighbor is assigned the right to peace and tranquility, then the noisy neighbor may offer something of value in exchange for the right to raise hell, including providing a quiet place somewhere else. It's all in the pricing and negotiation at the margins, starting with clear assignments of property rights. See the chapter "The Problem of Social Cost" in "The Firm, The Market and The Law".

- **Hernando de Soto: "The Mystery of Capital: Why Capitalism Triumphs in the West and Fails Everywhere Else" (2000)**

De Soto is a Peruvian economist who analyzed conditions in several third-world countries, as compared to the United States, Western Europe, Japan, etc., and came to the conclusion that what was missing from the former was an adequate system of documentation and defense of individual private property rights. The problem is not that the poor have nothing; they own assets whose aggregate value dwarfs all of the cumulative foreign aid to third-world countries. The problem is that ownership of assets is only recognized within narrowly constricted and informal social circles. Within a neighborhood, who owns what land or what house may be acknowledged by all neighbors (even barking dogs know where the property lines are), but the national government does not have a registry that can guarantee these claims.

To illustrate the point, imagine that a homeowner in Berkeley could not sell his house to a buyer from Miami because the latter could not be certain that the former's deed was legitimate, exclusive and enforceable. The result is that the world's poor own trillions of dollars' worth of assets, but as capital these assets are *dead*—not recognized, not leverage-able, not mortgage-able, possibly not even saleable. It is the ability to derive fungible economic media or financial instruments from physical assets reliably and consistently over the long term that has enabled people in the "first world" to increase their real wealth to such high levels, as compared to the rest of the world.

A very interesting aspect of de Soto's book is his analysis of the frontier experience of the United States during the eighteenth and nineteenth centuries. The pioneers of the American West were true pioneers in more than one sense of the word; they were the vanguard of the legal property system, refining the meaning and management of private property rights. The conflicting claims of "legitimate" landowners, squatters, miners, ranchers, farmers, railroads and native American Indians had an historically unique legal workout over the course of a century which resulted in the most advanced and effective system of property rights in the world. The Homestead Act of 1865 represented the United States Congress catching up with ground-level reality decades or even generations after the fact. The semi-literate pioneers had done the real, nuts-and-bolts work far in advance of the credentialed lawyers and legislators.

De Soto's book was originally written in Spanish, with the title, "El Misterio del Capital: ¿Por que el capitalismo triunfa en occidente y fracasa en el resto del mundo?" It is endorsed by Ronald Coase, Milton Friedman and Margaret Thatcher, among others.

- ## Thomas Sowell: "Basic Economics" (2015) and forty other titles

If you read none of the other books mentioned in this chapter, read this one. It is the best exposition of economics as it pertains to the citizen available, that I know of, written in non-technical language that the intelligent layperson can understand.

For the purpose of his common-sense layperson's book, Sowell defines economics as "the study of the use of scarce resources which have alternative uses." We don't live in the Garden of Eden. There is not enough of everything, whether bauxite or university economics course sections, to make everyone perfectly happy all the time. And if we could satisfy Susan in her appetite for ice cream, we might (in the short run, at least) have to deprive Janet of a certain amount of yogurt, unless Janet is willing to pay more to bid that use away from Susan's preference. Resources are scarce, and any one of them may be used in innumerable different ways, but typically only one way per unit of resource.

The principle of scarce resources which have alternative uses applies in many circumstances where no money is involved, such as medical supplies on a battlefield, where not only the quantity of resources is limited, but the probability of survival of the soldier receiving them. The implications of that simple expression can drive a lifetime of study. The refusal to acknowledge its central truth is the cause of every man-made disaster of history, the present day and the future.

Some more insights, courtesy of Sowell:

- o Price controls do not control prices.
- o Rent control does not control rent.
- o Public interest law firms do not serve the public interest.
- o For-profit companies lose money more often than they earn profits. Losses are at least as important as, and probably more important than, profits.
- o Not-for-profit organizations have to have an increase of revenue relative to expenses over the long term, just like for-profit corporations, or they eventually cease to exist, just like for-profit corporations.
- o Monopoly theory, upon which anti-trust regulation is based, is flawed in theory and bereft of supporting evidence in practice.

- o Regulations sold on the premise of preventing prices from rising are almost always, and deliberately, used to prevent prices from falling.
- o Minimum wage laws do not help the poor, especially young blacks, to earn more money.

Thomas Sowell would be a great, world-class economist, whether he were German, Russian or Chinese. The fact that he is American simply gives honor to America. The fact that he was born poor in rural North Carolina gives his work on wealth and poverty extra authority. And the fact that he is black and was educated in black public schools in Harlem during the 1940s serves both to enhance his credibility on matters of race while simultaneously exploding myths.

Sowell has been called "America's greatest living philosopher" by British historian Paul Johnson and others. In an article titled, "It's the Constitution, Stupid!,"[19] I advocated the adoption of seven new amendments. The last was the pinnacle:

Amendment 34: No person shall be found qualified to serve in either house of Congress, nor as a member of the federal judiciary including the Supreme Court, nor in a senior cabinet-level administrative position, nor as President or Vice President of the United States, who is unable to pass a factual examination on the contents of the book "Basic Economics" by Thomas Sowell.

Read it, know it, internalize it, then read it again. Then read "The Thomas Sowell Reader," gateway to his forty other works on economics, society, race, culture, migration and even child development. The crown jewel for the intellectually ambitious is "Knowledge and Decisions," inspired by a simple insight from Friedrich Hayek.

Above all, Sowell's writing on culture, history, geography, migrations, conquests and more exploded my mind, made me realize just how narrow and confined my understanding of the world and its history was. Through Sowell's work I came to appreciate how much more rich and vast the human pageant is

---

[19] http://www.citizenecon.com/2013/04/its-constitution-stupid.html

than the claustrophobic anti-American Marxist philosophy that my early mentors had provided me.

- ### David Horowitz: "Destructive Generation" (2005) and "Radical Son" (1998)

David Horowitz is the founder of the David Horowitz Freedom Center. From his page on FrontPageMag.com (where he is also a publisher), the DHFC publishes:

> David Horowitz was one of the founders of the New Left in the 1960s and an editor of its largest magazine, Ramparts. He is the author, with Peter Collier, of three bestselling dynastic biographies: The Rockefellers: An American Dynasty (1976); The Kennedys: An American Dream (1984); and The Fords: An American Epic (1987). Looking back in anger at their days in the New Left, he and Collier wrote Destructive Generation (1989), a chronicle of their second thoughts about the 60s that has been compared to Whittaker Chambers' Witness and other classic works documenting a break from totalitarianism. Horowitz examined this subject more closely in Radical Son (1996), a memoir tracing his odyssey from "red-diaper baby" to conservative activist that George Gilder described as "the first great autobiography of his generation."

Horowitz and Collier's works are among the primary sources for the chapter "Berkeley Redux," which follows this one, in which I review and re-interpret the events of the radical era of my hometown, which I had first outlined with minimal editorial comment in the chapter "Berkeley, California: My Home Sweet Home."

Piled Higher and Deeper (PhD)

That reading list should get you started on your way to earning your informal "degree" in Citizen Economics. The bottom line is this: all of those authors and their works did a far better job of explaining the world to me, and doing so in a rich, stimulating and mind-expanding way, than the socialist bromides and pieties and taboos had ever done for me at any time.

Berkeley Redux

With the benefit of my acquired conservative libertarian economic perspective, it is worthwhile to take a renewed look the events of the era and place from which I had naively emerged—the 1960s and 70s in general, and Berkeley in particular.

Radical Left vs. Liberal Left

Perhaps the most important insight from the study of this period is the sharp distinction to be drawn between the liberal Left and radical Left, and how this dynamic has played out in the ensuing campaigns and conflicts to the present day.

Throughout the heyday of the 60s movements, the battles, whether parliamentary or paramilitary, were not between Democrats and Republicans or between liberals and conservatives, but between the radical Left and establishment liberal Democrats. The term "liberal" in the context of the 60s meant a class of people who were comfortable with the government/university/corporate/military status quo, decidedly anti-communist. Their anti-communism was institutionalized in the Truman Doctrine more than McCarthyism. Their standard bearer and figurehead was President John F. Kennedy. In some ways, such as their positive view of America's role in liberating oppressed peoples around the world, they had more in common with what we more recently call neo-conservatives, than with the street protesters. At Berkeley, the liberals thus defined were represented by the administration in general and President Clark Kerr in particular. The professors came down on the side of the radical students, in one telling vote by a ratio of seven to one (begging the question of where the ideological impulses were really coming from).

Conservatives and/or Republicans were not entirely absent, of course. They had dominated the Berkeley city government for decades prior and sat on the university's well-heeled governing body, the Board of Regents. But their influence was waning, and they were less directly engaged than the establishment liberals, who effectively became the Right—the enemy to overcome—to the radical Left.

Red-Baiting Redux

It is tempting to "call a spade a spade" and say that they were all communists. But it is important to understand the difference between the New Left radicals of the 60s and the prior generation of American communists, even if the former's efforts to dissociate themselves from the latter turned out to be a futile exercise that came full circle in the 1980s.

The difference is captured in part in the famous 60s refrain, "You can't trust anyone over thirty," credited to Jack Weinberg of the Berkeley Free Speech Movement (the one held in the besieged police car on October 1-2, 1964). It is the expression of a youth movement, to be sure, but it goes deeper than that. The generation of American communists who came of age between the 1920s and the 1940s had always held the Soviet Union in highest esteem, considering it the vanguard of their worldwide movement, destined to overtake the United States in both power and general prosperity. American Leftists mercilessly ridiculed conservative's and Republican's concerns that the Leftists were loyal to and took their marching orders from Moscow to the point of treason. But then history, and more recently opened archives of the Soviet Union and its security arm, the KGB, have borne out the truth of many of the accusations.

These American communists endured over the years several severe challenges to the coherence and survival of their ideology and movement, from the murderous intrigue between Stalinists and Trotskyists (or "Trotskyites"), to the Hitler-Stalin pact, to the Nazi invasion of the Soviet Union, to the "treachery" of Whittaker Chambers, a once-communist who "turned" in a widely publicized memoir titled "Witness." But for the most part they closed ranks and held, even in the face of supposed "lies" about Stalin's purges of the 1930s, the starvation of Ukraine in which more people died than in all of the theatres of World War I, and the gulag archipelago of political prisons.

But in 1956 came a shock that the American communist movement could not survive intact. The premier of the Soviet Union and successor to Stalin himself, Nikita Khrushchev, denounced his predecessor for the crimes for which he had been accused, effectively admitting in a way that could not be spun away that the anti-communist anti-Soviets had been right all along. This revelation devastated the American Old Left, split communist communities, cells and families, set brother against brother and husband against wife.

And son against father. The generation coming of age in the late 50s and early 60s wanted nothing to with the crimes and failures of their parents. Or, at least, they didn't want to be stained with the dishonor of Stalin's crimes. For while they were disillusioned by the Soviet Union under Stalin, few of them made the leap to becoming pro-American pro-capitalists. From thence forward to this day radical Leftists insist that it is impossible and inappropriate to judge socialism by "actually existing" socialism, as opposed to the "true" socialism that they will finally succeed in building any day now, just around the corner.

And so, as David Horowitz put it, they invented a virgin birth for themselves. They disowned anything that might have gone wrong with the old Soviet Union before they were old enough to take any responsibility for it, and forged ahead undeterred with their Marxist-Leninist projects, disdaining the participation or advice of their elders, modifying their language from Marxist to liberal and "progressive."

This ability to start fresh, to never look back, gave the New Left the confidence that their generation would get things right, unlike their failed parents. But like restored virginity, after repeated cycles in the 60s, 70s and 80s, this ploy became evident to more and more for what it was: the inability to take responsibility—ever—for the real-world flesh-and-blood consequences of their social theories, to ever admit that they had been fundamentally wrong. Every time some third-world revolutionary hero that they backed in Asia, South America, Africa or even the United States would turn out to be a mass-murdering psychopath, they would simply move on and find a new beginning, a new generalissimo to champion. Love (of the abstract revolution) means never having to say you're sorry.

The Road to Serfdom

Insisting upon a distinction between liberal Left and radical Left is not to exonerate the former but rather simply to achieve greater clarity of understanding of what happened then and our predicament now. In light of the liberal versus radical Left division which characterized the upheavals of the Berkeley of my youth, one may fairly ask: why reject liberalism then? Why not just reject the proximate enemy of liberalism—Radical Leftism, Marxism, Leninism, Stalinism, Trotskyism, Maoism, Castroism—and re-embrace the (relatively) conservative political philosophy into which I was largely born? Why become an extremist? Why go whacko-tea-party-right-wing-nutcase on us?

The answer is that, apart from being nearly extinct in today's Democratic Party, I have come to believe that traditional establishment liberalism is fatally flawed, and those flaws are what caused it to be so ineffective against the radicals in the first place, and permitted the latter to take over the Party and eventually a majority of the nation's governing institutions in the second place.

I don't believe anymore that high taxes for the purposes of social or corporate welfare are a net benefit for the economy as a whole, least of all the poor. I have become convinced of the primacy of society separate from government; of the private entrepreneur and of private voluntary initiative and institutions, with neither privilege nor prejudice. These, not governmental power, result in the greatest prosperity to the greatest number (see "How Does Prosperity Happen?" and "The Entrepreneurial Cycle: From Scarcity to Abundance" in Part II for a more in-depth exposition).

The defining characteristics of contemporary liberalism, which are high taxes and the centralization of decision making, the top-down administration of economic activity, have the result of concentrating and amplifying power while reducing effectiveness and responsiveness to local or particular needs. This both increases the hazards of social conflict, where the desires of one group of citizens is given precedence by force over the preferences of other groups, and provides opportunities for ambitious men and women who crave power. Normal, humble and decent people do not lust for power over others;

avaricious people do. That is the central lesson of Friedrich Hayek's "The Road to Serfdom": that the worst men and women end up on top of power pyramids because they are the most strongly motivated by such enticements and most adept in the machinations of power. In this respect, the difference between the liberals and the radicals is one of degree, not kind; for all their supposed protests against power, hierarchy and conformity, the Leftists are the greatest creators of suffocating bureaucratic homogeneity ever. Signs carried by Free Speech Movement (FSM) protesters reading "Humanity or Unchecked Bureaucracy" ring hollow.

As for anti-corporatism, anti-corporate welfare and anti-crony capitalism (or more accurately, crony *socialism*), the Occupy Wall Street crowd needs to join the Tea Party. It is favoritism, "too big to fail" and excessive regulation that make corporations so much bigger and more prone to throw their weight around in the political arena than they would be in a free, truly capitalist market. If the smallest company that can survive in a particular industry has to hire a core of one hundred lawyers to ensure regulatory compliance and fight frivolous lawsuits, then only the biggest and baddest corporations can survive in that industry. It is government-chartered institutions like Fannie Mae and Freddie Mac that socialize the risks while privatizing the profits. It is "public-private partnerships" that create the rigged games in which the well-connected 0.001% make out like bandits at the expense of the 99.999%. Establishment liberalism has exacerbated rather than alleviated these challenges.

The answer, then, to "Evil Big Corporate America" is not socialism but a minimal interference in a libertarian political economy with neither privilege nor prejudice.

The Failures of Liberalism

Liberalism, and with it the Democratic Party, have been wandering in the wilderness for over forty years now because of its failure to differentiate itself from, and actively oppose, the radical Left.

Sincere liberals seem unable to do battle with radicals for three reasons:

- They accept too many of the radicals' premises, from the idea of the government as the appropriate arbiter of "social justice", to guilt over the accommodations they (the liberals) have made with American bourgeois values in their own lives, the feeling that the radicals are the "authentic" ones that they the liberals don't have the "courage" to be.

- They are cowardly afraid of being called the names that they abhor, such as "racist," "sexist," "imperialist," "homophobic," etc., and will grovel to any depth to avoid them, even if one radical faction damns them if they do while another damns them if they don't.

- They believe they have no alternatives because, in their minds, to seek common cause with or join conservatives or Republicans would be equivalent to joining Hitler and the Nazis (never mind that Hitler and his National Socialist German Worker's Party had at one time been the darling of international socialists before he "embarrassed" them).

The Content of Our Character

Heart surgery
Was first done successfully
By a black man

Friendly man who died
But helped the pilgrims to survive
Was a red man

Farm workers' rights
Were lifted to new heights
By a brown man

Incandescent light
Was invented to give sight
By the white man

We pledge allegiance
All our lives
To the magic colors
Red, blue and white
But we all must be given
The liberty that we defend
For with justice not for all men
History will repeat again
It's time we learned
This world was made for all men
Stevie Wonder, "Black Man"

Every race, every ethnicity, every nation has its heroes and its villains, its artists and its gangsters, its nobility and its thugs. The Italians have Luciano Pavarotti and John Gotti. The Scots-Irish have Elvis Presley and Timothy McVey[20]. For our society to live up to Martin Luther King's appeal to "the content of our character," we have to make distinctions between good and evil, beautiful and ugly, and act accordingly.

Vivien Thomas was a world-class pioneer in heart surgery in the 1940s, together with his longtime partner Alfred Blalock. Yet he struggled for years for recognition for his work because not only was he black, but he had not formally started, much less completed, medical school. Hired by a hospital to be a low-level technician, his improbable rise to partnership in the work of Dr. Blalock was entirely the result of applying his God-given intellect and showing up, observing, studying, participating, conversing and assisting under the supervision Dr. Blalock and other physicians. In other words, in a world that had effectively abolished the traditional apprenticeship, Thomas apprenticed to Blalock, eventually achieving the de facto status of peer. He was finally awarded an honorary doctorate and officially named an instructor of surgery for the Johns Hopkins School of Medicine at age sixty-five, thirty years after his groundbreaking work on open-heart surgery to treat Blue Baby Syndrome.

---

[20]   American terrorist who bombed the federal building in Oklahoma City, OK on April 19, 1995, killing 168.

If liberalism wishes to live up to its aspirations of honor and nobility, of human rights and justice for all men, or even just to ensure that medical and other sciences advance to give us all the miracles we depend upon for our lives, then it must strive to guarantee that the next Vivien Thomas should never go begging. It must ensure that the institutions that we construct—governmental, academic, professional—should facilitate and reward genius, invention, innovation, hard work and creativity no matter where it comes from, least of all excluding on the basis of race, ethnicity or national origin. In many ways, it has tried, but failure has followed on the heels of failure, as liberals seem unable to let go of their control-freak, Big-Brother-knows-best tendencies, and lack the capability to discern the difference between a Vivien Thomas (or a Ben Carson) and a street thug with a gift for inflammatory oratory. Instead, modern liberalism has built a world of metastasizing and evermore impenetrable bureaucracies, first implemented in government agencies and labor unions, and then imposed via regulations on private industries. More Americans, a higher percentage of the population than ever before, require a license from the government (the approval of authority) to practice their professions. Unions promote mediocrity at the expense of excellence. Corporate hierarchies limit the autonomy and accountability, and with it the creativity, of anyone working below the highest levels of what has come to be known as the "food chain." And liberalism seems to roll over and go comatose when black children in inner-city schools ruthlessly enforce a code of conduct among themselves not to deviate from self-destructive social norms, above all not to dare to "act white" by studying hard, being polite and considerate in class, speaking standard American English and striving for excellence and academic achievement.

Instead of celebrating and rewarding excellence, achievement and virtue, liberalism has in too many instances permitted radicals to elevate the basest elements of minority communities. For radicals, this is consistent with their anti-American, anti-integration/assimilation, anti-bourgeois and anti-capitalist ideology. For liberalism, this has corrupted and undermined their ability to build the harmonious society that they imagine will emerge when all vestiges public and private of racism, sexism, homophobia or other prejudice are purged from existence.

Thus did radicals first jettison Martin Luther King Jr. as their standard-bearer for social justice in general and progress for blacks in particular, and substitute in his place a descending order of rabble-rousers and thugs. Before the last echo of King's "I Have a Dream" speech had died out over the National Mall, and years yet before his assassination, the radical Left repudiated and renounced him, and elevated first Malcolm X of the Nation of Islam, then Stokely Carmichael of the Black Power movement and, eventually, the Black Panthers of Oakland, California, and its icons Eldridge Cleaver, Bobby Seale, George Jackson and above all, Huey Newton.

We Had a Dream

Liberals today are likely to assume (or accuse) that conservatives are racists because they don't support radical black activists and politicians and their policies and agendas. But this is a canard. Yes, many of the original Free Speech Movement students had volunteered for Martin Luther King in the South. But under the influence of radicals, King's influence waned. King's movement was (correctly) perceived to be essentially *conservative*, exhorting the nation to live up to its founding ideals and include everyone into the mainstream without regard to color. But this is not what the radical movement was about, it is not what Malcolm X, the black Muslim movement, the Black Power movement, the Black Panther party, the Weather Underground, the Symbionese Liberation Army or any other radical movement growing out of the 60s was about. The radical agenda was, and remains, changing America into something that it has never before been, of exacting revenge for real and perceived past grievances and for creating a distinctive and separate place of privilege for the leaders of the movement, with qualifications and credentials first measured by commitment to ideology, later to race and still later to sexual preference and/or gender identity. The president said it: It is about fundamentally transforming America.

It is a matter of serious debate whether Martin Luther King was a Republican or would be today. Whatever the case, it was the radical Left that denounced and renounced him before he was assassinated. And it is that radical Left that has had the greatest influence on the racial conversation of this country ever since, from Affirmative Action to Hands Up Don't Shoot, from the radical theories of Berkeley to the actual city politics practiced in Detroit and Washington D.C. (the municipality), to the #BlackLivesMatter Twitter hashtag movement. The disparate impact of social policies which have destroyed millions of black lives are not the natural outcome of Martin Luther King's civil rights movement or even of the segregationist policies that King opposed; they are the result of the toxic combination of liberal "compassion" through government welfare and radical politics that put the most outrageous political corruption beyond criticism or accountability, because its godfathers are black and therefore untouchable.

Here is the Black Panther's signature call/response chant, performed at public demonstrations in the 60s and 70s, standing or marching in formation in uniforms of black leather jackets, berets and dark glasses, sometimes holding shotguns:

> *Revolution has come! – Off the pig!*
> *Time to pick up the gun! – Off the pig!*[21]

The radical white intellectual elite Left bent over backwards to elevate Newton and the Panthers, deferring to them as the true vanguard and leadership of their movement. Liberal activists, politicians (like Governor Jerry Brown) and Hollywood types chimed in with public (taxpayers') and private donations to the organization and the community center and school that the Panthers established. Newton was hailed as a noble philosopher, by accident of birth and skin color born into an oppressive system in and for which violence had to be understood as his only recourse.

But Newton was a street thug, albeit a well-read and articulate one, and all that the Left's support and money did was to elevate him to the level of a Mafioso. The Black Panthers were a street gang elevated by Liberal-Leftist praise, influence and money to high respectability, but in reality to de facto status as a powerful organized crime syndicate. From the late 1960s to 1980, Newton and the Black Panthers would

---

[21]   "Off the pig," for the folks in Rio Linda, California, is a terse street-slang idiom signifying, "Let us—or anyone, for that matter—kill [Oakland] police officers whenever and wherever the opportunity arises. After all, they are no more worthy of humanitarian consideration than Nazi storm-troopers or the guards at Auschwitz." Remarkable how much meaning may be adeptly compressed into just three syllables.

be responsible for at least a dozen murders, including those of a police officer, a prostitute and an unknown number of their own "soldiers" suspected of collaborating with the police. Betty Van Patter, a white woman recommended to Newton as a bookkeeper by then-radical editor of *Ramparts* magazine (precursor to *Mother Jones*) David Horowitz, ended up floating on the opposite side of the San Francisco Bay, apparently for having asked too many probing questions about where the money was coming from and where it was going. Donations to the community center—arguably the most positive potential contribution to society made by the organization—went up Huey's and his friend's noses in the form of cocaine. The gang eventually even attempted to kill a woman who had been one of their most committed radical criminal defense attorneys—dedicated to them to the point of romantic and sexual involvement, even in prison—for the "crime" of refusing to aid and abet an attempted armed prison break attempt. Paralyzed by several bullets and in terrible chronic pain, Fay Stender participated in the successful prosecution—one of her few, if not only, prosecutions—of her would-be assailant, moved to Hong Kong and eventually committed suicide. Newton himself would ultimately be killed, not by an oppressor white police officer or FBI agent as his mythology would have written his destiny, but by a black drug dealer with whom he had had a "contractual dispute."

To believe that Huey Newton and his sometimes associates, sometimes mortal enemies, had no choice but to be and do as they were and did is to say that racism was more oppressive in the Bay Area than it was in the Jim Crow South, where it was ensconced in law. That doesn't pass the smell test.

Berkeley's Garfield Junior High School was renamed Martin Luther King, Jr. Junior High School. To get to school I rode my bike for part of the way on Martin Luther King, Jr., Way, renamed from Grove Street. Thus did Berkeley honor the civil rights leader almost immediately following his assassination. But by permitting the radical agitators of the race issue to define the parameters of public debate and political correctness, liberals—especially white liberals—put themselves in a schizophrenic bind. The black militants could criticize and repudiate King to their hearts' content, but no liberal could dare do so on pain of excommunication as "racist." But to embrace the radicals was to turn their back on King. And so, liberalism became trapped by its own confusion and lack of courage.

Not all liberal leaders have been ineffective against the radical racialists. Credit has to be given, oddly enough, to President Bill Clinton, for his neutering of rabble-rousers like the "Reverend" Jesse Jackson and the activist who achieved fifteen minutes of fame during the 1992 election cycle, going by the stage name "Sistah Souljah." Jesse Jackson never appeared so shaken and defeated as in one press conference early in 1993 where, having just conferred with the first lady at the White House, and apparently having been put in his place, he stammered her name as "Hillary *Rodman* Clinton."

Bill Clinton may or may not be a Marxist, but his political skills combined with his instincts for self-preservation—to pull back when he senses he has pushed too far—made of him a more pragmatic governor and president, negotiating in good (or at least practicable) faith with Republican Speaker of the House of Representatives Newt Gingrich on economic and tax policy and, on the third take, welfare reform. His lack of (radical) principles may be counted as virtues for what they are worth.

My Idols Reconsidered

To get inside the original zeitgeist of Berkeley in the 60s, to learn of the events of that time and how the participants understood them and perceived their own role in them, one of the best sources is the Leftist leaders' own self-congratulatory 1990 documentary film titled, remarkably enough, *Berkeley in the Sixties*, directed and produced by Mark Kitchell, co-written by Kitchell, Susan Griffin (who had been a founding member of the activist group SLATE) and Stephen Most. The film is narrated by Griffin and features interviews with several of the movement leaders themselves, twenty to thirty years after the fact, along with primary-source news footage of the era's major events, demonstrations and riots. Since these were the "heroes" thrust upon me as a young person without my informed or mature consent, I take here the opportunity to re-evaluate their movement and leadership from my evolved perspective.

First of all, the film has to be viewed with the awareness that many of these students and their fellow travelers went on to careers in politics and academia, some more successful than others, which collectively have fundamentally transformed if not all of America then certainly the Democratic Party and its agenda for the twenty-first century (a.k.a. Agenda 21). With the advantage of greater hindsight and mature conservative principles we may read between the lines and take the accolades with a grain of salt, if not a healthy dose of suspicion.

For example, all of the claims that the student leaders made in the demonstrations, in the documentary and in other recollections, have to be evaluated against their actions, now that they are no longer on the outside looking in but that they wield power from the inside top down in a majority of labor unions (public and private sector), administrative agencies, school boards, city halls, legislatures, the traditional press, broadcast media, university administrations, faculty lounges, the Supreme Court and even the White House.

The film opens with scenes of UC Berkeley students and others protesting across the bay in San Francisco, being dragged and pushed down the steps of city hall by police armed with clubs and fire hoses. The target of this protest was the hearings being held there of the House Un-American Activities Committee (HUAC), which was investigating communist influence in government, Hollywood and elsewhere, in 1960, years before the Free Speech Movement or JFK's moves into Vietnam. Susan Griffin narrates the scene, while Little Richard's upbeat "Keep a-knockin' (but you can't come in)" provides a festive background beat to an otherwise ugly spectacle:

"In the 1960s, my generation set out on a journey of change. Coming out of an atmosphere of conformity, a new spirit began to appear. One of the first signs was a demonstration organized by Berkeley students in May of 1960 against the House Un-American Activities Committee."

By opening with this scene they establish their point of reference— where they are coming from.

Conformity, and rebellion against the same, are favorite recurring themes for the 60s radicals. These students felt that the emerging knowledge economy that business guru Peter Drucker had written about just a few years earlier, and which UC President Clarke Kerr would laud in his speeches, was a trap, that the university was churning out robots—mindless IBM computer punch-cards with diplomas, feeding them into the military-industrial complex, washing out all attributes of individuality, creativity, freedom and justice. Just a few years earlier, William H. Whyte had written a book titled "The Organization Man," which spoke with alarm about the forces of conformity and sameness imposed in American corporate life with the too-willing acquiescence and approval of too many people. The book is a classic that sells well to this day.

Fair enough; we can agree that excessive conformity is un-American. I have written above about how bureaucratic institutions miss genius and crush creativity to the detriment of all of us. I will have more to say about this theme throughout this book. But now that the Left is in firm command of the government and its administrative agencies like the IRS, the EPA, the Department of Education, and the Department of Health and Human Services (HHS) with its signature mandate of Obamacare, has the Left brought us the Utopia of eliminated bureaucracy and liberation from conformity? What are the fruits today of their anti-conformism then? Answer: more conformity than ever, except that it is conformity with the norms and values that *they* command and approve. Revenge is sweet, I suppose; didn't realize that's what they were really after.

Moreover, the Left never owned any monopoly of concern on the issue of the country's economy and government becoming excessively dominated by the military-industrial complex. It was *Republican* President Dwight D. "Ike" Eisenhower who delivered a warning to the nation on this issue on the occasion of his farewell address in 1960.

Finally, the "atmosphere of conformity" of which Griffin speaks needs to be examined in the larger context of American history. What had the county gone through ten, twenty, thirty, one hundred, two hundred years earlier? Answers: The Korean War, World War II, the

Great Depression, the Civil War, and the American Revolution. Against that backdrop, compared with the sacrifices and suffering of prior generations, if your top complaint about America in 1960 was that it was too conformist, you might as well say it was the Golden Age.

Michael Rossman, one of the documentary's interviewees, made a comment on the Free Speech Movement which may be illuminating in this context: "Somewhere in the process of the FSM, for the very first time the young, privileged, affluent children of the culture began to see themselves as an oppressed class."

There may have been no one who expressed the spirit of rebellion (and, in my humble opinion, intellectual confusion) more forcefully than FSM leader Mario Savio, as exemplified by his speech on the steps of Berkeley's Sproul Hall on December 2, 1964, in response to the disciplinary action taken against leaders of the October 1 demonstration:

> We were told [probably meant to say "we asked"] the following: if President Kerr actually tried to get something more liberal out of the Regents in his telephone conversation, why didn't he make some public statement to that effect? And the answer we received, from a well-meaning liberal, was the following. He said, "Would you ever imagine the manager of a firm making a statement publicly in opposition to his board of directors?" That's the answer! Now, I ask you to consider, if this is a firm, and if the Board of Regents are the board of directors, and if President Kerr in fact is the manager, then I'll tell you something: the faculty are a bunch of employees, and we're the raw material! But we're a bunch of raw material[s] that don't mean to have any process upon us, don't mean to be made into any product, don't mean to end up being bought by some clients of the University, be they the government, be they industry, be they organized labor, be they anyone! We're human beings! [Rousing applause]

We're the raw material? No, you idiot(s), "we" students are the *customers*, who came here voluntarily, who wanted to be here in spite of having a thousand other choices all across the country and around the world. Indeed, "we" begged to get in, through a highly competitive admissions process. Many of "us" voluntarily paid handsomely for the *privilege* of coming here because we deemed what UC Berkeley had to offer to be of the highest quality and value.

This confusion is caused, again, by a colossal ignorance of economics, even among the educated classes, and even among the economics profession itself. Too many people believe that economics is just about money and materialism, market transactions and profits; it is not. Money comes only at the *end* of a long chain of analysis; it is not in any wise primary, and thinking that it is has led to innumerable catastrophes. Economics in the larger and truer sense is about people pursuing their interests according to their own values, in cooperation (or coercion) with other people, under the constraints of scarcity of both of the things that they want and of information about the things that they want, whether money is involved or not.

Ludwig von Mises understood the difficulty in defining economics to the public in this larger sense, and so he attempted to create terms which he thought better suited: "Praxeology" for the comprehensive study of human action, and "Catallactics" for the specific operations of markets and exchange. While these terms are utilized among economists of the Austrian school, they never made it into common popular usage (even Microsoft Word's spell-checker didn't recognize "Catallactics" when I typed it).

Calling students "customers" of the university may seem to cheapen the relationship, to express it in crass commercial terms. Acquiring an education is not the same thing as buying a gallon of gasoline, a Ford or a mortgage. Surely the value of a liberal arts education, imbued with an appreciation for the humanities, art, history, literature and culture, cannot be done justice in such vulgar terms as dollars and cents.

Nevertheless, in order to provide the buildings, classrooms, lecture halls, computers, laboratories and learned personnel qualified to teach all of the disciplines offered by the modern university requires setting aside tremendous quantities of resources for that purpose which could have been used for something else, but which presumably we value most in this use. The most effective and efficient way to produce and deploy these resources is through markets which provide information about the relative scarcities and abundances of products and services expressed in prices. And so, while the term "customer" as we know it does not seem to do the scholar-to-institution-of-higher-learning relationship justice, until we find a better one, it will have to do.

I attended five different universities during my undergraduate career before finally earning my B.A. (to the great relief of my parents), with a major in Music and significant concentrations in French and History. Yet for the discipline which eventually became my professional career, Information Technology, I took no undergraduate university classes at all, and just a handful in the MBA program I enrolled in later. Most of the classes I took in the field were offered by technology vendors—for-profit corporations. I got my foot in the door of this career by earning a Certified NetWare Engineer ("CNE") certification via classes, materials and exams offered by Novell Corporation. Similarly, over the years, I took classes and earned certifications from Oracle, Microsoft and Sun Microsystems. At none of these institutions was there ever a student protest demonstration, occupying the administration building, burnings in effigy of Bill Gates, Larry Ellison or Scott McNealy, rioting in the streets or police firing tear gas. The parameters of the relationship were clear: we were engaged in mutually beneficial voluntary exchange. If the relationship had been unsatisfactory in any way, either of the parties could have terminated it at any time with minimal fuss. If no one wanted to take these courses and exams, the vendors would have to adapt to the needs of the students or go out of business. The worst political harassment I was ever subjected to in this field were the hard-core communist rants of Steven Feuerstein, otherwise a worldwide guru of the very un-political discipline of Oracle PL/SQL programming.

As Ayn Rand pointed out in her essay, "The Cashing-In: The Student Rebellion," which specifically criticized the activities of the Free Speech (and the "Filthy Speech") Movement in Berkeley in 1964, the fact that the university is a public (i.e., government-run) institution, and that it has grown to such immense size, complicates the issue of private property but does not eliminate it. Mario Savio's indictment of the "firm" of UC Berkeley with the Board of Regents as the board of directors, professors as employees and university President Kerr as the manager is simply a narrow and ultimately ignorant reading of what those terms signify.

Savio isn't entirely ignorant, of course; he's disingenuous. As a virtuoso leader of a mass movement, he knows perfectly well the intricacies of organizational structure and parliamentary procedure and how models and protocols of organization must of necessity be applied to different types of entities. His indictment of the University as a corporation with a capitalist organizational structure is sophisticated demagoguery.

Savio continued:

> There is a time when the operation of the machine becomes so odious, makes you so sick at heart, that you can't take part! You can't even passively take part! And you've got to put your bodies upon the gears and upon the wheels . . . upon the levers, upon all the apparatus, and you've got to make it stop! And you've got to indicate to the people who run it, to the people who own it, that unless you're free, the machine will be prevented from working at all.

Eloquent. But, then again, any kindergarten kid in the sandbox who has just had his toy truck taken away could say (or at least feel, which is what counts most to liberals) the same thing. So, for that matter, could a grassroots Tea Party group leader who is dealing with a politically vindictive IRS. Was Savio truly speaking in terms of universal principles? What matters is the *substance* of your grievance, the question of whether it has merit. "Unless you're free"? Savio and his cohort are among the freest human beings ever to walk the Earth, as are most Americans—even those of us who didn't attend elite universities.

In hindsight, how shall we judge men like Mario Savio and, more importantly, what lessons should we learn from their lives and leadership?

One of the most important questions facing anyone seriously grappling with any matter of philosophy or religion is one of verification. How can we be sure something or someone is what it purports to be, is true or correct, or not? Jesus warned against the potential for deceit when he said in Matthew 7:15: "Beware of false prophets, which come to you in sheep's clothing, but inwardly they are ravening wolves." In the very next verse, he answers the question more eloquently than it has ever been answered: "Ye shall know them by their fruits."

Or, as Thomas Sowell or his mentor George Stigler might put it, "And *then* what will happen?" In other words, in order to judge someone's words, advocacy or advice, what's needed is to think through the arguments to their logical conclusions. If we follow Mario Savio, or Jimmy Carter, or Ronald Reagan, or Margaret Thatcher, or Barack Obama, or Hillary Clinton, where will it lead? After we have adopted their philosophies and implemented their policies, what will happen next, and after that, and after that?

In the case of Savio, it led, among other things, to the following honor, as reported by Wikipedia[22]:

> A Memorial Lecture Fund was set up to honor Mario Savio upon his death [in 1996]. The MSMLF hosts an annual fall lecture on the University of California, Berkeley campus. Past lecturers include Howard Zinn, Winona LaDuke, Lani Guinier, Barbara Ehrenreich, Arlie Russell Hochschild, Cornel West, Christopher Hitchens, Adam Hochschild, Amy Goodman, Molly Ivins, Jeff Chang, Tom Hayden, Angela Davis, Seymour Hersh, Robert F. Kennedy, Jr., Naomi Klein, Elizabeth Warren, Robert Reich, and Van Jones.

Not too many conservative Republicans or Tea Party activists in that group. Apparently, only Leftists are to be celebrated for putting their bodies against the gears.

Red-Baiting

There are plenty of people of goodwill, who are not hard Leftists, who feel that the House Un-American Activities Committee (HUAC) represented a low point in America's repression of innocent people, the manifestation of despised McCarthyism (named after the senator who made at times reckless accusations against many of his colleagues in the 1950s), to be buried alongside slavery, imperialism and the persecution of women, minorities and gays. But perhaps with the distance of time, a less emotionally charged analysis may be made.

In any time of conflict, mistakes and excesses are committed and innocent people get hurt, by the "good guys" as well as the bad. To say

---

22   https://en.wikipedia.org/wiki/Mario_Savio

the least, liberals and Leftists cannot claim to be exempt from guilt of collateral damage; to the contrary. So while some of the actions of HUAC and Senator McCarthy may have crossed the line from legitimate to erroneous to grievous, the question that remains is, was the whole enterprise unjustified? That is, was opposition to communism fundamentally misguided? Historian W. J. Rorabaugh makes the point more than once in his book[23] that Republicans and conservatives in Berkeley were out of touch with the times, carping about communism long after it had ceased to be relevant. This in the very early 60s, barely a moment past the construction of the Berlin Wall (which is to say, the conversion of East Berlin, if not all of Eastern Europe, into the world's largest maximum security prison) and almost thirty years before the same would be torn down after a long, exhausting struggle.

Communism is a political ideology with many flavors, variations and factions, many of which have waged bloody wars against each other but which share many common traits. It originated in the main with Karl Marx and Friedrich Engels and was put into practice by Vladimir Lenin and Joseph Stalin in the Soviet Union since 1917, by Mao Zedong in the People's Republic of China since 1949, the North Korean regime since 1950, Ho Chi Minh in Vietnam in the 1950s and 60s, Fidel Castro in Cuba since 1958, Pol Pot in Cambodia in the 1970s, and many others. The distinction that I draw between socialism as an economic system and Communism as a political one is that the latter tolerates no dissent whatsoever. People who stand in the way of "the people" (defined in the extreme abstract by the power elite) and their charismatic leader are arrested, fined, sentenced to labor camps such as the Gulag Archipelago or executed. Tens of millions of people, perhaps as many as *200 million people*, were murdered by communist regimes in the twentieth century. The indictments of slavery and persecution of the Native Americans, the poor, women, minorities and gays in the U.S. do not hold a candle to the crimes committed against humanity by the communists around the world. Already by 1950, the horrors of the Stalinist death camps were sufficiently well-known for people to be concerned about any possibility that the ideology or its policies and methods could take hold at home.

---

[23]   Rorabaugh, W. J. *Berkeley at War: The 1960s*. New York, NY: Oxford University Press, 1989.

94

In other words, Communism was, and remains, a terrible monstrosity to be feared and opposed by any rational, freedom-loving and compassionate people. The fact that some people took the threat seriously and took action first to evaluate its influence and second to root out that influence is not to be lamented. What is lamentable is how many people cannot see with their open eyes what a path we are being led down today by a Democratic Party completely in thrall to the radical Left, barely hiding, in plain sight.

From HUAC through FSM

Among the Berkeley radical student movement leaders' strongest claim to noble virtue is their stand for civil rights and free speech, the Bill of Rights and, by extension, the Constitution—patriotic, red-white-and-blue virtues. During the HUAC protests they sang "The Star-Spangled Banner." Above all they carried their activities and successes in securing greater civil rights for Negroes and other minorities as badges of honor. Student Art Goldberg (brother of Jackie) comments in one scene from 1964 that student groups that didn't normally speak to one another, such as the Youth for Goldwater and the Young Socialist Alliance, were forming a coalition for purposes of coordinated action on at least one issue. "I'm proud to say that American students are united on one issue, and that's the First Amendment privileges of Freedom of Speech, the right to advocate, discuss, at any time and any place as long as it doesn't disturb classes and interfere with traffic."

As long as it doesn't disturb or interfere. But when Dr. Edward Strong, Chancellor of the Berkeley campus, addressed the Sproul Hall sit-in demonstrators on December 2, 1964, with the aid of a bullhorn, saying—intended as preamble to his main remarks—that "this assemblage has developed to such a point that the purpose and work of the university have been materially impaired," the crowd of demonstrators broke out into spontaneous and raucous applause. When an administrator, addressing the December 7, 1964, outdoor convocation in the Greek Theater amphitheater, said, "There are a small number of individuals, I regret to say, who are interested in fomenting a crisis merely for the sake of crisis," the crowd of students again cheered in approbation of the foment. Interfering with traffic and more was very much the movement leaders' intention.

The fact is that all sides committed their share of innocent and malicious mistakes. The HUAC responses to the protests in San Francisco were inept, starting with holding the hearings there in the first place and including producing the anti-communist exposé film *Operation Abolition* that was so poorly directed and produced that the Leftists were able to use it for their own propaganda advantage and recruitment purposes. Blunders on the part of the university administration in general and UC President Clark Kerr in particular led to escalations of tensions and conflict rather than expedited resolutions. As Rorabaugh put it in his characteristically unbiased, dispassionate and impartial tone, "Throughout this period administrators resembled nothing so much as a group of five-year-olds gleefully tossing lighted matches into a jug of gasoline." But the crimes of the administration seem to have been less a true cause of grievance to the activists than as an intentionally provoked gift to be exploited to the activists' advantage. Speaking of glee, former FSM leader Jackie Goldberg can barely contain hers in her interview as she beams, "*Fortunately* the university committed another atrocity!" (My emphasis). Jackie Goldberg went on to serve on the Los Angeles City Council, in the California State Assembly and the Los Angeles School Board.

The film skips over the "Filthy Speech Movement" of early 1965, initiated when a student publicly and prominently displayed a sign with the "F" word scrawled on it on the steps of the Student Union. You can read about that in W. J. Rorabaugh's book (pp. 38-41) and in Ayn Rand's aforementioned critique. (Maybe the film skipped that episode because it was bipartisan; a conservative student group had had signs printed with slogan—fully spelled out—"F--- Communism".) In any case, the radical students (and the film director) had bigger fish to fry, which they took no time getting to.

"1, 2, 3, What Are We fighting For?"

> *1, 2, 3, what are we fighting for?*
> *Don't ask me, I don't give a damn*
> *Next stop is Vietnam*
> *And it's 5, 6, 7, Open up the pearly gates!*
> *Well, there ain't no time to wonder why*
> *Whoopee! We're all gonna die!*
> Country Joe and the Fish

That "bigger fish," of course, was protesting the war in Vietnam. Jentri Anders, one of the film's interviewees, quotes Mario Savio giving another speech on Sproul Plaza at a moment in 1965 where all of the tumult of the FSM and resulting trials seemed to be resolved, when life seemed ready to go back to normal: "Now, don't everybody go walking away, because we've still got a war to stop."

The transition in the film is as breathtaking as Ander's own shocked reaction. From one moment to the next, the entire tone changes. Suddenly, the United States is, and implicitly has always been, the most evil, murderous, genocidal, racist and imperialist nation on Earth.

Scenes of American soldiers burning villages and peasants weeping in terror of the occupying G.I. Joes are set to a moralistic speech by Students for a Democratic Society (SDS) president Paul Potter on Vietnam Day, May 1965:

> Most of us grew up thinking that the United States was a great and humble nation that only involved itself in the affairs of other countries reluctantly and as a last and final resort. But now the war in Vietnam has provided the incredibly sharp razor that has finely separated thousands and thousands of people from their illusions about the morality and integrity of this country's purposes internationally. Never again will this self-righteous saccharine moralism of promising a billion dollars of economic aid while we spend billions and billions of dollars to destroy them, never again will that moralism have the power to persuade people of the essential decency of this country's aims. What kind of a system is it that allows decent men, good men, to make the decisions that have led to the thousands and thousands of deaths that have happened in Vietnam? What kind of a system is it that justifies the United

97

States seizing the destinies of other people and using them callously for our own ends? We must name that system, and we must change it and control it, else it will destroy us.

So America's war in Vietnam, in which the United States took over from a defeated French colonial power to hold the line against global communist hegemony, the latter supported in various and alternating degrees by the Soviet Union, where Ho Chi Minh received his training, and the People's Republic of China, is not just an ill-advised adventure or a poorly planned fiasco; it's not even just plain wrong on its own merits, bad enough as that would be. *It exposes the inherent, pre-existing and irredeemable evil of the United States of America.*

Is that what liberals bought into when they opposed the war? People of goodwill may have disagreements and many honorable Americans opposed the American war in Vietnam, including Martin Luther King, Jr., the famous "Baby Doctor" Benjamin Spock and others. But for the Hard-Left radicals, it was never about the war or anything else that they claimed as their grievance. The war was their *opportunity* to win more people, including well-intentioned liberals, to their side, the side of anti-American revolution.

First they sued to "bring the troops home." Then they agitated to bring the *war* home, to the streets of America's cities. They would celebrate the defeat and humiliating withdrawal of America from Southeast Asia. And they would pile excuse upon excuse for the atrocities committed by the communists in the aftermath of that defeat.

If the issue were the issue, if the radical leaders of the antiwar movement were as sincere and principled as they postured to be, then they would be concerned about any violence, excesses or atrocities committed by any of the parties to the conflict. Instead, they demonstrated in the subsequent years and decades a remarkable consistency: America is always in the wrong, and America's enemies are always in the right. And so, following the fall of Saigon in 1975, when news of the persecution and trials of non-communist South Vietnamese by the communist regime began leaking out in testimonies of the Boat People, folk singer Joan Baez, who had been among the war protesters from the beginning, attempted to organize a protest to appeal to the conscience of the Vietnamese communist regime. She was shouted down by the radicals including Tom Hayden and Jane Fonda (about which more anon) and her efforts for peace and humanitarian activism on the other side went nowhere.

SDS and Tom Hayden

The Students for a Democratic Society (SDS), whose president could speak in such unequivocally anti-American terms to such an acquiescing audience, were a radical Leftist front group which had published in 1962 the "Port Huron Statement," authored by member Tom Hayden, at the University of Michigan at Ann Arbor. The Port Huron Statement was a political manifesto which, more than any other document, accomplished the aforementioned "virgin birth" of the New Left, dissociating it with the old guard communists and their stain of Stalinism, while rededicating itself to causes in the main inspired by Marxism-Leninism, clothed in the wool of "Progressivism" and liberal vocabulary.

Tom Hayden is one of the key radical activists of the 60s and 70s who is largely neglected by Kitchell and Griffin's film. Hayden had visited UC Berkeley in 1960 and modelled another student organization, VOICE, at UMAA after Berkeley's SLATE. He would have a long and storied career, serving in the California State Assembly from 1982 to 1992, in the State Senate from 1992 to 2000. But before that, his anti-Vietnam War activities, together with his once girlfriend and wife, movie-star actress Jane Fonda, are the stuff of legends. Together they travelled to North Vietnam, while the war was still on, to toast the enemy and generate sympathy for the cause of people who were actively engaged in war against American soldiers.

In the summer of 1968 the Democratic National Convention was disrupted by anti-Vietnam War protests, largely organized by Hayden and SDS. The film seems to paper over the deliberate provocation to violence, merely playing one speaker on the floor of the convention saying, "Thousands of young people are being beaten in the streets of Chicago." Instead, John Gage laments: "We . . . did not anticipate the arbitrary exercise of authority that Mayor Daly would bring to bear in Chicago . . . There was a side of politics in America that was vicious and violent, and that's what we saw in Chicago. Mayor Daly rolled over the antiwar forces. And it was the destruction of the Democratic Party . . . It seemed impossible that there could be any significant electoral path toward ending the war following the convention."

Susan Griffin: "The violence in Chicago triggered confrontations on campuses across the country."

Whose violence? The police? Or Tom Hayden and the calculated, violent provocation of the police? With all due respect to the honorable John Gage, his view seems naïve. The radical Left, represented by Hayden and his cohort, had no interest in preserving the viability of America's democratic and constitutional institutions. They wanted chaos and confusion, they provoked it and they got it. The events that followed played into their hands. The failure of liberals like Gage to see, even twenty years after the fact, how they had been manipulated by the radicals on their left flank, is the perfect example of what has been wrong with the liberal Democrat wing of American politics for the past forty years[24].

As for SDS, it would wind down in 1969, but not before spawning the metastasized Weather Underground, led by William "Billy" Ayers and Bernardine Dohrn. Their exploits were described briefly earlier in this book.

Bring the War Home

The Vietnam War was the first war whose images and sounds were brought directly into average American homes daily via television, and they were shocking. There was a sense among many people that nothing could possibly be worse than what we were doing there.

The Vietnam War having turned out the way it did, it may be natural to judge that it had always been, at best, futile. But that begs the

---

[24]   John Gage is one of the most conservatively appearing, soft-spoken interviewees in the film. He had worked on the Robert F. Kennedy campaign, later McGovern; he was critical of violent street protest tactics, advocated for change through the conventional electoral process and, years later, became an executive at the Silicon Valley high-tech corporation Sun Microsystems. In other words, he is one of the Knowledge Workers that UC President Kerr had lauded, and a liberal Democrat, like my parents—and me until 1991 or so.

question, why wasn't the war in Korea of 1950-1953 equally futile? That war also pitted hardcore communists who dominated the northern part of their country (closest to its patron, the Maoist People's Republic of China) against the more Western democracy-oriented South. Since that war had been fought to a draw, splitting the country in half at the thirty-eighth parallel, history provides us an almost laboratory case study to judge which system, communism or constitutional democracy, has been most successful. The North to this day is a Stalinist hellhole of stunted development, starvation and repression. But the South has thrived, not just surviving but becoming a world-class international economic powerhouse, nearly peer to Japan (up from the ashes of complete defeat at the hands of the U.S). Is that what SDS president Paul Potter meant when he said "seizing the destinies of other people and using them callously for our own ends"?

There is no doubt that thousands of innocent Koreans were caught in the crossfire and killed or injured. If in 1951 the suffering of these Koreans had been brought into American living rooms on a daily basis, if Senator McCarthy had already been disgraced and repudiated, if the Leftist student movement had been more further advanced in its development, then would an anti-Korean War movement have arisen to compel MacArthur's and Truman's troops to withdraw completely? (The movie and television series "M.A.S.H.," of which I was a regular fan during the 1970s, was, in part, an attempt to apply the Leftist morality of the Vietnam War retroactively to the Korean War.) In that case we would have today one Korea—one that resembles the actually existing North Korea far more than it would the South.

Whether the war in Vietnam could have had an outcome more like that of the Korean War is probably unanswerable. But one thing is certain: the Truman Doctrine under which we held the line against communism in Korea infuriated the Left, and their inability to do anything substantial against it was a major humiliation for them. With Vietnam, they got their revenge.

The Korean War was a terrible event that claimed the lives of 36,000 American soldiers and approximately two million Koreans and Chinese, three-quarters of them enemy combatants. But these terrible facts by themselves do not mean that the entire enterprise was futile. What must be considered are the alternatives actually available at the time, and everywhere that we have seen communism triumph, the alternatives have been manifestly worse[25].

In spite of the horrors that followed the American retreat from Vietnam, the radical Left has in the main been successful in maintaining the dominant doctrine of American foreign policy of "No more Vietnams," which stands in stark contrast to "No more Munichs," referring to the catastrophic appeasement of Adolf Hitler committed by British Prime Minister Neville Chamberlain in 1936, with the approval of all Leftists and most liberals in the West at the time.

The Panthers

There is coverage in the documentary film of the Black Panther movement. In Susan Griffin's words, "The Black Panthers came forward as the cutting edge of Black Power. Their militancy had a magnetic effect on the student movement."

Michael Rossman recalls: "We want the Panthers to be our friends. We want to follow their lead; in some fashion that's confusing, that's mysterious, all we are aware of, we want to go Black and White together into some kind of positive future against the oppressor who's feeling ever-more oppressive."

The film relates matter-of-factly that the student movement rallied behind Huey Newton in his trial for the murder of Oakland police officer John Frey, a charge for which there was credible evidence of Newton's guilt. The trial of former Panther David Hilliard is dismissed as simply "part of a government program to destroy the Panthers." In addition, the film papers over their internal divisions. Bobby Seale, one of the founders in 1966, is interviewed for the documentary in 1989-90 (Huey Newton, the longtime leader, at times in exile, died in 1989). While Seale regales in recounting the heroics of those heady early days, neither he nor the director or narrator mention the fact that Seale

---

[25]   I remember discovering a memorial to the Americans who served in Korea on the campus of Berkeley High School shortly after enrolling there in tenth grade. No doubt it had been dedicated prior to the 1960s. No ceremony was held or attention paid to the memorial by the faculty or administration during my tenure there that I can remember.

himself, although a prominent politician, had fled into hiding in the mid-1970s to avoid being murdered by his former partners.

The most honest assessment of the Panthers and their mesmerizing effect upon the Berkeley radicals comes from Michael Rossman, whose interview audio is played over scenes of a multiracial "Free Huey! Off the Pig!" rally: "The Panthers exercised a heavy influence in the *imagination* [my emphasis] of the White Left, partly because the White Left was confused about who it was and what it ought to do. They were fascinated by this tough macho image and they followed it, not so much willfully but involuntarily because *it was the projection out there of the thing in their own actions that thrilled them most*" [my emphasis again]. Even so, Rossman hedges in a convoluted argument to suggest that the Panthers "seemed worse than they [really] were" because of media sensationalism which gave the public the very image that the Panthers wanted to project and actively promoted. Huh?

Prague Spring

From there, the film shows images of disturbances occurring nearly simultaneously around the world in 1968, in France, Japan and Mexico. Included in this sequence are scenes from the Prague Spring, where Soviet tanks are crushing a pro-democracy rebellion by one of the Soviet Union's Eastern European satellites Czechoslovakia, just as they had in Hungary in 1956 just after the Khrushchev Report. But this uprising was of an entirely different nature, a rebellion against communism, which is inappropriately conflated with radical Leftist and student movements occurring contemporaneously in Western and Western-oriented nations, Jack Weinberg's glib equating notwithstanding.

Women's Liberation

The film's exposition on the women's liberation movement that budded in the late 1960s provides an interesting insight: again, it wasn't a clash between liberals and conservatives, but a revolt of young women within the radical left student movement getting sick of being gofers and taken for granted by the male leadership of the same movement.

The film's treatment of the women's liberation movement that emerged toward the end of the 1960s is revealing. Liberal mythology today would have most of us believe that women's liberation was a rebellion of liberal women against conservative, patriarchal society and that their movement had a direct lineage to the one spearheaded by Susan B. Anthony. But the proximate cause of their discontent, as expressed in their interviews for the film, was the condescension they perceived coming from their fellow radical male colleagues.

Conservative and Republican women seemed not to have this problem. Liberals may explain this away as conservative women being too oppressed and lacking in self-esteem to speak up. But an alternative explanation is possible: women on the Left were more likely than their sisters on the right to embrace the sexual revolution of the sixties that followed the invention of "the pill", with all of its libertine excesses. Maybe there is something in human nature (liberals hate that) which causes men to respect less the women that they consider too "easy." Could it be? Just asking.

As for Susan B. Anthony, she was a Republican (like her personal friend and Rochester, New York, neighbor Frederick Douglass), voted (illegally, in civil disobedience) Republican, dressed conservatively and urged her disciples to do likewise. And opposed abortion. Not quite the liberal Leftist icon.

People's Park

Mario Savio, who had always sported a clean-cut and clean-shaven appearance during the Free Speech Movement, reappeared during the People's Park controversy in a full hippie beard and slightly out-of-control (although already thinning on top) hair. His Marxist foundations showed through even more than they had during the prior events: "Property is not a thing to keep men apart and at war, but rather a medium by which men can come together to play—a People's Park."

So, with a wave of the hand, the entire institution of private property is dismissed as "a thing to keep men apart and at war." More people died in the twentieth century as a result of the ruthless enforcement of that notion than perhaps from any other cause.

Jack Weinberg, in his interview on People's Park, also reveals his Marxist roots, describing what the hippies were doing as "production for use rather than production for profit." The conceit, of course, is that under Capitalism, industry just produces stuff nobody can or wants to use, but they still manage to earn profits doing so. See "Human Needs Before Profits" in Part II for an in-depth examination of this fallacy.

Equal Time

The filmmakers did occasionally allow opposing views, and at times very insightful and true ones as that, to be played.

UC President Clarke Kerr states, "One of the most distressing tasks of a university president is to pretend that the protests and outrage of each new generation of undergraduates is really something fresh and meaningful. In fact, it is one of the most predictable controversies that we know. The participants go through a list of hackneyed complaints almost as ancient as Academe, while believing that what is said is radical and new." No doubt he won no friends among the radical student leadership with that dismissal of their grand visions of themselves. Then again, maybe it's just that the truth hurts.

There are a number of scenes featuring Ronald Reagan worth repeating here. For example, as candidate for Governor of California in 1966, he says, "It began a year ago when the so-called free-speech advocates, who in truth have no appreciation for freedom, were allowed to assault and humiliate the symbol of law and order of policemen on the campus, and that was the moment when the ringleaders should have been taken by the scruff of the neck and thrown out of the university once and for all."

...which drew responses from the film's interviewees, like this one from Michael Rossman: "He won by pandering to a citizenry that was outraged by what these terrible, ungrateful, insolent children were doing on the campuses." Substitute "appealing" for the gratuitously condescending "pandering," and that's about right.

Or, this one by Jentri Anders: "Ronald Reagan walked onto the political stage as a candidate for Governor in 1966. During the campaign he found that attacking what he called 'the mess at Berkeley' pleased the crowds." Translation: just having lived in California in the 1960s didn't make you a radical Leftist. There were plenty of conservatives, Republicans and reasonable liberals there at that time as well who were alarmed at what was going on in Berkeley and looking for leadership to deal with it appropriately. A public opinion poll taken in 1965 showed that three-quarters of Californians were opposed to what the radical students were doing in Berkeley.

Another example of an articulate conservative who made the documentary director's cut was John de Bonis, a Berkeley City Councilman, on the People's Park incident: "The Park issue is not the issue. The issue is, we must have a confrontation, a confrontation throughout the summer. They were out of confrontation issues. And as soon as you give them a park, they will dream up another confrontation. We have been invaded by people outside of the state, by people outside of the city, we have been invaded by militants. We are in a revolution . . . Now the question is, who is going to win it?"

Just prior to that, the one time in the film that an on-camera microphone is given to a conservative young woman, she had this to say about People's Park: "Roger Hines and the Regents and Ronald Reagan can't allow this to go on. If, um, there's one 'liberated territory,' people may get the idea that there can be other liberated territories."

The viewer must pay close attention to the voices that rarely get heard, what President Richard Nixon called the "silent majority." In Baltimore Maryland in 2015 they were the shopkeepers and business owners whose property was damaged or destroyed by the rioting and looting, with no high-profile campaign of sympathy supporting them, no members of the Congressional Black Caucus beating their chests on the floor of the House or in front of C-SPAN or CNN cameras on their behalf, even though the majority of the business owners are black. In Berkeley too, during at least one of the riot scenes, you can catch

106

for less than two seconds the image of a middle-aged non-political store owner frantically cranking the metal roller shutters of her shop closed to protect it from damage in the incipient People's Park riot. There would be no marches on her behalf, no protests in support of her civil—much less private property—rights. Yet many innocent people, black and white, of very modest means, had their property trashed by idealistic crusaders pinning medals of honor on each other's chests.

In the immediate aftermath of the People's Park riot, Governor Reagan met with the members of the University faculty. The documentary presents this scene:

Governor Reagan: "Those people told you for days in advance that if the university sought to go ahead with that construction on that property that they were going to physically destroy the university. Now, why did you—"

Professor: (inaudible, many speaking simultaneously) ". . . offered to negotiate, many times."

Reagan: "Negotiate? What is to negotiate? What is —" (Many talking) "Don't you—wait a minute! On that issue, don't you simply explain to the students that the university has a piece of property that it bought, for future construction of the campus, and that it was now going ahead with the plan? What do you mean, 'negotiate'?"

Professor: "Governor Reagan, the time has passed when the university can just ride roughshod over the desires of the majority of its student body. The university is a public institution . . ."

(Cut to a few minutes later) Governor Reagan: "All of it began the first time that some of you who know better, and who are old enough to know better, let young people think that they had the right to choose the laws they would obey as long as they were doing it in the name of social protest."

Then he got up and left.

When I had seen this film for the first time, when it was in its first run in theatres in 1990, in Santa Monica (a colonial outpost of Berkeley, thanks to Tom Hayden and others), I remember seeing someone sitting near me turn to his neighbor and say, "He's a fascist!"

John Searle, professor of philosophy at UC Berkeley (and active participant in at least the anti-HUAC demonstrations of 1960 in San Francisco, already as a professor then), perceived the deliberate provocation in the People's Park incident: "The fact remains that at bottom I believe the People's Park incident was extremely cynical on the part of the demonstrators. They *wanted* [my emphasis] a confrontation. What mattered was getting people out in the streets demonstrating." And later: "There was no vision, no articulate philosophy, no conception of social organization and social change. What there were, were a series of emotional moments, a series of passions, a series of desperately important issues. But you can't beat something with nothing. If you are going to fight this kind of long cultural battle, you really are bound to lose if you don't have a coherent, articulate, well worked-out vision of what you're trying to do, and that they didn't have."

But most of the views expressed are of the liberal or Radical-Left variety.

Susan Griffin: "The radicals of Berkeley and the hippies of Haight-Ashbury had a natural affinity. We were visionaries, critical of conventional society . . . In the 60s, we came at a certain point in the Cold War to reject the ideologies of both sides. And our declaration of freedom was a political freedom, but it had a larger dimension, that is, the freedom of imagination."

Both sides of the Cold War were equally wrong? To fail to distinguish between the imperfect and the evil may be forgivable in youth, but it is accessory to evil in adulthood. And regarding imagination, the Left has no monopoly except to the extent that it strives to *shut down* any creativity that it doesn't pre-approve (oxymoron) from the top of its now-entrenched bureaucratic redoubts.

Alienation

Jentri Anders: "[San Francisco] hippies exposed the chasm between our parents' generation and our own. By 1966, more of us were turning on [taking drugs], tuning in and dropping out. Our alienation ran much deeper than political protest."

Frank Bardacke on the anti-Vietnam War movement in 1967: "We were becoming much more alienated from American society and much more willing to be disruptive of that society. And, basically, we began moving to the view that we wanted to make the cost of pursuing the war abroad the un-governability of the society at home."

Jackie Goldberg seems to dissent with this characterization, saying, "The thing that irritated me the most in the stuff that came out about that period was the description of us as alienated and cynical. We were the absolute antithesis of that. We were so committed and so involved, we risked our careers, we risked our jobs, our education, and we did it because we were so tied into this system, to this country, to this culture. We believed in it so much that we were willing to take those risks at a time that it wasn't so popular to do so."

But Jentri Anders uses the word. And then, she displays the magnitude of their self-aggrandizing conceit:

> We were all beginning to see that it was much, much bigger than the war; it was much, much bigger than the civil rights movement. There were major things wrong, and I think the people who got involved in the counterculture on some level perceived that they did not want to be a part of what was wrong with a culture that was destroying the world . . . The point is that it was the culture that was sick. It was the whole American way of looking at things that was sick. And so, I think that we came to a realization that one way to change that is just to live it differently. Instead of trying to change the structure in a direct, confrontational way, you just drop out and live it the way you think it ought to be.

These words of wisdom are played over images of hippies going about their countercultural lifestyle in the Haight-Ashbury district of San Francisco, and followed by a scene apparently intended to drive the point home of what some people in that culture thought was the appropriate way to "just drop out and live it the way you think it ought to be." We see many hippie types milling about in a park-like setting, and a traditional, "square," middle-aged television journalist is attempting to interview a long-haired and peach-fuzz-bearded young man who is playing an ocarina (a short, stubby flute-like instrument made from clay or ceramic).

Journalist: "You don't play anything besides the sweet potato?"

Musician [letting his instrument out of his mouth and turning to the journalist with a glazed-eyed marijuana smile]: "Just the drums. Conga drums. And the . . . trumpet! Yeah. And I goupinthemountainsandyell now and then."

Journalist: "You . . . do what?"

Musician: "Go up in the mountains and yell. Go up in the high in the mountains and yell, as hard as I can."

Journalist: "What's the purpose of that?"

Musician: "Well, to greet the dawn, to greet the noonday sun and to greet the sunset."

Journalist: "You mean you stay up there all day, yelling morning, noon and night."

Musician: "Right. And standing on my head, and making gardens and . . . painting pictures."

Journalist: "Meaning you not only play the sweet potato, you also grow them."

Musician: "Right. Hee-hee-hee!"

In another man-in-the-street interview, a TV journalist approaches a long-haired man in a crowd who is wearing a Lone Ranger-style mask (as are many others around them). In the background the crowd may be heard singing the Beatles' song "Yellow Submarine."

Journalist: "They are singing about 'we all live in the yellow submarine.' What's this mean?"

Hippie: "Uh, it's difficult to explain. And I think, uh, we take this music seriously. And there's a meaning, a meaning which everyone can interpret it differently, about the yellow submarine. Uh, it's, it's a sort of, it's an understanding that we're banding together in the yellow submarine, and it represents a new way of looking at life."

Is this what Anders means when she says "much, much bigger than the war . . . much, much bigger than the civil rights movement"? The right to smoke marijuana, drop out, tune in, turn on and go-up-in-the-mountains-and-yell transcends all of the struggles and trials of Dr. Martin Luther King, Jr., and his people who exposed the evils and injustices of Jim Crow segregation to the world, in the face of Bull Connor's fire hoses? The fact that so many people were, in fact, free to live it the way they thought it ought to be without permission or coercion would seem to give the lie to the idea that America was a fundamentally oppressive society, much less "a culture that was destroying the world."

I shouldn't be too hard on Jentri Anders. As far as a cursory review of her biography can tell, she is no hypocrite; she lived her life according to her own values while making few demands on anyone else, living in a commune in Northern California, writing books about her experience and teaching at a college. Many of her contemporaries have not been anywhere near as willing to live and let live.

Coda

At the end of the film, the director gives an epilogue of what happened to his protagonists in the twenty years from the end of the era to the making of the documentary:

"Frank Bardacke left Berkeley in 1970 and spent the next decade working in the fields and canneries near Salinas, California. He is still a Leftist, active in labor and community politics. Now he teaches at Watsonville Adult School."

"Jack Weinberg turned to organizing in factories, eventually to become a steelworker. Due to a declining industry, he lost his job in 1984. Recently, he became coordinator for Greenpeace's Great Lakes project in Chicago."

Here you have a couple of well-educated, high-IQ, idealistic young people determined to "do good" in the world through, among other things, labor union organizing (it seems doubtful that either of them went to work in canneries and steel mills without a "higher" motivation). No doubt they were sincere in this. But if they truly wanted to help manual-working people, with their bright minds and elite educations, they could have initiated and/or expanded some project or enterprise which could meet human needs so well as to satisfy customers, investors and employees, allowing it to grow and increase the amount of capital invested per labor hour, thereby raising the productivity of labor and, with it, real wages, in a way far more substantial and enduring than any union organizing could achieve. Being labor organizers may have suited their talents and temperaments and brought them glory and honor, but I'm skeptical that it effected any fundamental improvement in the lot of working people. The best that most unions do is to achieve temporary advantages for their members and officers at the expense of other working people at other companies or in other industries or countries. If union organization and agitation were the key to the advancement of working people, then French, Mexican and Argentinian workers, with their formidable syndicates capable of shutting down their entire respective countries, should be the most prosperous in the world. But they aren't; that honor belongs to largely non-unionized American workers.

Due to a declining industry, he lost his job in 1984. Maybe if Weinberg had become a "capitalist pig" instead of persisting in acting the Marxist stooge, the industry he chose to work in might not have declined and his comrades might not only not have lost their jobs but might have found their wages, benefits and security increasing. (I treat these themes in greater depth in the essays "Where do Jobs Come From?" and "Why Does the Pay Suck?" in the Citizen Economics part of the book.)

"Mike Miller is a professional organizer. In 1972 he started the Organize Training Center, which works with labor and grassroots community organizations."

Ditto Miller what I said about Weinberg. I wonder how many of those "grassroots community organizations" have the words "Tea Party" in their names. I'm not hopeful.

"Susie Nelson started a successful restaurant in Berkeley, which she uses to support the Palestinian cause and promote peace in Central America."

So, she is a rising capitalist star, running a for-profit business fully subject to the discipline of the market, but she uses the proceeds of her capitalist enterprise to oppose Israel and to side with the Left against the U.S. in every one of the armed conflicts that are endemic to Latin America. Thus is "peace" defined.

Aftermath

People who succumb to totalitarian or fundamentalist cults lead extremely narrow and impoverished lives, even if their material existence is not deprived. Communism has terrorized millions of people through violent repression, murder and genocide, to be sure, but its hypnotic power over its devotees is even more remarkable. Stories are legion of Communist Party members excommunicated, with no power exercised against them other than being asked to leave, psychologically and spiritually devastated by the rejection.

I'm very grateful to have overcome a poisonous suite of ideologies, even if I perceive that my (and many of my compatriots') ability to better myself and my family materially has been severely impaired by the damage done to our economy and social fabric by the radical Left that blossomed so prominently in my hometown. For me, the antidote to the socialist and ever-shifting definition of "progressive" ideology was a straight and honest reading of a discipline that is rarely taught in any high school or university today: classical political economy (not to be confused with modern technical/mathematical economics or Keynesian macroeconomics). There are many sources of material about the era, and my account is certainly only one of many perspectives. The most insightful guides that I have found to the events of that time and place on my journey to discovering my politico-cultural roots are David Horowitz, Peter Collier and Ayn Rand. Horowitz and Collier are the most candid former radicals of the era who have written in exhaustive, firsthand detail about the people and times in the books *Destructive Generation* and *Radical Son*. Rand's essay, "The Cashing-In: The Student Rebellion" (at Berkeley in 1964-65), is a devastating dissection of a drama that had only begun to unfold at the time that she wrote about it. She, perhaps more than any other writer that I know of, recognized the Free Speech Movement for what it was—not decades later in hindsight, but immediately while it was ongoing. The piece can be read and re-read for its treasures, and a lifetime of study could be inspired by the leads that it offers, particularly in the currents of modern philosophy, of which the student movement was the natural, almost inevitably ordained, outcome.

My work here is a pale echo to Horowitz and Collier's nearly heroic opuses, but I hope it makes a legitimate contribution in the category of ordinary and modest heroism, the success of a mere pawn in other people's games to break away and define himself on his own terms. I especially hope it can provide comfort as well as ammunition to the millions of young people straining under the yoke of Leftist professors, political correctness, public fiscal irresponsibility for which they are on the hook, internal as well as external threats to the continuance of American civilization, and a severely dysfunctional economy.

The most trenchant insight into the nature of the radical movement that exploded onto the national scene from Berkeley in the mid-1960s is given by Ayn Rand in her 15,000-word essay, "The Cashing-In: The Student "Rebellion." I therefore give Rand the last word in this part of the book by excerpting her essay. While I do so at some length, what the reader should realize it that these are ultimately only teasers that should compel one to a hunger to read the complete work.

The Cashing-In (Excerpted)

By Ayn Rand[26]
[My occasional comments in square brackets.]

The so called the student "rebellion," which was started and keynoted at the University of California at Berkeley, has profound significance, but not of the kind that most commentators have ascribed to it. And the nature of the misrepresentations is part of its significance.

. . .

If a dramatist had the power to convert philosophical ideas into real, flesh-and-blood people and attempted to create the walking embodiments of modern philosophy—the result would be the Berkeley rebels. . . If that dramatist were writing a movie, he could justifiably entitle it "Mario Savio, Son of Emmanuel Kant". . . Ever since Kant divorced reason from reality, his intellectual descendants have been diligently widening the breach.

. . .

As in any movement, there is obviously a mixture of motives involved: there are the little shysters of the intellect to

---

[26]   From *The New Left: The Anti-Industrial Revolution.* New York, NY: New American Library, 1971.

a found a gold mine in modern philosophy, who delight in arguing for arguments sake and stumping opponents by means of ready-to-wear paradoxes—there are the little role players who fancy themselves as heroes and enjoy defiance for the sake of defiance—there are the nihilists who, moved by a profound hatred, seek nothing but destruction for the sake of destruction—there are the hopeless dependents who seek to "belong" to any crowd that would have them—and there are the plain hooligans who are always there, on the fringes of any mob action that smells of trouble. Whatever the combination of motives, neurosis is stamped in capital letters across the whole movement, since there is no such thing as rejecting reason through an innocent error of knowledge. But whether the theories of modern philosophy serve merely as a screen, a defense-mechanism, a rationalization of neurosis or are, in part, its cause—the fact remains that modern philosophy has destroyed the best in these students and fostered the worst.

. . .

[T]here is only one human discipline which enables men to deal with large-scale problems, which has the power to integrate and unify human activities—and that discipline is philosophy, which they have set, instead, to the task of disintegrating and destroying their work.

What does all this do to the best minds among the students? Most of them endure their college years with the teeth-clenched determination of serving out a jail sentence. . . And what they feel toward their schools ranges from mistrust to resentment to contempt to hatred—intertwined with a sense of exhaustion and excruciating boredom. . . This is the reason why a handful of Berkeley rebels was able to attract thousands of students who did not realize, at first, the nature of what they were joining and who withdrew when it became apparent.

. . .

The philosophical impotence of the older generation is the reason why the adult authorities—from the Berkeley administration to the social commentators to the press to Governor Brown [Edmund G. "Pat" Brown, Sr., 1959-1967]—were unable to take a firm stand and had no rational answer to the Berkeley rebellion. Granting the premises of modern philosophy, logic was on the side of the rebels. To

115

answer them would require a total philosophical reevaluation, down to basic premises—which none of those adults would dare attempt.

Hence the incredible spectacle of brute force, hoodlum tactics and militantly explicit irrationality being brought to a university campus—and being met by the vague, uncertain, apologetic concessions, the stale generalities, evasive platitudes of the alleged defenders of academic law and order.

. . .

If the rank-and-file of the college rebels are victims, at least in part, this cannot be said of their leaders. Who are the leaders? Any and all of the statist-collectivist groups that hover, like vultures, over the remnants of capitalism [*dwell on that for a moment: the* remnants *of capitalism, already over fifty years ago*], hoping to pounce on the carcass—and to accelerate the end, whenever possible. Their minimal goal is just "to make trouble"—to undercut, to confuse, to demoralize, to destroy. Their ultimate goal is to take over.

. . .

For its motley [L]eftist leadership, the student rebellion is a trial balloon, a kind of cultural temperature-taking. It is a test of how much they can get away with and what sort of opposition they will encounter.

For the rest of us, it is a miniature preview—in the microcosm of the academic world—of what is to happen to the country at large, if the present cultural trend remains unchallenged.

. . .

[T]he rebels chose Clark Kerr as their first target, not in spite of, but because of his [liberal] record.

Now project what would happen if the technique of the Berkeley rebellion were repeated on a national scale [*Answer: the campus unrest of the 21*ˢᵗ *century: Speech codes, "safe spaces," "trigger warnings," "social justice," "white privilege," free speech quarantine zones and entire departments dedicated to racial, ethic, sexual-identity, and other group grievances against traditional white Anglo-Saxon Protestant and capitalist America, with segregated housing and graduation ceremonies*].

. . .

[T]here is no justification, in a civilized society, for the kind of mass civil disobedience that involves the violation of the rights of others—regardless of whether the demonstrator's goal is good or evil . . . No one's rights can be secured by the violation of the rights of others . . . The forcible occupation of another man's property or the obstruction of a public thoroughfare is so blatant a violation of rights that any attempt to justify it becomes an abrogation of morality. An individual has no right to do a "sit-in" in the home or office of a person he disagrees with—and he does not acquire such a right by joining a gang . . . The attempt to solve social problems by means of physical force is what a civilized society is established to prevent.

. . .

To facilitate the acceptance of force, the Berkeley rebels attempted to establish a special distinction between force and violence: force, they claimed explicitly, is a proper form of social action, but violence is not. . . Consider the implications of that distinction as a rule of social conduct: If you come home one evening, find a stranger occupying your house and throw him out bodily, he has merely committed a peaceful act of "force," but you are guilty of "violence" and you are to be punished.

The theoretical purpose of that grotesque absurdity is to establish a moral inversion: to make the initiation of force moral, and resistance to force immoral—and thus to obliterate the right of self-defense.

. . .

There can be no such thing as the right to an unrestricted freedom of speech (or of action) *on someone else's property*. The fact that the university at Berkeley is owned by the state, merely complicates the issue, but does not alter it. The owners of a state university are the voters and taxpayers of that state. The university administration, appointed (directly or indirectly) by an elected official, is theoretically, the agent of the owners— and has to act as such, so long as state universities exist. (Whether they should exist, is a different question.)

In any undertaking or establishment involving more than one man, it is the owner or owners who set the rules and terms of appropriate conduct; the rest of the participants are free to go elsewhere and seek different terms, if they do not agree.

. . .

117

[N]o rights of any kind can be exercised without property rights.

There was no way for the Berkeley administration to answer the rebels except by invoking property rights. . . . There are no solutions for the many contradictions inherent in the concept of "public property," particularly when the property is directly concerned with the dissemination of ideas. This is one of the reasons why the rebels would choose a state university as their first battleground . . . The source of these contradictions does not lie in the principle of individual rights, but their violation by the collectivist institution of "public property."

. . .

As a trial balloon, the rebellion has accomplished its leaders' purpose: it has demonstrated that they may have gone a bit too far . . . but that the road ahead is empty, with no intellectual barricades in sight.

. . .

In the absence of intellectual opposition, the rebels' notions will gradually come to be absorbed into the culture.

. . .

The fact that the "non-liberals" among college students (and among the youth of the world) can be identified at present only as "anti-collectivists" is the dangerous element in today's situation. They are the young people who are not ready to give up, who want to fight against a swamp of evil, but do not know what is the good. They have rejected the sick, worn platitudes of collectivism . . . but they have found, as yet, no direction, no consistent philosophy, no rational values, no long-range goals. Until and unless they do, their incoherent striving for a better future will collapse before the final thrust of the collectivists.

. . .

If they seek an important cause, they have the opportunity to fight the rebels, to fight ideologically, on moral-intellectual grounds—by identifying and exposing the meaning of the rebels' demands, by naming and answering the basic principles which the rebels dare not admit. The battle consists, above all, of providing the country (or all those within hearing) with ideological answers—a field of action from which the older generation has deserted under fire.

Ideas cannot be fought except by means of better ideas. The battle consists, not of opposing, but of exposing; not of denouncing, but of disproving; not of evading, but of boldly proclaiming a full, consistent and radical alternative.

This does not mean that rational students should enter debates with the rebels or attempt to convert them: one cannot argue with self-confessed irrationalists. The goal of an ideological battle is to enlighten the vast, helpless, bewildered majority in the universities—and in the country at large.

. . .

You would be surprised how quickly the ideologists of collectivism retreat when they encounter a confident, intellectual adversary. Their case rests on appealing to human confusion, ignorance, dishonesty, cowardice, despair. Take the side they dare not touch: appeal to human intelligence.

Amen.

Berkeley, California: Too small to be a nation state; too big to be an insane asylum.

I love you, man. Let's get together some time soon[27].

---

[27]   The "insane asylum" quip is not my original, but attribution unknown. Berkeley may be only a 9 square-mile city, but it has its own foreign policy. Not very good at filling potholes, though.

Part II: Citizen Economics

Why the obsession over economics? Why the neurotic mania for a tedious, boring, dismal science? Why not take up stamp collecting or figure skating instead?

Well—quite apart from the fact that my knees are already shredded from trying to keep up with my daughter on the ice three days a week for five years—here is my tedious, boring, dismal answer: **It matters**.

It matters to me personally because if it weren't for economics, I might still be a liberal socialist progressive Democrat, and more importantly, I would still be groping futilely in the dark for answers to many of life's troubling questions.

It matters critically to you, our society and the continuance of our civilization. Consider: if our lawmakers were literate in economics, then millions more American would have jobs today than do, with better pay and lower costs of living, instead of suffering the worst employment and business entrepreneurship environment in two generations. If our public policies were based on rational economics, then we wouldn't have had a housing crisis and financial meltdown in 2008 (Canada didn't have one). If Bob Dole and/ or John McCain had known something about economics, they might have been elected President. If Richard Nixon had had a clue about economics, we would not have suffered from the simultaneous inflation and stagnation (high rate of inflation combined with high unemployment that the Keynesian-derived "Phillips Curve" had previously asserted to be impossible, a.k.a. "stagflation"), and long waiting lines to buy gasoline of the 1970s.

So, if you were expecting a straight Republican Party cheerlead, you've opened the wrong book.

Government policies and programs of Democrats and Republicans alike fail to the degree that they presume to be able to do the equivalent of repealing the laws of gravity, or of commanding the tide not to come in and wet the king's feet. Politicians presume that because their law says so, it will be so. They (or we who elect and support them) do not seem to understand or respect that there are natural laws in the realms of individual and social action that are beyond the reach of legislation, though they may be corrupted by it. We have seen too many times how well (not!)

that has worked out. It is indispensable for citizens and policymakers to become literate in supply and demand, incentives and constraints, knowledge and power, incremental marginal utility, private property, rule of law and the limits of what government may accomplish based on the very definition of what government is, in order to achieve the greatest liberty, security and prosperity for the greatest number. Political Economy, or Citizen Economics, is the key intellectual discipline required to achieve this.

Unfortunately, economic ignorance is bipartisan, and university economics departments and the economics profession have fallen short in providing a remedy. This book, its bibliography, and in particular this part, is one modest contribution to combating that ignorance, for citizens, student and public officials at all levels and from all walks of life.

The Tea Party for Doctors

Speech to the Annual Meeting of the Association of American Physicians and Surgeons (AAPS) in Denver, Colorado, September 28, 2013

This piece is as much about the topic of 'Part III: Obamacare' as it is about the broader mission of Citizen Economics, but I chose to put it here because it so well articulates the principles and rationale behind so much of my work, the definition of Citizen Economics, and why people like me—from outside the profession and lacking a PhD, or even a Master's—are showing up as the standard-bearers.

The AAPS is a group of brilliant constitutionally-minded doctors, exceptionally well-versed in classical liberal philosophy and economics, who advocate for free market principles applied in the realm of medical care policy.

To introduce me to the assembled group of about 200, the very conservatively-mannered board member Dr. Lawrence Huntoon, M.D., Ph.D., read deadpan verbatim from the About the Author page of my book 'Pull the Plug on Obamacare': "Howard Hyde has no formal credentials whatsoever qualifying him to write this pamphlet. He is neither a doctor, nor a public official, nor a professor, nor a professional economist. He holds no certifications or licenses in Medicine, Economics or Public Policy. He doesn't have any advanced degrees, and the B.A. degree he does have is in Music (University of Southern California Thornton School, 1990). For this reason the reader is cautioned not to believe anything herein contained on blind faith, but to check every fact, carefully analyze the logic of every argument and watch out for rhetorical slights of tongue and pen. Only by being vigilant, skeptical and critical can the citizen-voter prevent being misled by charlatans posing as experts."

I couldn't very well run away, so I mumbled some words of appreciation and forged ahead, deviating only slightly from my prepared text:

* * * * *

Thank you. It is a great honor for me to be invited to speak at your most excellent conference. I have to say, these past three days have truly been a breath of fresh air. I believe it was doctor Kendall on Thursday who was warning our medical students here not to get stuck working as an employee for some big hospital corporation, and as someone who has spent the better part of the last 20 years working for large corporations as an IT specialist, I can testify to that: In all of these past 20 years, I have not once experienced a speech or mission statement presentation by any corporate executive that was as intelligent, as substantive and as engaging as the speakers we have heard here this week.

I am Howard Hyde, Citizen-Economist, and I'm here to talk about defeating Obamacare, and I intend to speak until I can no longer stand![28] ... Oh, I guess they won't let me do that, but we'll do our best! Can I at least take off my shirt and dance?

[*Earlier, Charles Sauer, one of the event organizers, had shown a humorous YouTube- video of the 'Shirtless Dancing Guy', showing a young man dancing crazily in a public park and gradually attracting a huge crowd of imitators.*]

I can imagine that a number of you must be thinking, who is this guy, anyway? What does he have to offer us, we who have been fighting socialism in medicine for 70 years?

Well, we are here because the cause of free markets, constitutional government, private property rights and voluntary cooperation are under assault as never before seen in our nation's history. And unfortunately, liberty and the rule of law applied to any field, let alone medicine, has not been getting adequate defense from the credentialed, qualified professionals, the lawyers, the judges, or even the economists these days, to say nothing of the politicians that We the People have elected, and the administrative czars that we have not (but who exercise power over us).

Is it possible that the credentialed social scientists and power brokers have been corrupted? Say it ain't so! But when I meet attorneys and law students who have never even heard of Frederick Bastiat, I have to wonder at the very least what their system of legal ethics is based on, if it has any basis at all. (I have a hunch our General Counsel Andrew Schlafly knows who Frederick Bastiat is.) When I meet professional economists and college economics majors who have not

---

28   On September 24, 2013, just a few days before my AAPS appearance and six months after I handed him a copy of "Pull the Plug on Obamacare," Ted Cruz took to the floor of the Senate and declared, "I rise today in opposition to Obamacare. I intend to speak in opposition to Obamacare. I intend to speak in support of defunding Obamacare until I am no longer able to stand." He stood, and spoke – including reading Dr. Seuss's *Green Eggs and Ham* to his daughters – for 21 hours. My reading of Seuss is better.

read Adam Smith, Ludwig von Mises, Friedrich Hayek, Milton Friedman or Thomas Sowell, I have to wonder what their concept of their field even is. It would be as if doctors had never heard of Hippocrates, Galen, Harvey, Virchow or Lister[29]. And when I dig a little deeper I find an answer: economics to the economics Establishment (with few notable exceptions such as our dear friend Dr. Timothy Terrell at Wofford College and the Mises Institute), instead of being a study of how flesh-and-blood human beings come to grips with the fact that resources are scarce and have alternative uses, instead they think of their field as a discipline of sophisticated mathematical and financial formulas with charts and graphs of aggregate categories, where the individual human being economic actor, consumer or entrepreneur is melted into the batter. This is not political economy as it was known in the 19th century. And it is not the philosophy that will preserve, protect and defend that most scarce and precious of all resources, which is free human beings living under constitutional government and the rule of law. Today's mainstream economics profession seems to take as axiomatic the idea that the government is the prime mover in society and the economy; that it is the government's job to see to it that outcomes turn out correctly according to whatever defines correct in the political moment, and that it is the individual's job—your and my job—to do what is deemed correct according to what the experts in power determine. Buy more! Save less! Pay more taxes! Take more entitlements, eat more free goodies! Run your business as the IRS and Sarbanes-Oxley and Dodd-Frank tell you to. Run your medical practice as Donald Berwick or Kathleen Sibelius or Nancy Pelosi tell you to (...after you find out what's in it). Better yet, don't run an independent practice at all, because that's just selfish greed which doesn't serve the Greater Good. Work for a modest salary at a hospital corporation of Harry Reid's choosing, where if you are lucky you will at least have person with a medical background telling you what to do and evaluating your ... protocol compliance, albeit not a person as thoroughly trained and professionally experienced as you.

If hardly anyone can graduate from a law school, public policy or economics degree program without being so dis-informed, so indoctrinated into a government-centric worldview, so ignorant of the

---

29   Hippocrates, Galen, Harvey, Virchow, Lister: a few of the most historically significant physicians of the past 2400 years.

foundations and legacy of their own profession and of their country, then the defense of individual freedom, the Constitution, of private property and entrepreneurial capitalism (of which independent medical practice is an expression) will have to come from outside of the credentialed ranks. It will have to come from cowboys and outlaws and tea-partiers and misfits. It will come from former slackers like Andrew Breitbart and former communist agitators like David Horowitz and former New Dealers like Ronald Reagan and whacked-out libertarians like Ron Paul and ex-Liberal-Socialist-Progressive-Democrats-from-Berkeley-by-way-of-Paris like yours truly.

(*Digression*: Speaking of Ronald Reagan and economics, Reagan earned a bachelor's degree from Eureka College, an independent college in Illinois, around 1930-ish. At that time, they were still teaching classical political economy. Fast-forward 10 years and you have George Herbert Walker Bush learning *Keynesian* economics at Yale. And that's what made all the difference. Bush never bought into Reagan's understanding of free-market, classical economics, and that's why even during the primary in 1980 when they were competing for the nomination, Bush referred to Reagan's vision as 'voodoo' economics. And that's why the Republican Party has basically lost its moorings ever since it was infected with the Keynesian virus. Bush, Bob Dole, John McCain...say no more.

But I digress!

For these reasons I have dedicated evenings, weekends, vacations and holidays for the past 20 years to the study of classical and Austrian economics. I started my website HHCapitalism.com[30] several years ago to make my own modest contribution, to try to educate my fellow citizens, and economists, and lawyers, and politicians, and doctors and medical students in principles of economics indispensable for their understanding. For while one of the great principles of economics is the division of labor, whereby I do what I do best and you do what you do best and we exchange our surpluses with each other, making everyone infinitely better off than we could possibly be through self-sufficiency, yet the one thing that we cannot delegate to specialists is the foundational understanding of economics itself. Each of us must become a *citizen-economist*, able to discriminate between serious attempts to grapple with scarce resources which have alternative uses versus emotionally appealing political slogans that lead to destruction.

---

30   HHCapitalism.com is now www.CitizenEcon.com.

Because if we do not do our jobs as citizen-economists, then the politicians and power brokers will be only too happy to do it for us, to run our lives for us. That's what Benjamin Franklin was talking about when he said "a republic, if you can keep it."

[Turning to an individual audience member] Sir, what is your occupation? [He answers.] Ophthalmology? Wrong! You are a *Citizen-Economist* and Ophthalmologist! [Turning to another] what about you, ma'am, what is your occupation? [She answers "I am a citizen-economist, a revolutionary, and a physician!"] Class valedictorian, Ladies and Gentlemen! [Applause.]

I have written and published on a broad range of topics at AmericanThinker.com, FrontPageMag.com and HHCapitalism.com, including fiscal and monetary policy, immigration, energy and environmentalism. But when it emerged in 2009 that socialized medicine was once again a clear and present danger, I turned my attention to warning my compatriots that Obama-Reid-PelosiCare was 1) sold on fraudulent premises, 2) destructive and 3), doomed to failure, and 4) that much better alternative reforms are readily available.

When the unthinkable happened and the law passed in 2010, and then the Supreme Court re-wrote it and Obama was re-elected in 2012 along with 60 of his closest friends, I redoubled my efforts to complete the book, which I published in February of this year.

I have tried to give my friends, in a small but substantive package that may be read and comprehended in one hour, the logical and factual ammunition they need to have the necessary conversations with their Obamacare-supporter friends and family members, especially now as the creeping doubts fostered by the daily parade of bad news of Obamacare's destructive effects wears away at their fair-weather convictions and makes them open once again to considering rational arguments and alternative proposals.

We need to re-think this whole thing. After all, prior to 2010, for all of our problems it is not true that America lagged behind other more enlightened countries that have universal health care. What counts in the end is not how many people are enrolled in a government program but what the results are; how long is the waiting list for an MRI, a CAT scan or a knee or hip replacement operation; how many MRI machines are available per capita; what are the average survival rates for cancers, heart attacks, traumatic injuries and surgery? What country gets the highest marks for responsiveness to the needs of the patient? Which nation earns more Nobel prizes in Physiology or Medicine than the rest of the world combined for the past half century?

In all of these categories, because of freedom, through the dynamic and ongoing process of trial and error and re-trial, with power not concentrated but rather disbursed in the hands of those who have the knowledge and take the risks and do the work, the USA is the undisputed world leader. That is your legacy, the legacy of the country doctor on the frontier, informed by the academies of Europe but imbued with a distinctly American spirit of initiative, independence, entrepreneurship and generosity, operating under freedom and the Constitution and by the way, you really did build that! Contrary to the normal impulse of all government, which is to crush all competing sources of initiative and power, ours enforced the rule of law and otherwise stayed out of the way long enough so that you could build that. And that is the legacy of unprecedented achievement that we need to build upon, not tear it down, not administer it from Washington, not bottle it into a futile 'best practice' protocol flow chart of static codes to be enforced by bureaucrats and computers, not redistribute it by force for the sake of equalizing misery.

So how do we defeat the Obamacare juggernaut? After all, the top-down power has spoken.

But there is yet hope. The destructive effects are evident to all with each passing day, so that opposition to the law is no longer a partisan Republican game. Millions of people who had no idea this law would even touch them personally are seeing their premiums spike, losing their coverage, losing their jobs, seeing their hours cut or finding it impossible to find a job in the first place because John Galt Capital is on strike. Even the unions are up in arms about what the Law is doing to their members and to their own prestige. There are cracks in the edifice. We can now go on offense from the bottom up.

And the best way to do that, of course, is to get 'Pull the Plug on Obamacare' into every bookstore and newsstand and airport kiosk in the United States! Shameless, self-serving promotion of course. But if not my book, then take your pick from the fine books we have for sale in the hallway. Buy and promote Betsy McCaughey's book 'Beating Obamacare'. Get Sally Pipes' new pamphlet 'The Cure for Obamacare'. It's even better than mine; do you know why? Because it's only half as long! That's the kind of thing we need to change the minds of people who aren't inclined to read 10-pound economic

128

treatises but who may be ready to reconsider some of the socialist-progressive worldview that they have been spoon-fed their entire lives. [*At this point inspiration or nervous terror sent me careening completely off-script:* "When reality hits them in the face...you know, they had such great expectations for when they were graduating college, the job they were going to get, the money they were going to earn, the families they were going to start, the houses they were going to own, the businesses they were going to start -- it's all falling apart. What the hell is going on? I've got to think different. I've got to read something that I haven't read before. Okay? That's the opening that we have." *Soft landing...*] So make sure you buy 10 copies of the book of your choice and distribute them to all of your liberal friends and in-laws.

Now I would rather be asked "Why are you done talking" than "WHEN are you done talking?", so I will just say in conclusion that, AAPS, I am deeply moved by the graciousness with which you have accepted me into your family this week. I salute you and I am at your service. Thank you.

* * * * *

Video available on YouTube:
https://www.youtube.com/watch?v=LRMzHiofEJA

Where Do Jobs Come From?

[Published on AmericanThinker.com on November 1, 2013]

I have some bad news. No one gives you a job because you deserve one. No one gives you a job because you need one. Not because you are a good person, not because you are breathing, can fog a mirror, and/or are entitled. The "free market" doesn't mean you get stuff for free.

You get a job because someone needs some work done and is willing and able to pay you for it.

Let's elaborate just a bit. Someone needs some work done and is willing and able to compensate you with wages, working conditions, benefits, opportunities for advancement and intrinsic rewards just enough to persuade you to turn down all competing offers and accept the job; and willing to put up with your human deficiencies in getting the work done. He or she does this because you present the education, skills, experience, personal hygiene, judgment, grooming, intelligence and social skills adequate to get the job done *and* most important, to return to the employer value in all of the above that exceeds what it costs him/her to compensate you; and to do so consistently and for the duration of your employment, whether a weekend part-time temp fill-in contract or a 40-year gold watch career.

"Willing" and "Able" require some further explanation. Let's start with Able.

Employees typically cash a paycheck weekly, bi-weekly, or monthly. Entrepreneurs, strictly defined, don't cash a paycheck at all. They put up the capital for the enterprise, take responsibility for loans and other financing, pay the expenses (including payroll) and own the assets including revenue. If, over the course of months or years (or decades in the case of large-scale industrial projects such as oil drilling or computer chip manufacture), there is more revenue than expense, they enjoy profits which enable them to live well and invest in another round of entrepreneurship. If there is less revenue than expenses, and if the losing trend is not reversed, the enterprise eventually fails, and the entrepreneur goes bankrupt and has to go begging the banks or other financiers for capital to try again, or becomes the employee of some other more successful entrepreneur.

So "able" means someone with capital, with money. Someone who has been successful in a prior round of investing but who has no guarantee of success in the next round. What you get paid as an employee is *not* a share of the profits that your work makes possible, but an advance on the speculation of the profit potential of your work value, financed by the prior round of investment, profit, and loss. If you were paid out of the profits that your work made possible, then you would have to wait months, years, or decades along with the entrepreneur for those profits to arrive, with no guarantee that they ever would.

"Able" means someone with a dollar more than you. Such people have been characterized as evil, greedy, uncaring and/or undeserving rich, but in all likelihood in a free market without privileges or prejudice, such people are 40 to 60 years old, who were not born rich but who have prospered through hard work, thrift, savings, education, and sacrifice over the course of many years. Most such people have suffered failures and setbacks in their careers prior to achieving success, and that success is not guaranteed to continue just by doing the same thing over and over. In any case, you're not likely to get a job from someone poorer than yourself.

So get over the envy thing. It's listed as one of the seven deadly sins for a reason; it destroys the one who engages in it.

"Willing" means that the investment opportunity is more attractive than other projects or keeping the cash in a mattress. Investment, including hiring you, means giving up the use of the money it costs to pay you for any other purpose. Scarce resources have alternative uses. She could have used that money to bathe in Newcastle Brown Ale. But she pays you instead because over time, your work (combined with all the other elements of the enterprise) has the potential to enable her to bathe in Dom Perignon champagne. Or to invest in even greater and more interesting projects, like sending astronauts to Mars, curing cancer, producing a blockbuster movie, or caring for her ailing elderly mother.

In order for someone to be willing to give up the use of a resource forever (which is what investment in long-term projects is), what comes back or is likely to come back has to be more attractive than what is given up. Many billionaires would be willing to give up billions if they thought it could result in a cure some dread disease, just for the satisfaction of seeing it happen, even if there were no monetary profit. On the other hand, in a money economy, the lowest common denominator is that the expected amount of money that will come back over time has to be greater than the amount that would come back from a savings account, certificate of deposit (CD), or municipal bond. There has to be a more attractive upside. This is not greed; it's being un-stupid.

Investment (and with it, your job) is about the future, and the future is uncertain. There are more things that can possibly go wrong than there are characters in a Murphy's Law joke book. Earthquakes, floods, tsunamis, fires, hurricanes, tornadoes, landslides, epidemics of disease, and asteroids are among the natural hazards. Competition, (in)competence, effectiveness of marketing campaigns, reliability of suppliers and partners and fickle tastes and whims of consumers are among the ordinary business hazards. All of these and their relative likelihoods and risks have to be taken into account and hedged and/or insured against if possible. If the risks are too great, the investment won't be made and you will not get hired or get your raise.

But risk doesn't stop there. The greatest risk of all in a political economy is that government at some level will hamper or wreck the enterprise. Taxes on the activities, inputs and/or outputs of the business may be so heavy as to make it impossible to earn a return greater than a savings account, CD or muni bond.

Even if the enterprise is not committing murder, robbery, assault, fraud, theft, rape, persecution and/or conspiracy, government may treat the business as a criminal enterprise, with fines, confiscation of property or jail sentences handed out for non- compliance with regulations buried deep inside tomes of tens of thousands of pages, which even the regulating agency cannot explain in a consistent manner. Worst of all, governments and regulatory agencies like the EPA can change their minds in a week, while the entrepreneur has to plan years or decades in advance.

When heavy taxation, anti-business or anti-"rich" rhetoric from powerful politicians, instability and overbearing, unpredictable, and capricious regulation reaches a critical mass, the risks become too great for the investment to proceed. Capital goes on strike or looks for opportunities elsewhere, overseas. Kiss your job (or if you're lucky, your hours, your benefits and/or your raise) goodbye.

To recap then: Jobs come from successful entrepreneurs and investors willing and able to risk a buck on you in order to have the potential to eventually make two bucks for themselves and for the next round of investment, which in turn has the potential to create a new job or raise for you, or enable you to become an entrepreneur yourself. In order for that to happen, there has to be freedom of contract, respect and protection of private property rights, light and reasonable taxes and regulations, and political stability; the expectation that those conditions will continue. Those conditions have been deteriorating in the United States at an accelerating rate over the past dozen years.

Why Does the Pay Suck?

[Published as 'Why is the Pay So Lousy?' on FrontPageMag.com, November 12, 2013]

Even if you're lucky enough to have a job in the Sarbanes-Oxley-Dodd-Frank-Bernanke-Sibelius-Obamacare economy, and even if you've beaten the 31-year record and are still part of the 62.8% of American adults who are working even though job creation in October was less than the increase in the adult population (204,000 vs. 213,000), and even if your weekly hours haven't been cut to 29 or your health plan outlawed because it was, in the words of New Jersey Congressman Frank Pallone, "lousy," you still might be wondering what happened to your raise.

I have some bad news. You don't get paid much more because of how difficult your back-breaking labor is. You don't get a raise because you're so much smarter than everyone else in the world. You don't see an increase in your wealth just because you have an Ivy League degree.

You get paid more because of the quantity and quality of accumulated capital that is invested in your work.

When we talk about pay, we really mean the stuff—food, clothing, shelter, Newcastle Brown Ale, iPhones, super bowl tickets—that the wages that you receive can buy. It is futile to earn more money if the value of the money is collapsing due to inflation (that is, the price of everything is going up faster than your wages), or less stuff is being produced, leading to higher prices for everything that is still being produced. You could earn a billion deutschmarks an hour, but if that amount of money will only buy a single egg, as it did at one point during the hyperinflation of Weimar Germany in 1923, then you're not rich. If, on the other hand, entrepreneurial capitalism, with its division of labor, improvements in technology and automation and visionary leadership, is having the result that less labor is required in almost every industry to produce stuff than what was required before, then prices of stuff that wage earners buy will fall relative to the wages they receive. At the end of the day, it's not rising wages that counts so much as *the falling prices of the stuff people buy with their wages.*

If you take almost any professional [person], whether a plumber, a gardener, a computer programmer or a doctor, and transplant him or her from an advanced country like the United States to work in a second-tier or Third-World country, that professional will earn less than—perhaps only a fraction of—the pay he or she earned in the First World. In some cases, the relative loss of income may be offset by some elements of a lower cost of living, but that effect is limited; ultimately the material quality of life will be much lower.

Why is that? The professional is just as smart in Mexico or Rwanda as (s)he was in Germany or Singapore. But (s)he has less capital to work with. Just as a worker with a bulldozer is more productive than a worker with a shovel, all professionals depend on a developed infrastructure, state-of-the-art machinery, computers, technological instruments, information and transportation systems, communications networks and more to get their work done in the most productive way. Every worker in the First World sits on top of a gold mine of capital accumulated from prior generations, which he or she had no hand in building, to make his or her work that much more productive and valuable.

The capital that undergirds the economy takes many forms, from the obvious and tangible assets of land, factories and machines, to the less-obvious and intangible ones of management methodologies, technological processes and know-how, advanced and uncorrupted legal systems and private property rights.

Those last two are the make-or-break elements of a prosperous economy. Because if private property is not respected and defended, and/or if contracts are not enforced, and/or if the justice, tax and/or regulatory systems are corrupt, capricious and arbitrary, then the formation and deployment of capital will be retarded or destroyed no matter how many physical and intellectual resources are available. If you don't believe this American on this point, ask the Peruvian economist Hernando de Soto, author of "The Mystery of Capital: Why Capitalism Triumphs in the West and Fails Everywhere Else," who documented all of the "dead" capital that exists in the Third World, due to the lack of a system of recognition of ownership, in order to unleash its power to create wealth for all.

This point cannot be stressed enough: Physical assets like coal, oil, gas, timber, minerals etc. are worthless without a system of private property and prices in which unarmed, un-privileged and unpersecuted non-government entrepreneurs, large- and small-scale, may operate. The world is full of resource-rich countries, from Mexico to Nigeria and from Venezuela to Russia, which pathetically under-perform other nations like Japan, Switzerland and Singapore, which have no such endowments but which have well-developed legal systems of private property recognition and contract enforcement. Russia, with its 13 time zones and vast natural resources, has a per-capita standard of living that ranks roughly 50th in the world.

So if you are not seeing an improvement in the purchasing power of your wages or the material standard of living over time, and the same thing is happening to millions of people just like you and there isn't a major war on, chances are that intangible capital is faltering. And that in turn is probably due to attitudes and policies promulgated by politicians complaining that the "rich" aren't paying their fair share of taxes, closing off natural resources to development, and slapping so much regulation on businesses that they spend ever more time and energy on compliance instead of innovation, effectively working for the government instead of for their customers. That has been the trend in the United States since 2001 with Sarbanes-Oxley, accelerating since 2009 with Dodd-Frank and the Pelosi-Reid regulatory apparatus. Obamacare, with its effective abolition of voluntary cooperation between employers, employees, patients, doctors and insurance companies, is the single most destructive factor in this picture today.

High and rising wages depend on the quantity and quality of liberated capital invested in the labor. Whether you are a banker or a tree surgeon (and when I say banker I mean it in the traditional sense of a trusted conservative steward of customers' money as opposed to a politically-connected financial manipulator), the respect and defense of capital and private property matters to you, and you need to participate actively in the civic society for the furtherance of that respect and defense.

How Does Prosperity Happen?

[Published on CitizenEcon.com on June 1, 2013]

Your "progressive" politician—mayor, congressman, senator, governor, Liberator, Generalissimo, Beloved Leader—would have you believe that whatever wealth you have, you owe to Him, his programs and policies (with a cut for his allies in the media and academia). Through increasingly expansive and expensive social programs (welfare, public pensions, union privileges, labor regulation, health care, protective tariffs, bailouts for "too-big-to-fail" institutions, subsidies, giveaways, pork, earmarks, "cash for clunkers," etc.) He strives to transform that vague belief into a reality, to lock in your dependency, your vote and your submission to His authority. But as the examples of Greece, Spain, France, Venezuela, California and other basket-case nations around the world demonstrate, all the privileges, pensions, bread and circuses doled out by Santa Claus politicians do not sustain themselves; they have to be supported by other people who still produce stuff. Suppress the productive sector of an economy and the house of cards crashes to the ground.

Politicians don't create wealth; entrepreneurs do.

In the real world in which we live, the only constants are change and uncertainty. There are floods, wildfires, tornadoes, earthquakes, hurricanes, AIDS, volcanoes, swine flu and a million other unpredictable disasters. Even in the absence of natural disasters, economic activity such as farming or manufacturing products for sale frequently require long time cycles from initial groundbreaking until harvest and/or final sale to consumers. These extended time spans would leave people starving if they didn't have some food and other resources saved up or provided to them in the interim. For this reason, it would be extremely beneficial to most of us if some people were able and willing to assume for themselves a greater share of the existing risk, to store up food, shelter, Miller Lite and other goods, and in so doing, provide for the sustenance and reduce the level of uncertainty for others.

Fortunately, such people do exist. They're called entrepreneurs. They're called investors. They're called businessmen/businesswomen, speculators, and insurance companies; in a word, the rich.

In other words, the class (if "class" is the right word) of people most vilified by the political Left as evil, greedy exploiters are, in fact, the most indispensable material benefactors of their fellow human beings.

Too often we discuss entrepreneurs, investors, speculators or insurance companies in emotional terms. To some, these people are heroes to be put on a pedestal. To others, they are like disease-carrying vermin—parasites that reap obscene profits, destroy the environment and crush the rest of us with their monopoly power. But emotions aside, in the science of economics there is a critically important, objective role for a class of people who assume a greater share of risk in exchange for a correspondingly higher share of net gains—profits— when their forecasts, projects and decisions turn out correct, and a (negative) share that corresponds with the greater part of the losses when they turn out wrong. Unsuccessful entrepreneurs become the employees of successful ones. Successful entrepreneurs bid up the wages of employees with each round of capital accumulation and investment. Those higher wages afford more opportunities for employees to try their own hand at entrepreneurship and investment.

Employees do not directly enjoy the profits of the entrepreneur or investor, but neither do we directly risk the losses. The money that employees get paid does not come from the future profits that their work in the present makes possible (because by definition those future profits haven't been cashed in yet), but rather with the savings from the prior round of the investment cycle. The entrepreneur has to wait months, years or even decades for profits (or losses) that are uncertain, while the employee receives his paycheck every week or month, virtually guaranteed. Put another way, the employee's risk of not being paid for giving his labor to the entrepreneur is measured in days or weeks, while the entrepreneur's risk of not seeing a return on investment is measured in months or years.

Entrepreneurs may be big headline-grabbers like the founders of Google, Facebook, Apple, Microsoft or Standard Oil. But the vast majority are small, family-owned businesses: dry cleaners, local niche booksellers, auto repair shops, hardware stores, franchise restaurants. These are the people who make the economy work, provide vital products and services, and account for the lion's share of job growth.

We are all entrepreneurs to one degree or another. Every time we make a commitment to a certain course of action instead of another without a guarantee, betting on the outcome, we are acting as risk-taking entrepreneurs. Students act as entrepreneurs when they choose a major in college, betting on the future prospects of a career in a certain field to which they are personally suited.

To quote Rich Karlgaard of *Forbes* magazine, "Entrepreneurs are not just a cute little subsector of the American economy. They are the whole game." Or Tim Kane of the Kaufman Foundation: "When it comes to U.S. job growth, start-up companies aren't everything. They're the only thing."

The Entrepreneurial Cycle:
From Scarcity to Abundance

[Published on CitizenEcon.com on June 15, 2013]

We have been told over and over again that the world is running out of natural resources due to our short-sighted greed and overuse. This idea is nothing new; it has been preached not only in our own lives but for decades and even centuries on. Yet with every generation, the capitalist entrepreneurial cycle has proven these scares wrong. Whether it is food, clothing, shelter, minerals, energy, clean air, medicine, beer or university faculty parking spaces, the same pattern emerges under the free market:

- *Scarcity* leads to

- *Rising market prices,* which signal

- *Entrepreneurial opportunity*; there's money to be made ("There's gold in them thar hills!")

- Investors and speculators advance their own savings to fund *research and development* to invent new ways to extract and produce more, to drill deeper under the ocean floor using only one tower where five had been required before, to design new industrial processes, to genetically engineer seeds that multiply crop yields, to discover new and better drugs, etc.

- *Many entrepreneurs fail, at their own expense* (not yours and mine; not bailed out by the taxpayers)

- . . . but *others succeed,* and the result is *profits* for them and

- *Abundant products and services at lower cost than ever* for us, even cheaper and more plentiful than before the initial "crisis"[31]

In the final analysis, physical substances like minerals, oil, gas, water, food and a host of others are only as good, as useful and as available

---

[31]   This entrepreneurial capitalist cycle is described in detail by Julian Simon in his classic book, "The Ultimate Resource 2."

as the *people* who design the processes to mine, extract, cultivate, harvest, refine, market and distribute them. It is human ingenuity that takes icky gunk that oozes out of the ground and sickens your cows, and transforms it into energy—black gold. It is the entrepreneurial drive operating in a free market that responds to every shortage of anything by producing more than ever, at the lowest real prices ever. In the short run, physical resources are, of course, finite, but in the long term they are virtually unlimited, only constrained by human imagination, ingenuity, freedom and hard work. That is one difference between economics and physics.

That is why right now we have approximately thirteen years' known reserves of oil, whereas thirteen years ago we had . . . thirteen years' of known reserves then, and thirteen years before that the known reserves were good for . . . about thirteen years. The line keeps being pushed back by advancing knowledge, technological innovation and the entrepreneurial response to price signals in the market.

The fact is, it costs money to know how much oil (or any other resource) is available in reserve, because prospecting, locating and mapping deposits costs money. It's not worth it to anyone to know more than about thirteen years, but if the period drops to twelve or eleven, it starts to pay to know, and the companies that are in the business of knowing will renew their exploration efforts.

The concept of "known reserves" cannot be divorced from market prices. At $50 a barrel, there may be X trillion barrels of known reserves. But at $150 per barrel, the known reserves—that is, the quantity of the resource known to be profitably extractable at that price—may be 3X trillion or even 30X trillion. Moreover, after the investment is made to extract the more difficult-to-reach deposits, the tendency is for costs and ultimate consumer prices to fall once again. The market always finds a way to find more. Natural resources get cheaper and more abundant with every generation.

The only force capable of stopping this virtuous cycle is . . . force: controlling who may or may not engage in certain businesses or activities; interfering with the functioning of the market; controlling wages and/or prices so that signals and information about the true relative abundance and scarcity do not get transmitted accurately;

141

denying permits to explore for and/or extract available natural resources; awarding contracts and employment positions based on political favoritism, nepotism or ethnicity, rather than objective competence and qualifications; forcing taxpayers to prop up firms that have failed; expropriating profits lawfully gained by firms that succeeded; failing to enforce the rule of law consistently and fairly—these are the actions and reactions that can impede entrepreneurial capitalism from solving the universal problem of scarcity. Unfortunately, those actions are most often committed by the agency that should be defending individual liberty: government.

The world is full of wretchedly poor nations sitting on top of abundant natural resources. Russia, Venezuela, Nigeria and Mexico are examples of countries whose economic policies have stifled liberty, private property and the rule of law and thus have kept their people poor in spite of huge reserves of oil and other commodities. Meanwhile, countries with few or no natural resources at all (think Switzerland, Japan, Hong Kong, Singapore) crush the economic competition.

Capitalism, properly understood as a framework of individual liberty and responsibility, free markets, free trade and free people with neither privilege nor prejudice, is the economic system that has provided and will provide the greatest material abundance and prosperity to the greatest number of people of all nations and classes, whether measured relatively or absolutely. Capitalism is the solution.

"Human Needs before Profits!"

[First draft 1992; Published on CitizenEcon.com on March 9, 2007]

The alleged superiority of socialism (or communism or interventionism or anything-but-capitalism-ism) is that it somehow addresses the more noble goal of meeting human needs than the base, greedy, capitalist goal of reaping profits; hence, the political slogan, "Human Needs Before Profits!" Implicit in this slogan, which one can imagine an emotional crowd chanting at a demonstration, is the idea that capitalists are greedy pigs whose prosperity comes at the expense of the poor and that society should be organized (forced to behave) in such a way that true human needs (as defined by the slogan chanters) should have priority over the earnings of business owners.

This sentiment is the embodiment of multiple errors of reasoning, and I can demonstrate this by a very simple proposition.

I ask (defy) you, reader, to:
Design a business plan guaranteed to generate profits, while ensuring that no human needs get met. Or, if human needs are met, they are met only after profits have been earned and cashed.

Here are the rules: You may not kill, rob, rape, persecute or conspire; you must respect the lives and property of all other people, at least to the extent of doing no harm, committing no offense. But you must not provide any service that anyone needs, nor produce any product that is useful, nor add anything to a customer or beneficiary's well-being or happiness. Or, if you do, you must make sure you have pocketed your profit first. You must turn a profit consistently over the long term (say, eight out of ten years), without committing any crimes, and without subsidies, protective tariffs, or other government-bestowed privileges.

How would you do it?

Maybe you'd try the classic industrial capitalist model: build a factory, hire workers, produce and sell products. If your goal is to reap

143

profits without meeting human needs, you're already in trouble. First, you must accumulate the capital to build the factory. Let's pass over the implications of that and go to the next: hire the workers. Unless you are going to enslave people against their will (which is not permitted), you have to offer them wages and working conditions that are better than their alternatives, i.e., working on a farm or in a competitor's factory. You have to meet their needs at some level long before you can even dream of profit. In other words, under capitalism, human needs—the needs of the hired workers—already do naturally come before anything, and profit naturally comes dead last. Revenue generally can only be collected after the product has been delivered to the customer, which is after the product was manufactured, which was after the workers were hired (and paid, and paid and paid many times over), which was after the factory was built, which in itself required the hiring and paying of workers and the purchase of building materials and equipment. Profits come dead last, if they come at all. If the entrepreneur fails to meet the most urgent needs of his/her customers at a cost that is less than the prices customers are willing to pay, then the profits don't come at all.

It doesn't matter what business discipline or industry you chose. If you are operating within the laws of the free market, which require you to respect the lives and property of all other people and to only engage in voluntary cooperation, then there is no way to earn profit without meeting human needs, and no way to reap the profit before meeting just about all stakeholders' needs but your own—employees, managers, creditors, customers—first. If you go into a service business rather than industrial manufacturing, you'll have to serve the needs of customers in some way (hence, the term "service"). Whether you are an accountant, lawyer, physician, fashion consultant, beautician, personal trainer, software developer or masseuse, before you reap any profits, you're going to serve some customers.

But what about speculators? Now, there are some parasitic leeches, you say! Surely their profits come from no redeemable humanitarian activity!

Actually, speculators are no less virtuous than any other actors in the free market. They indeed do play a vital role in meeting human needs, through their research and assumption of risks, which they transmit to their "customers" through the price system of the market via their investments and trades.

An original equity investor provides funds to a company to enable it to get started or to expand operations: build a factory, hire workers, pay wages and salaries (meet human needs). Since the stock confers upon the stockholder an ownership claim to a portion of the assets of the company and, hence, the profits (and losses) thereof, it has a value of its own which can be sold and bought in the stock market. The price is determined by the average estimations of any number of investors as to how well the company is doing and its future prospects. The speculator's role is to put a reality check on all other speculators and investors and to correct errors before their magnitude becomes great. If investors bid a stock price up (or down) beyond reality, then eventually, fundamental business processes of profit and loss will inevitably bring it back down (or up). These price swings can be very painful, particularly for the investors who buy when the stock is overpriced and find the price sinking far below their original outlay. The speculator helps to smooth out these swings, mitigating the damage. If he is right, his short-sell puts the brakes on the excessive appreciation of the stock price; likewise, his buying the stock when it is undervalued influences the price in the right direction.

Speculators in the commodities markets provide a year-round, risk-mitigated market for agricultural products[32]. The farmer is not at the mercy of what the price of corn happens to be on the day he harvests his crop. Because of the commodity markets and the speculators who research market conditions around the world and express their forecasts by their own commitments, risking their own money, the farmer can be much more secure than he otherwise would be as to what price he will be able to sell for, and can make the decision any time of the year via futures contracts.

The speculator only wins (earns profits) if he is right. If he short-sells a stock at the wrong price point, he loses. So, you can't beat the human-needs-before-profits law by becoming a speculator (sorry!). Only in a market distorted by government intervention (high tariffs,

---

[32]   See also: "The Social Function of Call and Put Options" by Robert P. Murphy at http://www.mises.org/story/2417

taxes, corruption, regulations that have nothing to do with preventing murder, theft, fraud or conspiracy) can a speculator earn profits at the expense of the general population.

Profits are the reward—after the fact—of meeting human needs.

So the slogan is true after all, just not the way those chanting it understand.

Why We Don't Need Trade Wars

[Published on CitizenEcon.com on June 24, 2013]

In the movie *"L'Auberge Espagnole"* (*"The Spanish Apartment"*) a French college student goes abroad to Barcelona, Spain, to learn Castilian Spanish and complete his studies of economics, with the promise of an attractive job offer from his sponsor upon his return to France. In one scene, one of the economics professors insists upon teaching the course—to his students who come from all over the world—in Catalán, the historical language of Catalonia, the region of Spain of which Barcelona is the capital. "If you want Castellano [the language of Castile that came to dominate Spain as a whole and South America besides—what we call 'Spanish'], then go to Madrid!" he booms.

No doubt Catalán is a beautiful language with a rich literary and cultural heritage. But it is worth noting that while this business prof is training his charges in Catalán, the Chinese are teaching their business students (and 300 million of their closest friends, more than the population of the United States) . . . in English! Pop quiz: who's going to dominate the global economy in the twenty-first century?

This Catalonian professor was practicing what could be called cultural protectionism—insisting upon doing things his way, insulated from external realities. But his students will pay a price in diminished opportunity, for preferring the provincial to the global, blinders to eyes wide open.

And so it is with the more overt forms of economic protectionism and isolationism: tariffs, quotas, regulation that discriminates against imports, supposedly in favor of exports, etc. Most of these measures help only a few privileged or politically connected groups of people, and only for a short period of time, while injuring the welfare of the society at large, especially over the long term.

Trade Facts and Stats

Here are some facts and statistics which paint a picture of the globally interconnected economic world in which we live today[33]:

- International trade has tripled to quadrupled in the last fifty years.

- During the same two generations of expanding globalization, the U.S. workforce and total employment have doubled. Prior to 2008, the unemployment rate averaged 5-6%. Trade is not causing loss of the number of jobs (the employment crisis of 2009-2011 was not caused by trade, free or otherwise).

- Trade does not cause declining wages. Real hourly compensation in America, including non-wage benefits, increased 41% on average from 1973 to 2007, and 23% from 1991 to 2007.

- Over the past forty years or so, the median U.S. household income has increased 20%, from about $40,000 per year to about $50,000. The average size of a household was 3.2 people in 1967; 2.6 people today. Therefore, those household income figures translate into more dough per individual today.

- 20% of humanity lives in China, and trade with China constitutes 15% of all U.S. foreign trade.

- The U.S. spends about 2% of its GDP on goods imported from China; $260 billion in consumer goods and $60 billion in industrial goods. Two-thirds of that are products designed in the U.S., manufactured in Japan, Germany, South Korea, Taiwan, Singapore, Malaysia and/or the U.S., and finally assembled, at the end of the chain, in China. (Think Apple iPad.)

- The percentage of the world's population living in "absolute" poverty ($1.25/day or less) has decreased from over 50% in 1981 to 25% in 2005. In China, 600 million people have climbed out of absolute poverty in the last thirty years.

---

[33]   Most of these stats come from Daniel Griswold's book "Mad About Trade: Why Main Street America should Embrace Globalization" pub. 2009 by the Cato Institute.

- Quality of life has improved across the board in the developing world in this era of globalization. For example, since 1960:
  - Life expectancy: from 45 years to 65 years
  - Infant mortality: down 60%
  - Food: from less than 2,000 to more than 2,600 calories/day
  - Literacy: from less than half to over two-thirds
  - Child labor: down from 25% to 10%
- American companies employ 10 million workers outside of the United States. Fewer than 5% are in China; an equal number are in Germany, a country with 1/17th the population of China.
- More than two-thirds of American foreign investment flows to other wealthy peer countries, not Third World "sweatshops."
- Wage rates and labor costs are not the same thing. If Fatcatistan's workers get paid twice the ducats per hour of workers in Pauperia but produce three times the value output, then Fatcatistan has the lower labor costs.
- In 1776, 97% of Americans were farmers. Now only 3% of the population works in agriculture, yet we are the best-fed (overfed? most obese?) nation on earth and the world's leading exporter of food.
- Employment in the American manufacturing sector declined 20% in seventeen years, from 17.1 million jobs in 1991 to 13.5 million in 2008. On the other hand, employment in the service sector during the same period increased 51% from 37 million to 56 million. Thus, a decline of 3.6 million jobs in manufacturing has been offset by a 19 million job increase in construction, professional, business, financial, education, health and other services.
- American consumers spend 60% of their discretionary income on services today, whereas two generations ago, they spent more than that proportion on manufactured goods.
- Meanwhile, manufacturing output (productivity) increased by about 60%. We're making more stuff, producing more value,

with fewer people, just as we did in agriculture in past generations.

- America (a.k.a. 250,000 companies) is the world's #1 exporter. We make $380 billion worth of semiconductors, civilian aircraft, vehicle parts and accessories, passenger cars, industrial machines, pharmaceutical preparations, telecommunications equipment, organic chemicals, electric apparatus and computer accessories . . . and twice again as much more stuff. Not too shabby for a country that "doesn't make anything anymore."

- When imports go up, so do exports. When imports go down, so do exports. Anti-trade/pro-protective tariff theory predicts the opposite, and fails.

- The trade deficit is negatively correlated with unemployment. That is, when the deficit goes up, unemployment falls/employment increases. If you are pining for the good old days, those few individual years when we got the trade deficit "under control," you are a cheerleader for recessions: 1961, 1975, 1982, 1991, 2001.

- More than half of the imports into the U.S. are raw materials or intermediate products that American manufacturers use as inputs to their final product. Domestic American companies need imports.

- 97% of job displacement in the U.S. is due to technological change, not trade. Every year, 15 million jobs disappear and another 15+ million are created. Trade-related job churn accounts for up to 500,000 of those, which is to say 3%.

- Stuff that is traded in international markets gets less expensive all the time, whereas products and services protected or insulated from competition get more expensive. Think computers on the one hand vs. college tuition on the other; TVs vs. medical services; cell phones vs. Super Bowl tickets; clothing vs. car repair. Trade makes stuff cheaper for you and me.

- Two-thirds of GM and Ford's business is outside the U.S.

- With your outsourcing hysteria, get some *in*sourcing tranquilizer: For example, Japanese manufacturers employ about a third of all Americans who work in the automotive industry, in factories in eleven U.S. states. The 5+ million American employees of foreign-owned affiliates here earn, on average, 30% more than employees of domestic companies. Ask them if they think that's a bad thing.

- Americans own over $100 trillion worth of assets. Our negative Net International Investment Position (the difference between foreign assets that we own and American assets owned by foreigners) is less than 2% of that. 40% of that 'less-than 2%' are equity positions—stocks, real estate, direct investment—that is not a debt burden; it does not need to be "paid back."

- Price discrimination, like charging different prices for tickets to occupy the same movie theatre seats to adults, seniors, children and students, is a perfectly economically rational and legal practice. Yet, when a foreign company sells in the U.S. market below average cost, we call it "dumping," call the international police and slap fines on the "criminals." Someone please tell BMW that I would like a ~~2014~~ 2016 740iL "dumped" in front of my garage with the key in the ignition and a blue bow on top. In return, I promise: 1) I'll send a check for $100 to satisfy the "below average cost" requirement (including shipping, handling and gift-wrapping) and 2) I won't sue or lobby my congressman for a redress of grievance.

- About 100,000 Americans are employed in the steel industry. About 4 million (that's forty times as many more) work in industries that use steel to make products. The steel tariff of 2002 may have helped the few steel workers temporarily, but it screwed everyone else, like the steel-consuming industries and you and me, who buy or rent cars, machine tools, industrial equipment and office space. Thankfully, the tariff was repealed in 2004 under persuasion from that evil foreign menace to our sovereignty, the World Trade Organization (WTO).

Why we don't need a new New NEW Deal

[Published June 22, 2013 on CitizenEcon.com]

The last time the American economy was in such dire straits was over thirty years ago; perhaps seventy. Do the lessons of the Great Depression perhaps hold any explanations, let alone solutions? Let's recall a bit what happened all those years ago (it might even feel familiar):

- From September 1929 to July 1932, the Dow Jones Industrial Average (DJIA) fell from a high of 381 to 43, an 88% decline. In our time, that would be like the Dow falling from 15,000 to 1,800.

- Some of the most dramatic moments occurred in late October 1929, on the 24th ('Black Thursday': almost 13 million shares, or approximately 3 times the daily average, traded for a 6-point drop in the DJIA) and the 29th ('Black Tuesday': 16+ million shares traded for a 30-point drop).

- The market didn't recover its pre-crash level for 25 years.

- Chronic unemployment soared from a historical average of 5% to over 15% for almost a decade, peaking at 25% in 1933.

- Industrial production was cut in half.

- Business construction dropped 84%.

- Bank failures spiked from a historic average of 700 per year to 1,350 in 1930, 2,293 in 1931, 1,453 in 1932; 4000 commercial banks failed in 1933.

- The crisis rippled worldwide and contributed to the rise of Hitler and Mussolini in Europe.

- Four years into the Roosevelt presidency, in 1937-38, the economy sank into recession for a second dip.

- Only World War II in the 1940's resulted in increased production and put an end to high unemployment, at a terrible price; millions of lives lost in the war, all production being channeled into armaments with little left over for consumer goods or comforts. True prosperity would not return until the late 1940's or later.

The lessons to be learned from this calamity are indeed applicable to our present-day crisis. But the conventional wisdom about the Great Depression—that it was caused by the excesses of free markets that must necessarily lead to crisis by virtue of capitalism's inherent contradictions, abetted by the laissez-faire policies of a Republican president Herbert Hoover, and that the government-expanding New Deal policies of Democratic president Franklin Delano Roosevelt were the necessary and proper remedy which saved us from a worse fate—is entirely wrong.

The stock market crash of October 1929 was the direct result, not of free-market capitalism, but precisely of government interference in the market, transmitted via the political signal that the Smoot-Hawley Tariff bill, a protectionist monstrosity, would be made law. The market correctly estimated that this bill would substantially constrain international commerce, reducing the current market value of financial and other assets. The search for the right revaluation was a panicked activity; but that panic was rationally justified.

The subsequent government responses to the initial crisis dug the country increasingly deeper into the hole.

A Crisis of Intervention

Remember the Great Depression of the 1920s? Of course you don't, because it didn't happen. It might be because President Warren Harding ignored his Secretary of Commerce Hebert Hoover's advice to intervene in the recession of 1921, and that recession quickly recovered and was forgotten.

Herbert Hoover was no laissez-faire leader. In the early '20s, before either was president, Hoover collaborated with Franklin Delano Roosevelt in the American Construction Council, an attempt to turn the construction industry of the entire nation into one giant cartel. He participated in the drafting of the Railway Labor Act of 1926, a major step to collectivizing labor relations. He believed that high wages in an economy cause general prosperity, rather than—the other way around—that prosperity produces higher wages. From this premise much of Hoover's efforts as president would be targeted at maintaining pre-crash wage rates for those workers who still had jobs. Economic theory states that artificially attractive prices cause shortages. In this case, it led to a shortage of jobs: unemployment.

153

After the crash, President Hoover (1929-33) intervened aggressively in the economy. Hoover:

- Summoned the leaders of the largest corporations and business associations to a series of conferences for, in his own words, "the coordination of business and governmental agencies in concerted action." They acted in large part to maintain existing wage rates and continue expansion. Real wages for employed workers increased for most of Hoover's term, peaking at 11% above 1929 levels in 1931 and still a 'healthy' 8% in 1933 while unemployment simultaneously soared to 25% (in other words, nice work if you can get it; God help you if you can't).

- Urged public works programs in response to the crisis. The Division of Public Construction of the Department of Commerce was created in December 1929. Hoover urged state governors to follow suit at their level.

- Intervened in different directions at different times in commodity markets. When the Federal Farm Board's policy of price supports resulted in overproduction of wheat, cotton, wool and other products, thereby collapsing prices and bringing devastating losses, Hoover changed course to order acreage to be plowed under, taken out of production, and to destroy 'excessive' livestock.

- Authorized construction of Hoover Dam on the Colorado River, at a cost of $915 million (equivalent of roughly $45 billion of today's dollars).

- Signed the Smoot-Hawley Tariff into law in 1930.

- Weakened bankruptcy laws in favor of debtors and eroding the property rights of creditors.

- Imposed an immigration ban which effectively reduced legal immigration from Europe by 90% overnight. He deported as many as 20,000 'undesirable' aliens per year.

- Publicly assailed speculators and coerced the New York Stock Exchange to curtail short selling; campaigned against 'unpatriotic', 'traitorous' hoarders (or put another way, demonized frugal, risk-averse citizens who claimed the right to their property and thereby exposed unsound credit policies and institutions).

- In February 1931, signed the Employment Stabilization Act, creating the Employment Stabilization Board. Unemployment soared to 25% in 1933 and didn't fall to pre-depression levels until 1940.
- Massively increased government expenditures at a time when revenue to the treasury was falling, resulting in the largest peacetime deficits to date in American history. Federal expenditures rose 30% in 1930 alone, from $4.2 billion to $5.5 billion.
- In 1931, created the President's Organization on Unemployment Relief, effectively inserting the federal government for the first time into a sphere that had previously been considered the responsibility of private charities and religious organizations.
- In 1931-32, created the Reconstruction Finance Corporation, intended to centrally and comprehensively direct and manage the banking, lending, insurance and finance industries.
- Reduced the hours worked by government employees without reducing their salaries.
- Cancelled oil-drilling permits on publicly-owned land, in an effort to restrict supply and maintain a 'minimum fair price' for the petroleum industry.
- In May 1931, closed Federally-owned forest land to new logging, in order to defend timber prices.
- Urged the Federal Reserve to relax its lending and discount standards (in other words, engaged in artificial credit expansion). See: Glass-Steagall Act of 1932.
- Signed the Federal Home Loan Bank Act, creating the Federal Home Loan Bank Board, since 1989 the Office of Thrift Supervision, intended to promote home ownership.

One of the few of Hoover's acts which could be qualified as pro-limited government and individual property rights was his income tax rate cut of 1930, from the stratospheric height of 5% to 4% (a cut of

20%) for individuals, and 12% to 11% for corporations. Prior to the 1930's, the income tax had not taken anything like its modern bite in the daily lives and livelihoods of citizens.

However, in 1932 he reversed course and raised income taxes as well as prior wartime excise taxes and sales taxes on hundreds of consumer goods. The surtax on the highest incomes went from 25% to 63%. When businessmen suggested to Hoover that the tax regimen was detrimental to the general economic health and that the government would do better to cut expenditures by $2 billion, Hoover brushed them aside.

Roosevelt to the Rescue

Franklin Delano Roosevelt took office in March 1933. He would create hundreds of new interventionist agencies and embark on unprecedented projects, transforming American society on a massive scale. The following is only a representative sample of the alphabet soup of interventions, projects and agencies initiated by the Roosevelt Administration known in the aggregate as the New Deal:

- United States Bank Holiday / Emergency Banking Act: FDR ordered every bank in the country closed on the first week of his term. No one could make deposits or withdrawals, that is, have access to their own property.
- "Relief, Recovery and Reform": slogan of the early FDR administration
- Tennessee Valley Authority (TVA)
- Works Progress Administration (WPA)
- Wagner Act: Boosted privileges of unions and approved collective bargaining rights.
- Federal Deposit Insurance Corporation (FDIC)
- Federal Housing Administration (FHA)
- Securities and Exchange Commission (SEC)
- Agricultural Adjustment Association (AAA)
- National Recovery Administration (NRA)
- Works Progress Administration (WPA)
- Executive Order 6102, a.k.a. gold confiscation
- Farm Credit Act

- National Industrial Recovery Act / National Recovery Administration
- Public Works Administration
- Civilian Conservation Corps
- Federal Emergency Relief Administration (FERA)
- Reconstruction Finance Corporation
- Civil Works Administration
- Emergency Relief Appropriation Act
- National Labor Relations Act / National Labor Relations Board (the people who tell Boeing they can't open a new plant in a non-union state.)
- Fair Labor Standards Act
- Fair Employment Practices Commission
- Federal Project Number One (sponsoring artists, artistic works and productions)
- Committee on Economic Security
- Social Security Act

Finally, toward the end of his reign, FDR attempted to implement what he called the
- Second Bill of Rights

Many of these agencies and institutions are with us to this day and are likely to continue for generations. What these acts, agencies and institutions DIDN'T do is end the Depression.

The Depression lasted seven more years beyond Hoover, with a second, 'double-dip' recession in 1937-38. It didn't end definitively, with the return of full employment, until World War II production and mobilizations were well under way. World War II's destruction and death per se didn't fix the Depression. It was the return of relatively free-market policies and the END of the most aggressive interventions and the demonization of businessmen which permitted the economy to return to a more rational basis for functioning.

So what would you have done, smarty-pants?

Crises always look a lot simpler from a distance in space and time. But the response of Hoover and Roosevelt to the Crash and

Depression were not those of panicked, surprised men with no clue what to do. They were the premeditated strategies of calculating men, carried out in their moment of opportunity. Hoover and FDR were interventionists who didn't believe in free-market, laissez-faire capitalism and exploited every crisis for the purposes of implementing their own vision of governance, fully formed years earlier.

It's not that these were bad men; we can assume they sincerely believed, as many of our politicians to this day believe, that it is the appropriate role of the federal government, its hundreds of agencies and tens of thousands of bureaucrats, to micro-manage every aspect of our economic lives 'for the greater good'. To a degree they can be forgiven for being, as all mortal men are, imperfect and in this case, mistaken.

The same is difficult to say for the politicians who, 80 years later, insist upon leading us down the same path to government expansion, micromanagement and high taxation above and beyond the New Deal (and later, Lyndon Baines Johnson's Great Society) with the excuse that it's necessary in order to resolve or prevent the crisis and bring prosperity, security and health care to all. The evidence is overwhelming that regardless of political party, such intervention only amplifies and prolongs the crisis. Politicians and government, even 'good' ones, do not create wealth, produce high wages and low prices for workers, high revenue and low costs for businesses, or innovative and environmentally friendly products and services. They can't guarantee no one will fail and shouldn't guarantee that anyone succeed at the expense of anyone else. Only the market—entrepreneurs, business people, private firms big and small, investors, speculators, insurers and individual consumers—cooperating voluntarily, acting in their own interest within the rule of law, can accomplish the best production and distribution of wealth possible in an imperfect, physical world (as opposed to celestial paradise).

As a matter of economic principle, it was futile for Hoover or FDR to:

- Attempt to prop up wages. If the total amount of wealth and activity in an economy has diminished for whatever reason (natural disaster, war, contraction of trade due to protectionism—Smoot Hawley—and retaliation by partners, or other destruction of wealth), then someone's wages will have to fall in real terms. If one politically favored group's wages are artificially maintained above what they would be under un-coerced voluntary cooperation, then someone else's wages have to fall proportionately (and unjustly, including to zero—unemployment) to balance the aggregate accounts.

- Attempt to prop up commodity prices for farmers. If corn is too cheap, marginal corn farmers need to grow soybeans or take a higher-paying job in industry. This is how it has always been. When our nation was born, 97% of the population worked the land; now that proportion is reversed, with only 3% in agriculture feeding the entire US and much of the rest of the world. Low prices benefit the consumer and as such are not inherently bad.

  The futility of the intervention was brought to light when the Federal Farm Board's policy of price supports encouraged overproduction of wheat, cotton, wool and other products, resulting in even worse collapsing market prices and devastating losses. At that point Hoover intervened in another direction, to order acreage to be plowed under, taken out of production, and to destroy 'excessive' livestock.

- Attempt to prop up prices for the benefit of big industrial producers. If oil or lumber is too cheap, marginal oil/lumber companies have to get into a different business where they have a relative advantage and/or where the consumers are clamoring for the product. No subsidy or privilege is required, let alone justified, to bring the economy back into balance.

- Attempt to 'protect' domestic industries from foreign competition via protective tariffs such as the Smoot-Hawley bill. Such actions always hurt domestic consumers and invite retaliation from foreign governments and their favored industries. The Smoot-Hawley bill was arguably the single most important trigger of the October 1929 crash, as investors and economists correctly re-estimated the value of their investments under a reduced-trade market.

- Herd workers into unions that they would not join under conditions of voluntary cooperation. Favoring unions at the expense of free labor is a violation of liberty; it raises wages for some at the expense of others who receive less (or nothing) and undermines the ability of workers to develop as independent entrepreneurs. Independent-minded Americans have always resisted unionization compared to other western nations, for good reason.

- Manipulate money and credit prices / interest rates. Monetary manipulation by private individuals is prosecutable as counterfeiting and/or fraud, and is no less evil or destructive when practiced by government. Forcing interest rates too high chokes economic activity; forcing them too low makes longer production cycles—and with them higher investment returns—appear like mirages in the desert, deceiving investors to make bets that are destined to fail.

- Embark on public works projects for the purpose of 'putting America back to work'. If a road or bridge needs to be built, let the agency most impacted by it (municipal, country or state government, or private firms) build it. If an electric company sees a business opportunity in building a dam, let them buy the property, indemnify 3rd parties and other stakeholders, carry plenty of insurance, clean up their messes, reimburse anyone they harm, and finance the project with their own investor's resources (and reap whatever profits the market may bear without having it taxed away). But spending capital for the sake of busy activity does not increase wealth; it sucks wealth away from where it is more desperately needed. The 1930's Autobahn in Germany was a glamorous showcase, but an economic and social disaster.

- Weaken protection for creditors in bankruptcy proceedings. This is a classic case of attempting to make a balloon smaller by squeezing it at one end; it always bulges out at the other. What person with money to lend wants to risk their capital in an environment in which the government has signaled its willingness to arbitrarily change the terms of any loan contract? Such uncertainty leads to a contraction of credit. How does that help future borrowers/debtors?

- Threaten and demonize innocent people. In different times and places, this has meant Christians, blacks, Jews, merchants, bankers, gypsies, homosexuals, whites, Hutus, the mentally deficient, the culturally undesirable, browns, union workers, strike breakers ('scabs'), foreigners, rich people, poor people, good people, bad people and ugly people. Corrupt and despotic politicians have employed this base technique for millennia, but it is unworthy of an enlightened leader of a free people today to do so. The only justification for any accusation is specific allegations of criminal wrongdoing targeted at the specific individuals (not groups) who committed them. Investing and/or speculating against the market outcomes desired by a political party or government program does not qualify as justification for group persecution.
- Increase government spending in time of diminished tax revenue.
- Micromanage businesses.

As a solution to the economic crisis, Roosevelt's interventions and the alphabet soup of agencies created to implement them were equally or more futile than those of Hoover. The Social Security Act and system will require its own in-depth discussion. But make no mistake, Bernie Madoff could not have done worse in the long term.

Conclusions

- The Great Depression was a crisis of government intervention, not one of free-market capitalism. Government intervention is the problem; free-market capitalism under the rule of law is the solution.
- The Hoover-Roosevelt administrations constituted a continuum, not a fundamental change of policy direction. Herbert Hoover was not a free-market, laissez-faire capitalist, limited-government president.
- As long as the interventionist philosophy prevails in our nation's capital and in state capitals, we can expect more economic crises, as bad or worse. It doesn't matter that the

interventions are 'for the greater good' or that the people leading the intervention are good, well-intentioned, virtuous, upstanding citizens. An impossible task is still impossible when undertaken by a mortal saint.

It is remarkable that the myth of the 'success' of the New Deal lives on to this day. The Depression lasted seven more years beyond Hoover, with a second, deep recession in 1937-38. The depression didn't end definitively, with the return of full employment, until World War II production and mobilizations were well under way. In other words, a calamitous event in which tens of millions of people worldwide were killed and hundreds of cities, with all of their wealth and assets, were completely destroyed, was by one measure less damaging to the economy—perhaps even beneficial—than the policies of Hoover, FDR and the New Deal.

It is dangerous to hold the thought that war is an antidote to economic depression, just as is it is to consider war and conquest a solution to economic challenges such as securing reliable supplies of materials that your country lacks (from Caesar's conquests to Hitler's 'lebensraum').

World War II's destruction and death didn't fix the Depression. What happened was that many government interventions of the New Deal, including the demonization of businessmen, were abandoned and not reinstated after the war was over. The end of the Hoover-FDR New Deal ended the Depression. It would have ended 10 years sooner if this tragic blunder had never been attempted. Moreover, some of the worst tragedies of the War might have been avoided if not for the worldwide ripple effects of the economic malaise. May we never again be tempted to repeat such a disaster.

That depends on YOU, citizen-economist.

Understanding the Financial Crisis of 2008

[Published on CitizenEcon.com on June 21, 2013]

The housing market—prices and lending behavior—went irrational in the first half of the first decade of the 2000s, then crashed in 2008, sending seismic financial shock waves around the world which are still reverberating late in 2013, with stubbornly high unemployment and massive increases in public spending and debt which haven't improved the situation at all.

Since housing was the spark that set off the fire, let's take a closer look at that.

Not all housing markets (by geography) experienced the same wild gyrations. As a national average, the rise in purchase prices paid was only 38% from 1999 to 2005, and the "collapse" only 10% from 2006 through 2008 (in other words, home prices were still higher in 2008 than in 1999 by 28%—hardly a crisis). But in certain local markets in Nevada, Florida, Arizona, coastal California and a few others, the rise and fall was much more amplified, with prices more than doubling in some places during the boom and falling almost as far or farther in the crash. Most of the rest of the country was not going nuts. In places like Houston and Dallas, Texas, for example, there was hardly any extraordinary rise in prices and therefore no traumatic bust. Moreover, housing in general has been more affordable in those markets, taking a substantially smaller share of an owner or renter's income to maintain than in the "hot" markets.

In other words, the housing market surge and collapse was, at its root, a localized phenomenon, not a general or national one.

So, why did prices rise so dramatically in these particular markets? It's a question of supply and demand—mainly for land on the one hand, and for mortgage loans on the other.

The supply of loans (price/interest rate and availability/approval) is principally governed by the lender's perception of the risk of getting paid back (or not) for the cash advanced to the borrower. In a free market, banks that lend to deadbeats will soon be bankrupt, unable to recoup the money they've advanced (bankers consider that a bad thing). So, traditionally, these have been very conservative and prudent, wearing their bowties and green eyeshades, scrutinizing and documenting every potential borrower's credit history, good character and sources and amounts of income, as well as general economic conditions that may affect the continuance of the same. The higher the perceived risk of lending, the more constrained the supply of lendable funds and the higher the interest rate (credit price) charged. The calculation of risk and supply are made on the basis of general market conditions, the amount of cash that each bank has available and case-by-case particulars centered on the individual borrower or co-borrowers.

In the 1970s, the price of housing in Nevada, Florida, Arizona and coastal California were not that much different from the rest of the country, neither in absolute terms nor as a percentage of the owner/renter's income required to maintain a home (which is to say, affordability).

Two contradictory and not fully thought-through political goals kicked off the long march to disaster: ***wilderness preservation*** and ***affordable housing***.

Wilderness Preservation
Beginning in the 1970s, the environmental movement and its political allies promoted increasingly extensive and rigorous land-use restriction laws. These policies were always promoted under the slogans of preserving wilderness, saving farmland, creating open space, "smart growth," rescuing endangered species and/or habitat and other happy, desirable outcomes.

News flash! Reducing the supply of a good puts upward pressure on its market price! In the markets and geographical regions where such laws were passed, real estate prices began to climb out of previously "normal" ranges. The cost of real estate—and with it, housing—skyrocketed in relation to other regions where the legal environment favored full, unfettered private property rights. Housing became less affordable.

Affordable Housing

> *Neither by comparison with the recent past nor by comparison with other countries today is most housing in the United States unaffordable. The median-priced home in the United States as a whole is 3.6 times the median income of Americans. For Great Britain, the median-priced home is 5.5 times the median income and in Australia and New Zealand, the ratio of home prices to income is 6.3.*
>
> Thomas Sowell, "The Housing Boom and Bust"

Nevertheless, the federal government and its appendages have been on a decades-long crusade to make housing in America more "affordable."

The Community Reinvestment Act of 1977 gave the federal government an unprecedented foothold in micromanaging the business practices of lenders, telling them to whom they should lend, how much and on what terms. In the 1990s the power of this act was amplified, with banks having to establish racial and ethnic quotas, both in their lending and in their hiring practices, and ask permission before merging or opening new branches (permission which might be denied on the political grounds of not having done enough "socially responsible" work or lending in their communities). In 1993 the Department of Housing and Urban Development, or HUD, began suing banks over race-based statistical disparities. The implicit assumptions seem to have been that a) bureaucrats in Washington (and community activists at ACORN) know better than bankers in Peoria what are the "correct" lending criteria and practices for their local markets, what is the best and soundest "socially responsible" policy for what to do with their depositors' money, b) lending is somehow doing someone a favor, as opposed to being a mutually beneficial exchange, and c) unless Washington keeps a close vigil on greedy, racist bankers, they would discriminate unfairly against racial minorities, denying them loans more often than white/European majority applicants.

Point A—Washington bureaucrats know best—is laughable on its face, yet its premise underlies most government economic policy today. Point B—lending is a one-way favor—seems to ignore the fact that lenders are in the business of lending and benefit from it; they *want* to lend.

Point C—banker's racism would run amok if not put on a short leash—is easily refuted:

- Bankers' favorite color is not white or black, but green. Any banker offended by receiving a monthly loan payment from a brown or yellow person will soon find himself in the red. The natural mechanism of the market is for gaps in supply to be eagerly filled by entrepreneurs, however greedy or racist they may be. Customers missed by one supplier will be eagerly served by another. Take race out of it, and it's called market segmentation, specialization, and niche opportunity exploitation.

- Statistical differences between racial groups are not proof of unfair discrimination against individuals. When controlled for credit ratings, wealth, income, employment history and other factors, no material discrepancies remain.

- Black-owned banks have been shown to turn down black applicants for loans at a higher rate than white-owned banks.

- Chinese and Japanese Americans have suffered discrimination and even internment as de facto prisoners of war in the past. But, today, Asian applicants in the aggregate are turned down for loans less often than white/European Americans. This fact does not support a theory of white racism among bankers.

So, banks were under increasing pressure to make loans to satisfy politicians rather than depositors and borrowers—to loosen lending standards, to *not* scrutinize and document the individual applicant's creditworthiness, good character and sources and amounts of income, but to focus their attention on rectifying the supposed evils of "redlining" and "disparate impact." Thus, the non-traditional, or "subprime," market grew from 7% of all loans in 2001 to 19% in 2006.

But how could the banks do this (neglect their lending standards) without cutting their own throats?

The politicians, who did the bankers no favors by bullying them into making millions of loans that they might not have made, gave them a way out: flip the loans, and with them, the risk of default—good, bad or ugly—to someone else.

Over the past forty years, the privileges and obligations of two government-sponsored companies, Fannie Mae and Freddie Mac, have been significantly beefed up, again for the laudable purpose of promoting "affordable housing." These companies have CEOs, stockholders and profit-and-loss statements like private banks and other publicly traded companies, but they were chartered by the federal government for the purpose of doing "good" in their markets (as opposed to merely raking in obscene profits for their greedy shareholders and CEOs like Franklin Raines and his $90 million compensation package), in exchange for which they enjoy preferential tax treatment and the implicit guarantee that if anything goes wrong, Uncle Sam (that's you and me, the taxpayers) will pick up the tab.

Since at least 1992, Fan and Fred have been under orders to buy up more and more "affordable housing" mortgages from the originating lender banks. By 2007, Fan and Fred had purchased 40% of the sub-prime and/or non-traditional mortgages (a.k.a. "Liar Loans," loans made with minimal or no documentation, due diligence, credit checks, character references, etc.) originated in the United States, or about $1 million worth. The total value of their debt outstanding, as of 2010, was over $8 million; that's two-thirds the magnitude of the national debt of the United States in that year.

Fannie Mae and Freddie Mac have long enjoyed unwavering support from cheerleaders in positions of significant power in the federal government, among them Barney Frank, Christopher Dodd, Maxine Waters, Joe Baca, Nancy Pelosi, Charles Rangel and Kit Bond, among others.

In any event, the inevitable happened. In 2006, loan default rates, especially in the sub-prime market, reached record levels. In 2007 Countrywide Home Loans' share price collapsed and it was acquired by Bank of America. B of A itself was one of several targets of the Troubled Asset Relief Program (TARP) to the tune of $45 billion, along with several other financial dominoes that were deemed "too big to fail": Citigroup, $50 billion; AIG, $40 billion; Wells Fargo, $25 billion; J.P. Morgan Chase, $25 billion.

In spite of TARP and multiple rounds of economic "stimulus" spending plans by the Bush and Obama administrations (or perhaps because of them), the employment rate and general economic health of the country has sunk to lows not seen in at least thirty years, with hardly an exit in sight.

The natural economic forces of supply and demand were derailed in housing markets in America in the early years of the twenty-first century, leading first to the craze, and then inevitably to the crisis. Like all crises of this magnitude, this was one of government interference in the natural, self-correcting mechanisms of the free market, building one intervention on top of another until it collapsed of its own dead weight.

- - - - - - - - - - - -

Recommended reading/primary sources for this chapter: Thomas Sowell's The Housing Boom and Bust, Revised Edition *2010 by Basic Books; John A. Allison's* The Financial Crisis and the Free Market Cure, *2013 by McGraw-Hill;* 'Fanny Mayhem: A History", *a compendium of 30 Wall Street Journal articles documenting the cozy corruption of Fannie Mae, Freddie Mac, Senator Christopher Dodd, Congressman Barney Frank and others in the years leading up to the 2008 crash: http://www.wsj.com/articles/SB121599777668249845*

For a deep dive into business cycle theory, see Murray Rothbard's chapter 'How the Business Cycle Happens' in America's Great Depression, 1963 by D. Van Nostrand *and/or chapters XX and XXXI of Ludwig von Mises'* Human Action, 1998 by the Ludwig von Mises Institute.

Why Obamacare Will Fail

[Excerpted from the book "Pull the Plug on Obamacare" and published on FrontPageMag.com, October 30, 2012. Included in this part because the principles presented are especially universal, not limited to health care.]

Medicare, when proposed in 1965 was expected to cost $12 billion by 1990; it cost $90 billion in that year—seven and a half times more than expected (or more accurately, sold to the public). Medicaid was projected to cost $238 million per year. In its first year, the actual invoice came in at $1 billion—four times greater than advertised. The hospitalization program was supposed to cost $1 billion by 1987; instead the tab was $17 billion that year. The program has been expanded to the point of being 37 times more costly (inflation-adjusted) than originally sold.

Yet we are supposed to believe that we have an unfettered virgin market in health care ruled by the law of the jungle, that insufficient regulation is causing all of the problems and that the only rational solution is for the federal government to take command of a sixth or more of the entire US economy; a brand new, original idea.

Obamacare, being the most ambitious social entitlement program ever conceived, much less attempted in the US, will only magnify and multiply the failures of prior interventions.

The failures of Medicare, Medicaid and socialized systems around the world are not accidents, rounding errors or bad luck of unanticipated complications. Rather, they are the inevitable, predicable result of forceful interference in the voluntary cooperation of free citizens. Obamacare will fail for the same reason that the Soviet Union did: command-and-control economies cannot function rationally.

When President Ronald Reagan famously declared "Mr. Gorbachev, tear down this wall" in 1987, few people believed that the concrete and razor-wire barrier separating the communist East from the free West Berlin, Germany, would in fact be demolished, liberating the citizen-inmates not only of the eastern sector of Berlin, but of most of Eastern Europe and Russia itself just 2 years later. But Reagan understood that a system conceived in the denial of individual liberty as both the fundamental moral principle of civilization and as the only rational basis for functioning economics, was doomed to collapse

169

under its own weight. He understood this in part because the downfall of the Soviet system had been predicted a few years earlier … in 1922.

Ludwig von Mises, the Austrian (later American) economist, demonstrated that socialism could never fulfill its promise no matter what variation was attempted nor how wise and virtuous the men running it. In his book "Socialism" he demonstrated logically that every wage and price control, every tariff, tax, privilege, prejudice, manipulation and regulation that does *not* derive from government's legitimate need to prevent and punish murder, robbery, assault, fraud, theft, rape, persecution and conspiracy distorts and destroys information necessary for rational economic planning and action. If some collective entity like the state owns or otherwise controls capital goods, land, natural resources, factories, machinery, services, licensing etc. then there is no market for these goods. There is no buying and selling, no bargaining and haggling, no competition to compel lower prices, higher quality, better service and the division of labor where each finds the role they are best suited to, and no supply and demand.

If there is no market, then there are no prices in the real sense of the word. Prices constitute the indispensable information system for signaling the needs and scarcities in an economy, and the cost of available alternatives. There are a hundred different ways to build a building, and dozens of alternative materials and techniques for each component. Which combination is the most economical? Who knows? Without prices, there is no way of knowing. There is no other metric that can adequately substitute for market prices. Economic planning cannot function without these numbers.

That is why socialism fails every time it is tried: Economic calculation is impossible under socialism.

And then there's the bureaucracy, which von Mises also wrote about. With no markets there is no competition, neither incentive nor reward for better customer service or to provide a higher quality product at a lower price. The entire economy becomes like a giant Post Office or Department of Motor Vehicles, with self-serving, inner-directed bureaucracies with languages and cultures of their own, foreign to the rest of us, with iron-clad privileges, job security and pensions that do not vary with how well or poorly they serve willing customers.

As applied to the health care market, those same principles apply. The more the government commands and controls services, insurance, physicians and other health professionals, drugs/pharmaceuticals, equipment like MRI machines, devices like defibrillators etc. then the less flexible and innovative is the market for these. There is: less buying and selling between parties commanding their own resources on their own account and for their own benefit, less bargaining and haggling (apart from government bullying from its position of monopoly power, as in price controls shrinking Medicare payment schedules etc.), less competition to compel lower prices, higher quality, better service and the division of labor and less operation of supply and demand.

Furthermore, this system leads to: the abolition of profit and loss, whether for providers, insurers or patients as legitimate regulators of behavior or scorecards of success or failure; a reduced scope of the operation of prices, therefore a breakdown of the indispensable economic information system of abundance, scarcity and alternatives; reduced possibility to recover research and development costs of breakthrough drugs (why bet billions when success makes you a target?). Shortages, waiting lists and government-imposed rationing of services, doctors, medicines etc. are the inevitable results.

With the market-based economic model suppressed, the only alternative is bureaucratic management based on politically-derived values. The opinions, concerns and desires of physicians, patients and families take a back seat to functionaries who are completely removed from personal economic or emotional involvement in the patient's case. What matters to him is that he faithfully executes the rules dictated to him by the dominant political party and union bosses.

"Progressive" politicians love to feed on people's resentment of "faceless" bureaucrats at private insurance companies as evidence of the failure of the free market. But when there is only one insurance company left, the government, with the right to tax you rather than face its own bankruptcy no matter how poorly it is run, people aren't going to love that insurance company more than the few nominally private ones we have now. Even if private insurance companies survive Obamacare, they will be taking their orders from the bureaucracy and the czars, not from patients, families and physicians.

Socialized medicine is not a new idea. It has been tried again and again in many advance countries yet has never achieved results to compare with the relatively free United States. Obamacare, the biggest such initiative of them all, will be the biggest failure. The most passionate sincere supporters of the Patient Protection and Affordable Care Act will be the most disappointed.

Part III: Socialized Medicine and Obamacare

As I mentioned in my speech to the AAPS earlier, it was Obamacare that got me out of my armchair and onto the streets handing out pamphlets in front of town hall meetings to warn my fellow citizens that socialized medicine was a really bad idea whose time must never come to America. This work culminated in the publishing of my short book, "Pull the Plug on Obamacare" (2013), articulating for the lay reader the reasons for our opposition. In a nutshell, in the book I warned Obamacare was deceptive, destructive and doomed.

I won't re-travel too much territory here already covered by that book, but this part contains some of my other published articles on the topic whose fundamental insights have stood the test of time.

Post-Obamacare Reform

[Published on FrontPageMag.com, February 20, 2014]

For all of the daily noise about the latest casualties of the Obamacare train wreck (Senator and Obamacare author Max Baucus' term), from the nonpartisan Congressional Budget Office (CBO) predicting major long-term damage to employment markets to the President's illegal delay of the black-letter provisions of the employer mandate, there is very little public discussion of what to do about all of it. The time is overdue to get alternatives into the public consciousness.

Obama and the Democrats love to say that Republicans never offered any alternatives to the Patient Protection and Affordable Care Act, a.k.a. Obamacare. They pretend to ignore the proposed Patient's Choice Act of 2009, the Empowering Patients First Act of 2009, the Patient Option Act of 2013, the American Health Care Reform Act of 2013, and now the Burr-Coburn-Hatch plan, a.k.a. the Patient Choice, Affordability, Responsibility, and Empowerment Act, a.k.a. the Patient CARE Act (PCA), to name a few. They get away with this feigned justifiable ignorance because they know that the dominant media will hardly give those proposals any ink, tweets or air time, even to let the public know that they exist.

There are plenty of options for healthcare reform besides the ACA, as even Obama tacitly acknowledges every time he issues another royal decree in contradiction to the law's (rare moments of) plain, unambiguous language; and we will have to discuss them in order to repair the damage left behind by this law and renew the world's best medical system. Let's first take a look at what is perhaps more important than the individual proposals themselves: the principles upon which reform should be based.

Principle Number One: Incremental (as opposed to comprehensive, all-or-nothing, take-it-or-leave-it) reform. Each policy should be a net positive in and of itself, a move in the right direction rather than a costly kludge that has to be offset somewhere else in the tangled web of taxes, fees, accounting gimmicks and legalese.

One of the biggest problems with Obamacare, as with the immigration reform and too many other bills besides, is their sheer size and scope. No one can read it apart from a handful of unaccountable 'experts' to whom we are supposed to surrender our common sense, our money and our liberty. We're still learning, four years later, what's in the Obamacare 'law'. And then when we do look at individual elements, whether actually in the law or made up after the fact, they are almost all negative: taxes, penalties, prohibitions, exemptions, delays, arbitrary and capricious power granted to unaccountable officers and boards, cost shifting (or it is SHAFTing?) to those least able to protect their interests by hiring lobbyists.

An important aspect of the policy proposals that I list below is that each of them can be taken on its own as a stand-alone bill, to be proposed, debated in the light of day, and voted up or down more or less independently of the others. If one seems less important or less urgent than others, we don't have to get bogged down; we can come back to it later while we pass the low-hanging fruit. Let the political horse-trading be expressed by the ordering and prioritizing of policies in separate bills, rather than in Cornhusker Kickbacks buried in the omnibus bill cooked in the smoke-filled back room.

Principle Number Two: Empower consumers, patients, families, physicians, insurance companies, counties and states — in that order — not the federal government and the Department of Health and Human Services (HHS). At this point in our big-government evolution, solutions consist largely of divesting power from Washington and returning it as far as possible to the individual citizen.

Principle Number Three: Free markets. Private property and limited interference from government results in the best products at the lowest prices for the largest number of people. Think iPhone; apply to health care. We need a market environment for healthcare that is just as free and dynamic and innovative as that for computers and orange juice and mutual funds and automobiles and beer. Consider that the reason we have such contention over immigration policy is that America, because of Capitalism, has become the most attractive place in the world for people to live and work. The US healthcare system, for all its warts, was until 2010 the best in the world because it was the freest.

Principle Number Four: Use the 'Bush/Romney Standard':
That is, we should not give any powers to Barack or Bill or Hillary that we wouldn't be equally eager to give to President Bush or President Romney, to say nothing of President Cruz. You wouldn't let them raid Medicare to the tune of $760 billion or make the rules up as they go along.

Discretionary powers should be clearly and explicitly enumerated, and those not so enumerated must be assumed not to exist; in other words, to require the legislation and/or approval of the people's representatives in Congress.

Principle Number Five: Get out of the way of the unmatched generosity of the American people to help each other.

Private, voluntary charity is not a failure; it is a blessing to be honored and cultivated. Americans donate more of their time, talent and treasure than any other nation, through their churches, synagogues, non-profits and other voluntary organizations. They serve the poor and the disadvantaged that they know personally, with neither need for nor interference from bureaucratic codes and protocols. They do this without demanding salaries, benefits, job security and unfunded defined-benefit pensions that are demanded by our public employee unions who run our government programs. Voluntary giving is many times more effective and efficient than government-run poor relief and creates no burden on the economy or public finances. It is an important and integral part of the solution for which we make no apologies.

Principle Number Six: Envy is not a principle.
Period.

With these principles in mind then, the specific policy proposals include but are not limited to the following:

Promote competition among insurance companies across state lines without interference or dictation from state insurance commissioners. If we can buy oranges from Florida, mutual funds from Tokyo and wine from France we should be able to buy financial products like insurance from whomever gives us the best deal. As I have written before, those products are relatively freely sold in highly competitive markets across not just state lines but national borders.

177

Health insurance, on the other hand, for decades prior to Obamacare, has been sold in severely and increasingly constrained markets, dictated to by 50 different state insurance commissioners, each with his own favorite list of mandatory coverage provisions. Competition and innovation have been crushed under the jackboot of bureaucracy and compliance. Patient-consumer choice has been reduced. If any plans are "sub-standard", "lousy", "cut-rate" or "bottom-feeding", as Obama and his supporters like to say, that's why.

In a truly free market, many more people than today would be able to find a plan that works for them at the intersection of their needs and their means, with consumer reports, reviews on social media and word-of-mouth from friends and family members to guide them. Companies that offer products and services in free markets live and die by their reputations. In the era of Facebook and Twitter, no insurance company could survive if a significant number of its customers assessed its products and services as "sub-standard", "lousy", or "bottom-feeding". We need competition, not control, to bend the cost curve downward.

Eliminate the mandates and let consumers negotiate with insurance companies for the features they consider essential (or not).

In particular, re-open the market permanently to low-premium, high-deductible catastrophic coverage plans which are the baseline standard for all true 'insurance'.

Not everyone needs coverage for maternity services, contraception, fertility treatments, quitting smoking, acupuncture, hair plugs, chiropractic, naturopathy or massage therapy. But by mandating these services and more, regulation drives up the cost of plans unnecessarily while potentially denying consumers access to things they need and want more urgently, like better customer service, lower prices, coverage for other conditions not mentioned in Obamacare or greater catastrophic coverage —or just more insurance companies willing and able to participate in the market.

Mandates are a dead weight on the economy, causing costs to rise unnecessarily, making us all (especially us 99%) poorer. In 2012, the 6 most expensive states (average family premium per enrolled employee for employer-based health insurance) had premiums on average 28% higher than the 6 least expensive states ($17,167 vs. $13,387) and 43%

more mandates (48 vs. 34)[34].

If the consumers want something covered, they will demand it anyway by their buying and not buying, preferring the offerings of one company and plan over those of others. If consumers don't want it, it's an extra unnecessary expense, no different economically or in terms of moral hazard than compelling Jews and Muslims to eat pork; might as well pig out if it's 'free'. Moreover, the cost of bureaucratic staff required to enforce the mandate, must be covered somehow. Mandates are taxes dishonestly imposed. We should have no taxation without honest representation.

Repeal the medical device tax, the Medicare tax, the new 2014 tax on small-business and individual-market health insurance premiums and all the other taxes that only serve to destroy innovation and make healthcare more expensive to everyone now and forever.

Promote Health Savings Accounts (HSAs) and Flexible Spending Accounts(FSAs). These help people pay for medical expenses with pretax dollars and encourage people to spend health care $$ wisely.

No one spends other people's money more wisely than they spend their own. The cost curve will be bent downward to the degree that resources and decision-making power are pushed back to the people to whom it makes the greatest personal difference.

Reform the tort liability legal casino so that doctors don't have to spend a hundred thousand dollars apiece fighting frivolous lawsuits (which 90% of malpractice suits are found to be). Doctors should only order costly and/or hazardous tests if they are in the patient's best interest, not because they need to triple-cover their own legal backsides.

Texas put a cap of $250,000 on non-economic damages in 2003 and reduced the number of cases by over 80%, and the number of physicians attracted to practice in the state increased 18% in four years.

Implementing 'loser-pays' laws, in which any plaintiff filing a claim found to be baseless must pay the legal costs of the defendant, would bring restraint to this out-of-control arena of legalized extortion.

---

34   Sources: Kaiser Family Foundation and Council for Affordable Health Insurance

Make all health plans and medical expenses tax-deductible from the first dollar. Level the playing field between individuals and employers, because World War II is over and we thought we won.

Our current model of employer-provided health insurance dates from WWII when wage and price controls led employers to resort to non-wage benefits to attract workers (now where's a great law like that when we need one? —MAXimum wage laws!). There is no moral or economic justification for letting one group of Americans deduct medical expenses from taxable income and others not.

Allow physicians to take a tax deduction or credit for services rendered pro bono (serving the poor and/or uninsured), without micromanaging their work. If we want the poor to be served, encourage it.

Eliminate government subsidies for unhealthy products like sugar, corn syrup and tobacco (yes, you read that right; in spite of all the government anti-smoking campaigns, tobacco growers received $1.3 billion in subsidies between 1995 and 2011).

Abolish the IPAB. This is the Independent Payment Advisory Board, created by the ACA. Its members are as unaccountable —by design—as members of the Fed (the Federal Reserve Banking system) and all they can do is issues price control edicts and deny care. There's a reason they are called the 'death panel'.

Reform Medicaid according to the terms of its own mission.

If you ask the average intelligent Joe what Obamacare was supposed to accomplish, he might reasonably answer, provide health coverage for the very poor, uninsured and uninsurable. Well guess what? That's what Medicaid was supposed to do! Only problem is, it's a failure. A recent study demonstrated that people with no insurance at all had better health outcomes than those covered by Medicaid. If we insist upon helping the poor through a federal government program, then let's fix the program that has been targeted at the poor for almost 50 years.

Medicaid does best in the states where it is block-granted rather than micromanaged by the Feds. And States that take the money and buy insurance for the poor do even better.

Finally, **Honor the Medical License**.

There is a reason we confer licenses of different degrees of authority and responsibility upon people who have dedicated decades of their lives and hundreds of thousands of dollars of debt to medical education, training, internships, residencies and professional practices. In economic terms, it is a cost-saving mechanism. We do it precisely because no matter how well the website works or how brilliant our genius leaders in Washington and their cadre of lawyers are, there is no way that they can know everything about medicine and every patient in the country. We need trained professionals that we can trust to make the correct judgments in the field better than anyone else possibly can, regardless of what the computers and MBA's flowcharts say.

The Nobel laureate economist Milton Friedman was opposed to government licensure of physicians. Most physicians and many right-thinking people consider that view to be ludicrous; of course we need a recognition of the highest levels of professionalism; otherwise, who will protect us from charlatans and quacks? But the government seems increasingly uninterested in using licensure as a way of delegating and trusting, and more as a sucker's game; a means to controlling, micromanaging and manipulating. It's about power, not about doing the right thing.

Traditionally in America, doctors have been self-employed, running their own practices and referring within a circle of reputable colleagues. But the overwhelming trend now is herding the majority of doctors into employee roles at big hospital corporations and Accountable Care Organizations or ACOs (anyone on the anti-corporate Left paying attention?). A provision of the ACA actually prohibits doctors from pooling their resources to be owner-investors in new hospitals. Lawyers and hedge-fund managers are welcome, but physicians need not apply.

In other words, those with the most knowledge of medicine in general and their own patients in particular are being stripped of their power by those with the most ambition and the most Harvard Law degrees. This is not an improvement for the American health care system or for patients.

We must eliminate the mandates that require doctors to suppress their own professional experience and judgment to comply with cookie-cutter protocols, Electronic Medical Records (EMRs) and codes dictated by Washington bureaucrats who are without any medical training or knowledge of the individual patient.

Right now as you are reading this, individual doctors and patients, churches, citizens, foundations and insurance companies are finding the solutions all across this great country of ours. That is the solution, not Washington D.C.

Conclusion

Obamacare is now a dead letter. If its 2,700 pages of 'law' and 20,000 pages of regulation do not mean what they say but only what Obama or Sibelius say that they say depending upon their transient mood and the shifting political winds of the moment, then it means nothing and doesn't even have to be formally repealed in order to be gotten past. We can ignore it and move on. The task for us, citizens and our representatives, is to construct an alternative system, one brick at a time, major priorities early, improving with each increment, without Rube Goldberg contradictory constructions, violations of the sovereignty of the individual and of the patient-doctor relationship, or massive and dangerous concentration of centralized power. The greatest health care system the world has ever known can yet be greater than it ever was.

It begins with We the People. It begins with liberty.

The Unaffordable Mandate Act

[Published on FrontPageMag.com, December 10, 2013]

"If you like your (sub-standard, lousy, bottom-feeding) health plan, you can keep it, period. No matter what. Unless it changed. Unless we change the rules. Unless you can't."

Right. We all heard that loud and clear, twenty-how-many times in 2009 and 2010. Those Republicans (and non-political citizens, and union members…and Democrats) who are shocked by the millions of policy cancellations forcing people into dysfunctional government exchanges need to just get over their misunderstanding of the president's unequivocal words (no doubt taken out of context) and talk about the real issue. What really matters is how sub-standard, lousy and bottom-feeding the old plans were and how much better the plans offered on the exchanges are… going to be, once a few minor bugs are ironed out of the crony outsourced half-billion-dollar no-bid dot-com/dot-gov product.

Stage-4 cancer patient Edie Sundby, whose United Healthcare plan has paid over $1 million without hassle but which has now been cancelled due to non-compliance with the ACA, leaving her without recourse to continue treatment from the three medical centers in two states that have kept her alive for the past seven years, might disagree. So might millions of others.

But let's take them at their words: "Sub-standard", "lousy", "bottom-feeding". Are they talking about iPhones? Toyotas? Oranges? Mutual funds? French Wine? No, these products are relatively freely sold in highly competitive markets across not just state lines but national borders. Nokia (Finland) has to be better at making cell phones than Apple (California) or it will lose customers and could get acquired by Microsoft (oh, wait—that really did happen). Florida oranges dominate the juice market, even in California. French wine makers cannot rest on their laurels in a world market that includes California.

Health insurance, on the other hand, for decades prior to Obamacare, has been offered in severely and increasingly constrained markets, forced to comply with the dictates of 50 different state insurance commissioners, each with their own favored list of mandatory coverage provisions. Competition is limited; bureaucracy and compliance are king. Patient/consumer choice is reduced. If any plans are "sub-standard", "lousy", or "bottom-feeding", that's the reason why; serving regulators is not the same thing as serving customers.

Not everyone needs or wants pre-paid maternity services, contraception, fertility treatments, quitting smoking, acupuncture, chiropractic, naturopathy or massage therapy. The top priority of insurance has always been and of necessity must be: protection against health and financial catastrophe, something that Obamacare is rapidly banishing from the market. Hair plugs don't qualify for that definition (I know I'll get hate mail for that).

People who want additional non-catastrophic services could have the choice to pay for them directly without having their costs added to their insurance premiums. But by mandating these services and more, state insurance commissioners and now Obamacare drive up the cost of plans unnecessarily while potentially denying consumers access to things they need and want more urgently, like better customer service, lower prices, more choices of doctors—or just more insurance companies willing and able to participate in the market and compete for the patient/consumer's dollar.

The key word is choice. Mandates are the choice killer that drive competitors out of the market.

Mandates, whether pre- or post-Obamacare are a dead weight on the economy, forcing costs to rise unnecessarily, making us all (especially us 99%) poorer. In 2012, the 6 most expensive states (average family premium per enrolled employee for employer-based health insurance) had premiums on average 28% higher than the 6 least expensive states ($17,167 vs. $13,387) and 43% more mandates (48 vs. 34) [Sources: Kaiser Family Foundation and Council for Affordable Health Insurance].

In a free market, if the consumers want the coverage, they will demand it anyway and the mandate is superfluous except to enable the rooster (government) to take credit for the sunrise. If consumers don't want it, it's an extra unnecessary expense, no different economically or in terms of moral hazard than compelling non-smokers to buy cigarettes; might as well smoke 'em if they're 'free'. Either way, the army of bureaucrats needed to enforce the mandates, with their guaranteed salaries, iron-clad job security and (unfunded) defined-benefit pension plans—not to mention health care—must be paid for

184

somehow (hello taxpayer and grandchildren). Mandates are just one more way that politicians can pretend to be Santa Claus to some, buying votes along the way, while imposing hidden costs on the less well-organized and connected.

In a free market, instead of having just a handful of insurance companies and plans available, toeing the line to the extensive rules and regulations of the particular state government, consumers would be able to choose among dozens of providers from any state in the union. And for that matter, from any nation on Earth: insurance is a *financial* product, and the British, Japanese, Singaporeans and Swiss are rumored to have some financial skills. Many more people than today would be able to find a plan that works for them at the intersection of their needs and their means, with consumer reports, reviews in traditional and social media, and word-of-mouth from friends and family members to guide them. Insurance companies, operating under uniform and stable rule of law and under no mandates other than what consumers demand, with neither subsidies nor presumptions of guilt, like companies in any other industry competing in open markets, live and die by their reputations. In the era of Facebook and Twitter, no insurance company could survive if a significant number of its customers assessed its products and services as "sub-standard", "lousy", or "bottom-feeding", unless it operated within a government-protected so-called "exchange".

Which is why real reform that actually has the chance of bending the cost curve downward for consumers must increase competition among a multitude of providers, nationally and internationally, rather than herding wholesale swaths of the population into increasingly restrictive regulatory corals at Healthcare.gov.

The President's and his supporter's sales pitch seems to have shifted to "If you like your health plan, you can change the subject." But harping on the failings of the status quo ante is an indictment of government intervention, not of free-market capitalism. We're going to have to move in the direction of the latter if we ever hope to achieve anything super-standard, un-lousy or top-feeding.

Health Care Solutions: Patients in Command

[Published on FrontPageMag.com, August 21, 2013]

In a scene from the movie "Monty Python's Meaning of Life," a pregnant woman in labor is seen being wheeled down hospital corridors at freeway speeds, with the bumpers of the gurney crashing through swinging fire doors inches from the top of her head until the delivery room is reached, where an excess of necessary and unnecessary equipment momentarily obscures the location of the patient. While the doctors and nurses prep for the procedure, a crowd of ostensibly qualified strangers (but not the patient's husband) are invited to observe from a strategic viewpoint. The woman asks, "what do I do?" to which John Cleese's doctor replies "Nothing darling, you're NOT QUALIFIED!"

Which is about how our discussions of the controversies of health care reform, health management, Accountable Care Organizations, Scope of Practice Expansion, etc. go. The patient is rarely consulted for an opinion, much less approval.

And why should patients be consulted? They're not experts, like doctors and nurses, or more to the point, like the MBAs, executives and employees of federal departments who exercise the power. Even more to the point, the patients aren't the ones paying, at least not directly.

American patient-consumers are not permitted to control how their insurance premium dollars and medical expenditures are spent without interference from government. There is one set of (tax) rules for employees who may get a health plan through an employer, and another set of rules for people purchasing plans individually. With few exceptions, Americans who are not in an employer/employee relationship are not at liberty to freely associate under the First Amendment for purposes of creating health insurance pools. Farmers, ranchers and other self-employed individuals are forced to fend for themselves alone.

Unlike the normal rules of freedom of commerce whereby any American may buy or sell from or to anyone in any state or country, in health insurance there is one elaborate and rigid set of rules for Californians, another set for New Yorkers, another for Mississippians and so on. Consumers and medical insurance companies are not free to negotiate on mutually agreeable terms as they are (relatively) with auto, home, earthquake, fire or flood insurance. In essence, the consumer's money is not his or her own but the government's, to be directed as the elected representatives and unelected administrators and czars determine.

Is it any mystery, then, that costs are out of control and billing patterns and practices are irrational, even diabolical? The people who have the greatest stake in the game—the patients—are hardly consulted in how much they are willing and able to spend on what.

Most of us, if presented with a choice of a BMW 740iL luxury performance sedan or a KIA Forte, would prefer the BMW. But not all of us can afford a BMW, while the KIA is perfectly adequate for getting from Point A to Point B. How many BMWs and KIAs get produced and sold, and to whom, depends upon the resources and preferences of millions of individuals acting on their own account and commanding their own resources, which, at least in the West and to the degree that the free market is permitted to function, are substantial. There is no runaway inflation or gross imbalances of supply and demand of automobiles, bicycles, flat-screen TVs, personal computing devices, clothing or a thousand other products and categories where the footprint of government, regulation and taxation treads relatively lightly. People of the most modest means today have a cornucopia of products and services from around the world available to them at affordable prices, thanks to capitalism. No king, or emperor, or even secretary general of the Supreme Soviet ever enjoyed such abundance even 50 years ago.

What if there existed in the USA a truly free market in health insurance and health care services, that is, what if the government did not interfere in favoring and then dis-favoring employer-provided insurance? What if the government did not mandate what benefits had to be included in insurance plans; did not interfere with interstate commerce in financial products, thereby limiting consumer choices; did not monopolize medical residencies through Medicare and Congress (number of residencies frozen since 1997 in spite of growth and need for more doctors); did not monopolize medical services to the elderly and then cut reimbursements to a level that makes it a losing proposition to many doctors to accept Medicare patients; did not deliberately put Health Savings Accounts and Flexible Spending Accounts at a disadvantage relative to Health Maintenance

Organizations (HMOs) and Accountable Care Organizations (ACOs); and a thousand other interventions, prohibitions, taxes, favoritism, prejudices, fines, penalties and taxes? Then patients and their families would be in far greater command of their own resources and of those being spent on their behalf. Then they, through their choosing and rejecting, spending and withholding, could sort out which of the brilliant ideas of the experts truly have merit, which are nice tries and which are losers. They could and would determine whether mid-level providers may substitute for fully-licensed physicians in the operating room, and whether compliance with evidence-based protocols enforced by bureaucrats and computers or hard-earned professional experience and judgment should govern physician behavior. They will fine-tune to what degrees medicine is a scientific discipline, a production process to be administered, or an art.

The mess that we are in with Medicare (looted), Medicaid (failed; statistically better to have no insurance at all than to be enrolled) and now Obamacare (train wreck, according to one of its prominent sponsors) underscores the perils of "solving problems" instead of pursuing opportunities. Controlling costs by denying treatments and steering patients away from the most trained and qualified professionals, rationing, death panels, the Independent Payment Advisory Board (IPAB) etc. all "solve problems." On the other hand, our dedicated physicians, nurses, specialists, pharmaceutical research, and medical art, science, creativity and innovation, along with patients in command of the resources that are to be spent on their behalf, are our opportunities. Freedom, voluntary cooperation, liberty of contract and the generosity of American neighbors and friends—unmatched anywhere in the world—are our opportunities. If we Americans will pursue those, we will once again pull ahead in our lead as the world's foremost medical innovator and most responsive to the needs of the patient, as we have been for at least 50 years.

How Dare We Claim America Is #1 in Health Care?

[Published on FrontPageMag.com, March 20, 2013]

It outrages some that conservatives and Republicans claim that the USA's health care system is the best in the world and that the proper goal of reform is to continue to extend our lead, not "catch up" with more "enlightened" countries that have universal, government-directed health care systems. This assertion has been vigorously challenged by individuals citing anecdotal evidence and presumably scientific studies, such as the World Health Organization's World Health Report 2000, which served as one of the key justifications for Obamacare. The WHO study specifically ranked the USA 37th of 191 industrial nations.

Yet Sally Pipes of the Pacific Research Institute, Scott Atlas of the Hoover Institution and many others have meticulously gathered and crunched data demonstrating that, at least prior to the current administration, the best country in the world to find yourself diagnosed with cancer or in need of a knee replacement operation or MRI exam, is the USA. This holds equally true for Saudi princes as for individuals without insurance. In fact, the ultimate irony is that patients without insurance undergoing treatment for serious conditions have better outcomes on average than those covered by Medicaid. The government-run medical program with the worst record is being aggressively expanded by force and by bribery to be the default system for the majority of Americans.

Among 16 types of cancer, the U.S. men's 5-year survival rate is 66% and the U.S. women's survival rate is 63%, versus 47% and 56% respectively for European men and women. The USA has 81 Nobel laureates in Physiology or Medicine in the past half century compared to 67 for the rest of the world combined. Your risk of death on the operating table is 4 times higher in Britain that it is in the USA. Canadians wait 9 months on average for orthopedic surgery like knee and hip replacements.

But we're number 37?

Yes, of course we are, if your criteria for the ranking is how well we conform to a politically-correct ideal of universal, government-run health care. If such hard, scientific and incorruptible measures as "financial fairness" and "equality" as reported by the "impressions" of

189

WHO staff members are your guide, then the USA falls short of the glory of Eternal Truth. That turns out to be the true nature of the WHO study, as exposed by Pipes, Atlas and others.

But if you're looking for actual outcomes, with or without insurance, sorry, America is #1.

Or has been. As Obamacare forces us into conformity with socialist ideals, our outcomes may well place us 37th or worse among industrialized nations, in which case the anecdotes alluded to earlier will become increasingly common. We have already embarked upon that path since ratification. The only question remaining is why Republican office holders seem now so eager to pre-emptively surrender what power they have remaining to stop it.

Fire the Real Boss of the VA

[Published on WesternJournalism.com, June 2, 2014]

So Eric Shinseki, Secretary of the U.S. Department of Veteran's Affairs, has resigned, and...so what? What will that change? Next to nothing substantial will change at the VA, and nothing will prevent the VA fiasco from becoming the fate of all of us under Obamacare–until the real boss, the 800-pound gorilla that we don't speak of, not only resigns, but is removed permanently without replacement.

A random survey of two dozen recent articles on the VA in the *New York Times* yields not a single hit on the word 'union'. Kimberly Strassel of the *Wall Street Journal* makes up for the deficit with 28 mentions in a single column ('Big Labor's VA Choke Hold, Potomac Watch, March 30').

The unconscionable and unconstitutional power and privileges of the public employee unions is the single most significant driver of the crisis at the VA, as it is with state and county budgets from New Jersey to California. Two-thirds of the VA's 300,000+ employees are members of the National Federation of Federal Employees, the American Federation of Government Employees International Union, and other unions. In 2012, 258 of them actually worked full-time only for the union, while being paid full salary and benefits by the VA–that is, by you and me the taxpayer. Of those, 17 earned between $100K and $132K; and it's a safe bet that their benefits and pensions are at least twice as generous as those received by anyone earning comparable salaries in the private sector.

We don't begrudge anyone earning $100K, $1 million, or even $10 million if it is earned honestly and paid for voluntarily by informed customers or clients who are free to take their business elsewhere. Doctors, nurses, teachers, and even union professionals should be paid seven figures if the consensus of their peers and those who write their own checks is that they merit it. But the minute someone's haul becomes an ironclad privilege subject to no accountability beyond pleasing an equally unaccountable cabal of cronies, corruption multiplies until the inevitable results—long waiting times, neglectful care, needless deaths—become too glaring to ignore. Such is the nature of the public employee unions' claim on taxpayer dollars irrespective of performance today.

More money is not going to solve the problem. The VA's budget has tripled in the past 13 years, while the number of veterans served is either flat or has increased a maximum of 30%. It's how the money gets spent, by whom, and under what incentives and constraints that counts.

The current ratio of 'in-house' to 'outsourced' care should be inverted, such that 90+% of the dollars spent by the VA pay for service delivered outside of the agency's facilities and employee network. There is no reason why the U.S. government itself has to directly run 152 hospitals and be the primary care provider for veterans, any more than it has to be the monopoly manufacturer of furniture, appliances, or cell phones for them. Uncle Sam contracts out development of weapons of war and aircraft to hundreds of for-profit companies like Boeing, Lockheed Martin, and Glock Ges.m.b.H. As a middleman manager of taxpayer resources, it can set up a voucher system that enables veterans to purchase health insurance on the private market and to pay for catastrophic care provided by Casa Colina, the Kessler Rehabilitation Center, Johns Hopkins, and others. Veterans who fought for our freedom should not be captives of any single monopolist, whether the government, a union, or a political party (imagine the outcry if this scandal had broken under a Republican administration).

General Shinseki's ouster is not justified based on the performance of a system beyond his control, unless he is a cheerleader for the status quo. There is little Shinseki or anyone else could or will be able to do about the agency's dysfunction until Congress, with the support of the American people, asserts its authority over the agency's business and revokes all privileges that create the moral hazard of giving the interests of unionized employees preference over those of the veterans they ostensibly serve.

But that's just an extremist, right-wing Republican view, right? Perhaps. Or perhaps it's just a measure of how far we have come, or fallen, since before the current hostage crisis became business as usual. Consider these icons of right- wing extremism and what they had to say yesteryear:

New York mayor Fiorello LaGuardia: "The right to strike against the government is not and cannot be recognized."

AFL-CIO president George Meany: "It is impossible to collectively bargain with the government."

A.F.L.-C.I.O. Executive Council's 1959 advice: "In terms of accepted collective bargaining procedures, government workers have no right beyond the authority to petition Congress — a right available to every citizen."

President Franklin Delano Roosevelt: "Meticulous attention should be paid to the special relations and obligations of public servants to the public itself and to the Government. The process of collective bargaining, as usually understood, cannot be transplanted into the public service."

FDR again: "a strike of public employees manifests nothing less than an intent on their part to prevent or obstruct the operations of Government until their demands are satisfied. Such action, looking toward the paralysis of government by those who have sworn to support it, is unthinkable and intolerable."

Colby Buzzell, an Iraq war veteran writing in the *New York Times*, reminds us that the VA motto, taken from Abraham Lincoln's Second Inaugural Address, reads: "To care for him who shall have borne the battle and for his widow, and his orphan."

How we accomplish that requires respect for economic principles, with a bias toward the free market that is no small part of what our veterans were defending when they served.

Obamacare: And Then a Miracle Happens

[Published on AmericanThinker.com, July 8, 2013]

So the administration has delayed implementation of the employer mandate for one year in what must be a desperate move to avoid an immediate train wreck, a tacit acknowledgment that the mandate is unworkable, or a shrewd and/or cynical political move to get safely past the 2014 election cycle, depending on which theory you find most plausible.

But none of this should cause any of us to doubt that the complete Patient Protection and Affordable Care Act will ultimately triumph and become a beloved part of our Way of Life, deeply appreciated by a grateful citizenry, right?

Let us put aside for a moment the fact that regarding Obamacare, most Americans have no clue what they are supposed to do or what the law is going to do to them, even though the *individual* mandate is still officially to go into effect in January and the exchanges are supposed to launch just three months from now (and that's a big "supposed"; try contacting your state insurance department or the HHS and asking for specifics). Never mind that the estimated price tag for the exchanges has doubled since last year to $4.4 billion. Pay no attention to the absurdity of using Hollywood and sports celebrities, none of whom will ever be caught dead in an Obamacare clinic, to sell young, healthy people on the idea that it's *cool* to spend money (that they don't have because they can't find jobs in Obama's economy) on inflated health insurance premiums to subsidize their older, sicker compatriots.

Don't worry about the complex software, electronic medical records, and other technology required to make all of this work as smoothly as bidding for dirt-cheap travel on Priceline or Orbitz.com. Trust your friends at the IRS and HHS to enforce compliance fairly and kindly.

After all, these are all mere sideshows, normal growing pains of any large project. Nobody said it would be easy, right? Keep our eyes on the Big Picture. In the end, we're all going to love it and thank Obama, Reid, and Pelosi many times over for their great visionary wisdom, compassion, and courage.

To achieve enlightenment on why this is so, we can examine a few of the actual discrete elements of the program.

For instance, Obamacare mandates that insurance companies may not discriminate on the basis of industry or the health of employees (with the exception of smokers) to set premiums for company plans. Good, right? Discrimination is bad, and non- discrimination is good in the Kindergarden of Eden (thank you, Evan Sayet). Of course, if you happen to be a small company in a low-health risk industry that employs mostly younger workers, your premiums will have to rise to compensate higher-risk industries and/or older employees. Not more affordable for you.

You have to spend 10% of your taxable income on medical care before you get a tax break under Obamacare, whereas the threshold used to be 7.5%. Flexible Spending Accounts (FSAs) and Health Savings Accounts (HSAs) similarly receive more unfavorable treatment under the new law than before. How any of that makes health care more affordable to anyone who pays income taxes has not been explained.

Medical device manufacturers are taxed at 2.3 percent of gross sales. This obviously raises the cost of medical devices, inhibits investment in innovation to produce the next generation of life-saving gadgets, and puts domestic manufacturers at a disadvantage relative to foreign ones (giant sucking sound of jobs heading offshore, anyone?). This may seem like not quite a step in the affordability direction until you realize that the $29 billion that the government expects to collect from the tax will be much more wisely spent than it would be by the greedy profit-mongers, and therefore will lead to more affordability on the other side, somehow. Good thing the tax is still in force in spite of 33 Democrat senators joining 45 Republicans to repeal it.

Sarcasm aside, to believe that Obamacare will all work out in the end is to believe that the whole is not only greater than the sum of the parts, but 180 degrees the polar opposite of the sum of the parts.

In the fields of science and information technology, numerous cartoonists have produced variations of a confusing process design diagram, with dozens or hundreds of geometric shapes connected by crisscrossing lines, swim lanes, and arrows, and including at least one module labeled "Then a miracle happens." That is what we are being expected to believe: that in spite of Obamacare's unprecedented massive complexity and every discrete thing that it actually does, it's going to turn out for the best for everyone (or at least Democrat voters and office-holders) in the end.

Rather than accept this proposition like sheep, perhaps we should pay attention to the fact that the weak fines and guaranteed issue for patients with pre-existing conditions are unlikely to persuade people to pony up the premiums in advance. We might consider that increasing numbers of unions, normally reliable allies of Obama and the Democratic Party, are partnering with their erstwhile adversaries in business to oppose portions if not the entirety of the law, because they see how it is hurting their worker members. (Per Sally Pipes: "Union firms and workers will have to shoulder the entire cost of their health plans—while their non-union competitors will be able to get subsidized coverage through the exchanges." Oops.) Maybe there's something to the story that there are 99 things that have to happen in the next (less than) 99 days in order to guarantee a successful launch, assuming that that's desirable (see Sarah Kilff writing for the right-wing *Washington Post*).

The fact is, these are not just accidents or normal growing pains, but the inevitable consequences of excessively complex legislation born of corrupt politics and no sound economic principles. Perhaps the majority of Americans, who now disapprove of the law, are on to something.

Part IV: Politics and Foreign Policy

All of the preceding notwithstanding, I was for many years reluctant to practice my civic participation in an overtly partisan way. Like Milton Friedman, I hoped to persuade people of the validity of principles which transcend petty party politics. For a while, a few times a year during the early 2000s I hosted luncheons with colleagues at the Very Big Corporation of America where I worked, where I would present economic concepts in a purely academic, non-partisan way, and we had interesting and enlightening (and respectful) discussions, even though many of us were from different political persuasions.

Nevertheless, politics and the party system are the organs through which action in political economy is taken, and in order to accomplish more than intellectual gratification, it is necessary to define oneself, choose friends, allies and adversaries, organize and act.

For these reasons I grew over time increasingly to define myself as a Republican, and when that label was insufficiently precise, I honed it down to Constitutional Conservative Libertarian Republican. Whatever that means. Well, read on...

Townhall Root Canal

[Published on AmericanThinker.com as "Townhall Follies", February 10, 2014]

Citizens' townhall meetings with members of Congress can be painful.

A college professor asks, what are you going to do so that our students can pay off their loans? Another citizen asks whether the budget will be increased for this or that social program. A third asks for unemployment benefits to be extended, again. The officeholder is compelled to promise ever-increasing benefits, goodies for all, increased spending with no considerations of cost, competing demands, prioritization, trade-offs or the constitutional appropriateness of the expenditures.

Where do the constituents making these earnest pleas think the money for all of this comes from? It comes from themselves—from the rest of the people there in the junior high school auditorium. To say that the money comes free from "Washington" is to be deluded by the Big Lie. Washington DC, the federal government, has nothing except what it takes from the states and the counties and cities and the citizens, taxpaying or otherwise. For any district to ask for more money is either to ask for its own money back less Washington's commission or to ask for other districts to run a deficit for the former's benefit, also less middleman fees. Should Mississippi support the San Fernando Valley? Should Beverly Hills underwrite Anchorage? Why shouldn't Denver subsidize Appalachia and Bel Air, if their respective representatives demand it?

Set aside for a moment the immorality of politicians and their supporters constantly jockeying for advantage at each other's expense (for this *is* truly a zero-sum game), money extracted from other districts and dispensed by political favoritism does not create wealth. Senator Robert Byrd, the once member of the Ku Klux Klan of West Virginia, was a master at bringing home the political bacon. Nevertheless, West Virginia remained poor overall. Other states and districts with less adept politicians have nevertheless thrived without being beneficiaries of a political gravy train. What counts in order for a district, a state, or a nation to prosper is individual initiative, hard work and the "creative destruction" of capitalist enterprise operating under liberty, private property rights, rule of law, low taxes, and light regulation.

What if a congressman/woman or candidate were to say to his or her constituents the following?: "*No! I'm not going to try to rob the pork from a richer or poorer district. There is no moral justification for robbing the poor, and if the great wealth of some other district is so attractive, then let's do what they do! Instead, I'm going to fight to see to it that our money doesn't leave our district in the first place. Because even if we could get back 100% of our share of the pie, that 'share' will end up being much less than what we had paid out because of Washington 'public servants' extracting their piece of the action. We have capable experts in business, technology, medicine, charity, and administration right here. We don't need Washington 'experts' to do it for us or tell us what to do. We don't need bureaucrats usurping power over our own job creators and demoralizing our people with dependency. We don't need them crowding out our churches and synagogues that deliver charity and aid to the less fortunate on a personal and voluntary basis, replacing them with armies of salaried and pensioned functionaries in whose interest it is to increase the number of their 'clients' to the highest possible volume. No. What is needed is to take responsibility for ourselves and to demand our own lives, liberty, and property back; to reduce the federal government's jackboot print on our lives and economy; to cut federal tax rates to low, flat levels, and to lighten regulation to the point of simply preventing and punishing murder, assault, robbery, theft, fraud, rape, persecution, and conspiracy; and even then only to the degree that states and counties are unable to do so for themselves. To go back to the model where the largest line item in the federal budget is the Defense Department, because that is the most important of the few and constitutionally enumerated responsibilities of the federal government which the states may not take on independently; keeping our citizens safe from foreign aggression.*"

The answer to this "what if" of course is that any congressman or candidate who refuses to play Santa Claus and promise unlimited candy for all if only the "rich" would pay their "fair share" would be routed in the next election, unless a plurality of the voters are private-sector property and/or business-owning, responsible, and intelligent working adults and parents. The current administration and its supporters are not only rapidly extinguishing this category of Americans through their policies, decrees and executive orders, but celebrating their own success in doing so.

Now if you will excuse me, my teeth hurt. What is my congressman going to do about it?

India Gets It - But America Doesn't

[Published on WesternJournalism.com, May 19, 2014]

India is still a third-world country, with half the homes still not having plumbing and a large percentage not having electricity. But even more significant than its dynamic technology sector growing into a world-class destination for contracts and capital is the fact that India has the most intelligent electorate in the world right now.

For the first time in 30 years, India's voters have given a decisive majority — 336 of 543 seats in the lower house of Parliament — to one party. And it is not the dynastic Congress party of Jawaharlal Nehru (and now Rahul Gandhi) that has dominated Indian politics for the 67 years since independence from Great Britain; it's the Bharatiya Janata party (BJP) and its Prime Minister-elect, Narendra Modi.

A closer look at what Modi's platform is and the obstacles he had to overcome will have California Republicans weeping and gnashing their teeth that they didn't draft Modi to run for Governor of the (once) Golden State. Modi's agenda is precisely what is needed to rescue California (if not the United States) from its self-inflicted disaster.

The Congress party ran on a social welfare platform, promising more goodies, more subsidies, and more government programs for the poor.

The poor rejected it. They want economic growth and expanding opportunity, and lots of it. A 5% growth rate, which would be considered miraculous if it could be achieved anywhere in the West, is not good enough; they want 8% or better. They've tasted that in the last decade, and they want more of it. Modi and the BJP declined to play Santa Claus; refrained from stirring the identity politics of religion, region, caste, and ethnicity; restrained their more strident Hindu nationalist wing and tendencies; and instead focused on economic principles and basic good governance. The voters rewarded them for these principles and for their courage in proclaiming and defending them.

American Republicans might learn a thing or two about how an effective modern campaign is run, as the BJP left the Congress party in the dark ages with savvy use of technology and social media. Just because people don't have electricity in their homes doesn't mean they don't have iPhones, Facebook, and Twitter. Modi even appeared as a holograph at events where he was unable to be physically present.

Manmohan Singh, prime minister of India for the past 10 years, Finance Minister from 1991-96, and Leader of the opposition party from 1998-2004, has been a potent pro-free market voice and force in India's rise over the past 20 years to the status of international technology powerhouse. But his party, as too often happens with parties that get too cozy with unchallenged power for too long, has been rocked with corruption scandals in recent years. Apparatchiks have been feathering their own nests while the roads and bridges crumble (sound familiar?) The voters have had enough and want a party that can credibly promise a cleaner and more accountable regime—and modern highways and ports too.

Someone wake me when California voters demand the same.

Half the voters in India are under the age of 35, and they aspire to a modern Indian Dream of upward social mobility and universal nationality. They chose Modi over his rival Rahul Gandhi in spite of the fact that Modi is 63 and Gandhi 20 years younger.

While most Americans, when pressed, would admit hoping that the United States would continue to lead the world in prosperity, growth, and world influence, the rise of India is not America's loss. A robust India is an indispensable asset to the United States and the West, as a counterweight to China and an ally with no rose-colored illusions about the challenges of coping with Islamic nationalism—whether emanating from Pakistan, Iran, or elsewhere.

No party or leader is perfect, and it remains to be seen how long Modi can sustain the momentum after the initial euphoria wears off, his party comrades begin to succumb to the temptations of power and perks, the opposition party regroups, and/or the inevitable shortcomings become Modi's to own. The reality of the policies that will be required to bring India's economy out of the doldrums will almost certainly offend some by taking away a subsidy or a privilege. Social upheaval in a fragile nation of dozens of linguistic, ethnic, and religious groups is a constant hazard. Modi has had to fend off charges of complicity in riots in 2002–in which over 1000 people died. Some of his own policies may fail to deliver the promised results, such as his lukewarm attitude toward foreign direct investment, a mistake in the eyes of most free-market economists.

But the fact that the electorate itself, across class, caste, ethnic, and linguistic lines, have come down so decisively on the side of pro-growth free-market economics, rejecting the siren song of socialistic welfare, shows greater hope for the long-term prospects for India than any one minister or party. Politicians always fail to some degree to live up to their promises. But Indians are choosing the right promises, with pretty good odds.

India gets it. I wish I could say I thought we did.

Throw the Bums...In!

[Published on AmericanThinker.com as 'Making the Best of the Bums', May 19, 2014]

The latest backlash against over-privileged public officials is taking the form of a bill known as the "If our military has to fly coach then so should Congress" Act.

While these are noble and understandable sentiments, IMHO[35] they miss a larger and more important point.

Congressmen at least have the one redeeming quality that they are the directly chosen representatives of the people, nominally accountable through the election process. We may argue about how to make that accountability felt more acutely in light of the high recidivism, um, re-election rate for incumbents. But that is the basic definition.

A much more serious problem with our government is the directorate class of our administrative agencies, ostensibly under the supervision of the Executive branch but in practice acting as an unaccountable and extra-constitutional branch of the federal government. No voter has the opportunity to recall a Secretary of Energy, Health and Human Services, the Interior, or the EPA. Moreover, the senior staffs of these agencies pocket salaries, benefits, and pensions that dwarf what any congressman makes. They directly command tens to hundreds of billions of dollars' worth of taxpayer-funded resources. HHS alone is several times larger than the Defense department (dwell on that for a moment).

When the people's most constitutionally legitimate representative confronts one of these czars to bring them into line with representative republican (small 'r') governance, the latter can just laugh, like Godfather Vito Corleone confronted by a petty shopkeeper. What's some pathetic congressman compared to the wealth and arbitrary power of an executive agency czar?

Thomas Sowell has suggested a constitutional limit on congressmen to single, six-year terms with a seven-figure salary but no pension (separately, I have suggested a constitutional amendment that would

---

"IMHO" = In My Humble Opinion.

require public officials to pass a factual examination on the contents of Sowell's *Basic Economics* as a condition of their taking office—but I digress). This would have the virtues of attracting a high caliber of candidates and focusing office holders' attention on their jobs rather than their re-election and fundraising, putting them on an equal prestige footing with their peers while erasing hope of feathering a long-term nest.

The cost of business class and first-class travel for congressional staffs is a drop in the ocean compared to entitlements and unfunded public employee (union) pension liabilities. The citizens have an interest in their representatives being productive and not inconvenienced while they cope with the extraordinary demands on their time. The fact is that rank-and-file military have an honorable but different role to play. But I would support upgrading entire cabins of military aircraft to first class for all before I would tear down the constitutional representatives of the people to make the shared inconvenience 'fair'. Tearing down one side for the sake of fairness is an idea that comes from somewhere else.

Bums should be thrown out. But as long as they are in, we need the best.

Libertarianism and Republicans

[Published on WesternJournalism.com, July 10, 2014]

Below is a speech I delivered to the Southern California Republican Women and Men, of which I am President, on April 26 of this year. Since being published on my website www.CitizenEcon.com, it has risen into the Top 10 all-time most-read posts (of almost 300 posts over 8 years) on that site.

Today, our meeting competes with the California State Convention of the Young Americans for Liberty at USC; and coincidentally, my talk today is about Libertarianism and Republicans. I did not know about that event before I planned my presentation. I don't pretend to know anything in detail about that organization, but I do know something about Libertarianism from my own perspective; and with just enough serendipity today, I hope to make a positive contribution to the discussion.

People sometimes ask me if I am a Libertarian, to which I reply, well, yes, I have some libertarian tendencies—but it's not like I have a meth lab in my Winnebago or anything[36]. To clarify, I say that when I am elected President of the United States, Ron Paul will be my Czar in charge of the decommissioning of Fannie Mae, Freddie Mac, The Community Reinvestment Act, Dodd-Frank, Sarbanes- Oxley, Section 1706 of the 1986 Tax Equity and Fairness Reform Act (or TEFRA), and the Fed. On the other hand, as it pertains to foreign policy and geo-politics, my nominations for Ambassador to the United Nations and Secretaries of Defense and State are, in no particular order, John Bolton, John Bolton, and John Bolton. In the unlikely event that Mr. Bolton is unequal to all three commissions simultaneously, my alternates are Allen West and Benjamin Netanyahu (it shouldn't be difficult to procure a credible birth certificate for Ben, considering precedent).

Almost half of the attendees of CPAC (the Conservative Political Action Conference) were under the age of 26, and a plurality of these are libertarians or members of the liberty caucus. This is an

---

[36]   A reference to the award-winning and highly popular AMC television series "Breaking Bad".

international movement of youth who have opened their eyes and realized that as a generation, they have been screwed by the collectivist members of their parent's generation and are determined to do something about it. In libertarianism, they see the solution.

Is this good or bad for Americans in general and Republicans in particular? In my opinion, it is on balance very good, with the caveat that like anything else, it needs to be understood by all at a greater-than-sophomoric level, failing which, like anything else again, it could just as easily lead to catastrophe.

So, what exactly is libertarianism? What do we need to understand about it?

The modern libertarian movement has its roots in the Austrian School of economics, which began in the late 19th century with Carl Menger and reached its apogee in the works of Friedrich Hayek (Nobel Laureate) and his mentor Ludwig von Mises, whose 93-year lifespan overlapped with Menger's from 1881 until 1973–after Nixon had declared that "we're all Keynseyans now" (come to think of it, that's probably what killed him).

Like classical liberalism and modern American conservatism, libertarianism holds that the best model for political economy is that characterized by the most limited interference in the decisions of citizens, low taxes, and light to no regulation beyond preventing and punishing murder, assault, robbery, theft, fraud, rape, persecution, and conspiracy. Conservatives may call this being guided by the Ten Commandments; Libertarians might consider it plain common secular sense.

The Austrian school was the most radically minimalist in its view of the appropriate role of government. And that minimalism was taken to its radical extreme in the work of Mises' disciple Murray Rothbard, who posited that government wasn't even necessary for police and defense, as these services could be bought and sold on the free market just like bread and haircuts.

In 1963, Rothbard wrote a book on the Great Depression that I consider absolutely required reading for anyone wanting to know just how President Franklin Delano Roosevelt did NOT save the country from the Great Depression but rather worsened the crisis, and how Herbert Hoover was no free-market, laissez-faire pro-capitalist president. In the same book, Rothbard also wrote the most clearly articulated presentation of Austrian business cycle theory (or the theory of booms, busts, and crashes), a theory to which the financial crisis of 2008 fits like a textbook case.

The two dominant branches of Libertarianism in America today are represented by the Cato Institute on the one hand (based in Washington D.C. and focused on practical, policy-oriented research and lobbying) and the Mises Institute on the other, deliberately based away from the centers of power in Auburn, Alabama in order to remain more purely focused on theory and academic freedom. While Murray Rothbard and Mises Institute president Lew Rockwell have carried Mises' theoretical torch forward in many ways admirably, in many other cases they have made assertions that Mises never did and probably never would have, and have done so dogmatically and intolerantly.

My infatuation with Rothbard ended abruptly when I read the op-Ed piece that he had written at the conclusion of the Reagan Administration. "Eight years, eight dreary, miserable, mind-numbing years of the Age of Reagan, are at long last coming to an end," he groaned in a piece titled "Ronald Reagan, an Autopsy"—fifteen years before the Gipper's actual passing. It was a litany of accusations worse than Thomas Jefferson's indictments of King George III in the Declaration of Independence. Nancy Pelosi could not have penned a more bitter diatribe. The only thing Rothbard gave credit to Reagan for was lifting the 55 mph federal highway speed limit.

Now, Ron Paul is derived from Rothbard, and in many respects in a good way. It was Rothbard who first penned the academic "*The Case Against the Fed*," from which Paul's more populist "End the Fed" is derived. I am mostly in agreement with these positions on domestic economic issues, as is John Allison, current president of the Cato Institute, bank president for 25 years, and author of "The Financial Crisis and the Free-Market Cure."

So again, while I am wary of extremists of any stripe, my only quarrel with Libertarianism as such is the role and character of America's diplomacy and armed forces in the world; on the latter, I stand firmly with Ronald Reagan. Otherwise, I look forward to the day when we'll say that "We're all (conservative) libertarians now." That's much better than being all Keynseyans, or progressives, or all socialists. Maybe the young people can help us bring that about.

Our Intolerable Success in Iraq

[Published on WesternJournalism.com, June 18, 2014]

Of the opportunities in Iraq squandered in our national insistence on our own inadequacy or even evil, few rank as highly as religious freedom and plurality.

The United States did not enshrine religious liberty in the Constitution because all of its people were tolerant, fair-minded, or secular. The colonists were as intolerant of religious difference as people anywhere in the world, no more and no less. But we came to recognize that in the interest of national survival, we had to put aside our differences—or at least ensure that no single sect of the 13 intolerant sects that dominated each if the 13 colonies would have the chance of becoming the official state religion, enforced by a tyrannical king or pope. Shared recognition of the higher principle of religious tolerance as a virtue in and of itself was a collateral outcome, not a primary cause, of the First Amendment.

It is a principle sorely needed in many parts of the world, not least of all the Middle East; and it was within our grasp to achieve it in Iraq 6 years ago. We owned the country. We operated the oil fields. Saddam Hussein was dead; his murderous Baath party was defeated; and Al-Qaeda and the jihadis, if not gone, were neutralized.

At that point, we could have drafted a Constitution based on the principle of separation of powers such that conflict between Sunnis and Shias and Kurds took a back seat to aggregations of citizens along different dimensions, neutralizing the religious one. We could have supported a leader who was able, ready, and willing by principle and conviction to govern across sectarian lines; we didn't have to settle for the partisan Shia autocrat prime minister Nouri Al- Maliki; and we could have imposed the time-honored practice of term limits (even on the one we chose.) We could have given every adult Iraqi citizen, men and women, equal shares of common and preferred stocks and bonds of a fully privatized formerly national oil industry, giving them a direct stake in the defense of peaceful free-market capitalism and private property rights, as well as a sense of sharing in both the national purpose and its bounty. And we could have stayed until the job was truly done, or at least until after we had pulled out of those other countries where we had overstayed our welcome, like Germany and Japan (the Philippines kicked us out over 20 years ago; but due to the recent Chinese reality check, they want us back). At the very least, we could have negotiated a realistic and appropriate Status of Forces agreement.

But all of that would be Imperialism and Ugly-Americanism, of course. Unacceptable! At the very least, too expensive!

Right, until you consider the alternative: the world that is re-emerging before our horrified naive eyes, of a world where American constitutional principles do not reign, where religious difference is grounds for brutal summary beheading, where American influence is weak or non-existent, and where our enemies do not fear us and our friends do not trust us (for good reason). A lot more barbaric and expensive in the end than if we had the confidence of our actual virtues.

Instead, by our abdication and premature withdrawal, we have achieved the worst possible outcome: an all-out civil war drawn categorically along religious sectarian lines. The Iraqi Grand Ayatollah Ali al-Sistani, who has maintained a restrained posture for ten years, is now rallying the population (young men especially) to defend Baghdad and the current regime—not in terms of patriotic nationalism, but motivated by religious holy jihad against the rival sect. As Charles Krauthammer put it, these are "two devils, different stripes." And the biggest winners are the Shiite Ayatollahs of Iran.

In the Fall of 2008, with the domestic economy melting down with the housing market crash and the TARP bailouts for the 'too-big-to-fail' banks, a majority of Americans, including a plurality of Republicans, were eager to get beyond George W. Bush and their weariness of his Iraq misadventure. That scorn may soon turn to nostalgia as the American people realize how much has been lost in the squandering of the real gains and opportunities afforded us at the height of our success in Iraq in that year.

Argue if you want to that we never should have gone into Iraq in the first place. But what mission was accomplished by our pulling out?

Answering the Libertarian Indictments on Iraq

[Published on WesternJournalism.com, July 9, 2014]

Some Libertarian readers of my June 17 and 18 articles on Iraq, 'Peace Requires a Permanent Commitment' and 'Our Intolerable Success in Iraq,' have interpreted them as apologia for George W. Bush's initial invasion and have taken the occasion to excoriate them on that basis. I stand accused of defending a permanent commitment, not to peace, but to war. I hear of the many Iraqis now nostalgic for at least the stable and predictable times under Saddam Hussein. I am told that our over-extended global adventures must ultimately lead to the collapse of our global empire, as they did with (now not-so-Great) Great Britain. I am asked to consider how people from around the world, in particular South America and the Middle East, feel about our interventions in their countries. They tell me that to be pro-free-market, and to be logically consistent, requires being non-interventionist if not isolationist. And finally, the whole notion of fearing 'the terrorists' (their quotation marks) is ridiculed as so much irrationality, comparable to the communist 'red scares' of yesteryear that turned out, according to them, to be groundless.

While I do defend the decision to invade Iraq in 2003 as arguably the best that could have been made under the circumstances—with virtually the entire world, including prominent Democrats like Hillary Clinton as well as the UN, France, China, and Russia in unanimous agreement on the facts about Saddam Hussein, his crimes, and his intentions—that wasn't the primary point of my articles. My point was that given the stable status quo of 2008-2011, the decision to withdraw in 2011 and pretend that Barack Obama had masterfully achieved the peace and triumphed over Bush was a short-sighted and politically-motivated blunder of colossal magnitude, if not a crime.

That said, having unleashed the Libertarian furies, so to speak, a decent respect for the opinions of mankind requires that we respond to at least some of their more thoughtful comments.

By "permanent commitment," I mean keeping the peace that has been won at the cost of blood and treasure in police patrol mode. What city in the United States today decommissions its entire police force once the murder rate (temporarily) drops below some threshold?

213

Would we try that in New York City, Los Angeles, Chicago, or Detroit, and then congratulate ourselves, proclaiming that "Our urban war in America's cities ends this month"? If the peace is kept more effectively and justly by us than by anyone else, then we are the ones who must do it. This doesn't mean we charge into any and every unstable country to impose our will. But it certainly means we stay where we find ourselves the only thing standing between relative justice and open kill zones, even if it wasn't our political party who got us there. The decision to pull out of a former theatre of war is at least as serious as the decision to go in in the first place, perhaps more so if recent experience is any guide. The next Republican president will have to deal with the world as Obama left it, not as he should have or as President Romney would have.

Senator and presidential candidate Rand Paul makes hay out of the acknowledged fact that "Today, the Middle East is less stable than in 2003". But what does that really demonstrate? That Bush was wrong to lead us in, or that Obama squandered our success there? The Middle East, Iraq in particular, was more stable in 2008 than it was in 2003. After 5 years of Obama, the entire world is less secure and holds the USA in lower esteem (enemies don't fear us and friends don't trust us) than before 9/11. Far from indicting Bush and neo- conservatism, these facts repudiate the isolationists, anti-Americanism, and the Left—Barack Obama in particular.

After 2008, Iraq had fallen off the radar. For five years, stories about Iraq rarely made the front page of any American newspaper. The number of U.S. servicemen and women killed dropped two thirds from 904 in 2007 to 304 in 2008, fell by half again in 2009, and by more than half yet again in 2010 to just 60. No news is good news; Joe Biden was ready to take credit on behalf of Obama for this foreign policy success. ExxonMobil and Royal Dutch Shell were partnering with the Iraqi national oil ministry in Business-As-Usual mode. As Fouad Ajami, the Lebanese-born American, put it in his January 9, 2008 article in the Wall Street Journal, 'Bush of Arabia', "There is Shiite primacy, Kurdish autonomy in the north, and a cushion for the Sunni Arabs—in fact a role for that community slightly bigger than its demographic weight." This is about as close to success as foreign policy ever gets on an imperfect planet Earth, as opposed to a Kindergarden of Eden.

As for the Iraqis' presumed nostalgia for Saddam Hussein's stable and predictable regime, Iraqi citizens who were suspected of being insufficiently in love with their leader could rely on the stable
214

predictability of their eventual torture and/or extermination. The hundreds of thousands of victims of Saddam Hussein's genocide and their families do not miss him. If they are unhappy with us, it is because in their estimation, we botched the job.

The Libertarians go far beyond just Iraq or Vietnam to indict the USA and Great Britain for the crime and folly of colonialism. But was Britain's 'intervention' in Hong Kong for 100 years an abject failure? More broadly, was the entirety of the British Empire's world dominance a colossal mistake, if not evil? Certainly we can cite many failures and even atrocities committed by the British around the world in the past 300 years. But is that the same as saying that on net balance, the alternatives actually available then would indisputably have been better? Today, 8 of the top 12 most prosperous and free nations in the world are former British colonies and/or English-speaking nations— the heirs of the Magna Carta. Chile is one of the noted exceptions, thanks largely in part to its adoption of free- market principles that originated in the Anglo-Saxon world. More people speak English (or study it at least) in China than the entire population of the United States. Former British colonies have thrived in proportion to how well they have adopted the principles learned from their former overlords. This is not a lost experiment.

The Libertarians tell me that in foreign policy as in physics, Newton was right when he observed that for every action, there is an equal and opposite reaction; therefore, all of our interventions are folly in defiance of the Law of Unintended Consequences. But the mechanistic view of political economy and human action as analogous to Newtonian physics is perhaps the weakest pillar of sophomoric libertarianism. Honest Libertarians should re-read Ludwig von Mises and not the inferior pretenders who claim His legacy. Human beings are not inert atoms or asteroids; they have complex cultural, religious, and moral patterns. Was Japan's emergence as a pillar of peace in East Asia an equal and opposite reaction to Hiroshima? Was Mohammar Khadafi's abandonment of his nuclear program an equal and opposite reaction to our invasion of Saddam Hussein's Iraq? Was the escalation of the Palestinian attacks against Israel an equal and opposite reaction to the latter's surrender of land, presumably in exchange for peace?

Of course there will be unintended consequences and reactions. Hitting someone might make him want to hit back. Displacing one tyrant might draw even worse elements into the vacuum. Rebelling against a tyrant could bring repression. Declaring Independence from

Great Britain might lead to a long and bloody Revolutionary War. Buying an SUV might enrage an environmentalist who then makes it his life's mission to take away your private property rights and freedom. But this does not mean that we can hide behind our oceans. We are engaged in the world and have to make the best choices that we can and take action with imperfect knowledge, building into the plan the ability to respond to the unexpected. In 2003, that imperfect knowledge included the concurrence of such right-wing warmongers as John Kerry, Bill and Hillary Clinton, Harry Reid, Al Gore, Ted Kennedy, Nancy Pelosi, John Edwards, Robert Byrd, the bipartisan Robb-Silberman commission, Bill Clinton's CIA director George Tenet, Kenneth Pollack (Persian Gulf expert on the National Security Council for Bill Clinton)... and the list goes on. It meant coping with the undeniable fact that Saddam Hussein stood in open defiance of at least 16 United Nations Security Council resolutions. He could have come clean and avoided the invasion, but chose not to.

The free market requires defense; it doesn't just spring up spontaneously and peacefully. Private property, freedom, and enforcement of private contracts, rule of law etc. all require a benevolent force to restrain the bandits, the thieves, the murderers, and those who deem others unworthy of life due to ethnicity, religion, or other characteristics. It requires someone to prevent and punish murder, assault, robbery, theft, fraud, rape, persecution and conspiracy. It requires protection of the rights of minorities, women, and homosexuals. If no one can do that better in Iraq or anywhere else than we can, AND the bandits threaten us and the wider world besides, then sooner or later we will have to justify *not* getting involved.

One reader put the word "terrorists" in quotes, apparently to imply that they don't really exist, that they are just figments of us paranoiacs' imaginations. We should not fear terrorists because Americans die of heart attacks and traffic accidents? We should not declare war on Japan because on the day of December 7, 1941, more Americans died of natural causes than of the attack on Pearl Harbor (and besides, we had no business being there in the first place)?

We should not fear the terrorists because, like the communists before them, they are weak and ineffectual, not really a threat at all? Has it escaped the Libertarians' notice that the anti-liberty, anti-capitalist, and anti-libertarian agenda of the communists is being realized in America today at an accelerating rate, that America has never been less free or less Capitalist in its entire history than it is now? From the local (Los Angeles) city council banning plastic bags and ordering businesses to charge their customers money for a product (paper bags) that they would rather give away for free, to the President issuing executive orders contradicting the letter of his own signature legislation, to job- killing Global Warming taxes, to out-of-control regulatory agencies, to the politicization of the IRS—the encroachments on liberty and prosperity should terrify any sane and informed citizen. Are we supposed to blame all that on Bush's foreign policy? While we are asking people how they feel, let us ask the former refugees from communist Poland, Czechoslovakia, Cuba, and the People's Republic of China how they feel about creeping communism in America today.

The terrorist threat today is as great as it was on September 10, 2001; and it increases with our weakness abroad and with the encroachment of Sharia law into our American government, education system, and society. Osama bin Laden and his band of merry men were no doubt disappointed that their attack failed to kill 30,000 Americans, as it well could have, instead of a 'mere' 3,000. Did they attack us because of our foreign policy? No. There is nothing we could do or not do, short of SUBMISSION (the literal translation of the word 'Islam') to the Caliphate, with "Dhimmi" (second-class non-Muslim legal) status at best. They hate us precisely because of who we are, as embodied in the Declaration of Independence, the Constitution, the Bible, Liberty, and Capitalism. Libertarians, homosexuals, and single mothers will be the first to be stoned under the Sharia that is creeping into the West.

But, let us concede for the sake of argument that we never should have invaded Iraq in the first place. That still doesn't justify the decision to withdraw in 2011. In light of the circumstances of 2008-2011, the pullout borders on qualifying as a high crime: a betrayal of the U.S. servicemen and women who had paid the ultimate price to secure the gains; against Iraqi leaders (official and unofficial) who tempered their own extremist constituencies and tendencies to compromise and cooperate for a greater good; and against the ordinary Iraqis who welcomed us, trusted us, and assisted us in securing the nation against Baathists and terrorists.

Obama may simply have been naive, believing in his own press clippings and the validity of his pathetic Nobel Peace prize. Some of his allies certainly had to know better. But they supported the withdrawal anyway because nothing could be worse to them than permitting it to be thought for an instant that Bush might have succeeded after all. The Leftist narrative of America's — and especially G.W. Bush's — failure trumped all other considerations, including the lives of our soldiers. The American project in Iraq had to fail, even if by political force from within America.

It pains me to quarrel with Libertarians because we are indispensable allies in the struggle for limited government, liberty, low taxes and reduced regulation domestically. If Republicans (or Libertarians) propose to cut income tax rates, privatize Social Security, or repeal and replace Obamacare, will Libertarians (or Republicans) undermine the other because we disagree about foreign policy?

I hope not. Our freedom, prosperity, and, yes, military strength depend on getting it right at home. Let's achieve the libertarian dream of limited government so that ordinary Americans can exercise appropriate oversight of our military and foreign policy. Maybe we can agree on that.

Hillary's Path to 9/11

[A shorter version of this was published on AmericanThinker.com on April 10, 2015]

We will probably never know specifically what was on Hillary's email server (unless, as suggested by the Wall Street Journal, we subpoena China's military intelligence). But if the spell is finally and definitively broken, as the willingness of less-than-right-wing pundits at the New York Times, Time Magazine and others to criticize Hillary without restraint suggests it might be, then we may yet learn many things about the world in which we live that we had no idea were being suppressed out of rapturous worship, or mortal terror, of the Clintons. We may emerge into a world of freedom and democracy that we had almost forgotten existed.

As just one example: Imagine for moment a world in which any of the movies Flight 93, World Trade Center, Zero Dark 30 or American Sniper had been produced but never screened in theaters, because some cabal of politicians had objected to it and seen to it that the film would be censored, censured and suppressed.

Stop imagining. That is exactly what happened to the prime time miniseries "The Path to 9/11", written by Cyrus Nowrasteh, directed by David Cunningham and featuring possibly the performance of a career by Harvey Keitel as John P. O'Neil (FBI special agent and later chief of World Trade Center security, who died in the twin towers on 9/11). This film is arguably the most significant of the post-9/11 set, as it connects the dots between the first World Trade Center attack of 1993, the failure to off Osama Bin Laden in Afghanistan despite multiple opportunities, and the ultimate tragedy of September 11, 2001.

Yet this 5-hour docudrama was aired only once on ABC TV in September 2006, with edits and cuts demanded by partisan censors, and then buried under orders of Robert Iger, president of the parent company, Disney. To this day it has not been released to the public on DVD. Why? The ostensible reasons are summarized by Wikipedia as

"The film was controversial for its alleged misrepresentation of events and people, that some people called inaccurate, biased and included scenes that never happened". One would be hard-pressed to name a single historically-based or documentary film that couldn't be accused of the same to some degree, except that the bias of most that get produced emanates from the left. "Fahrenheit 911", "Sicko" and "An Inconvenient Truth" come to mind. Yet the controversy surrounding these and similar films never remotely caused, or are ever likely to cause, anyone to contemplate the possibility that they might be banned (or "voluntarily withdrawn") from the public square.

What then made the case of The Path to 9/11 different? Was it a precursor case of Charlie Hebdo Stockholm Syndrome appeasement? Suppress the film out of sensitivity to our Muslim friends, or so as not to provoke our not-quite friends the jihadis into committing murderous atrocities against innocent people? No. No peep was ever heard from any Islamic organization in objection to the film.

The reason for the unprecedented censorship may be summarized in two words: The Clintons. The Clinton machine, jealous both of Bill's legacy and Hillary's 2008 White House ambitions, saw the film as a right-wing hit piece against them and mobilized all of its heavy artillery to make Disney/ABC offers it couldn't refuse, first to edit and then to completely withdraw the film.

Following a partial pre-screening of the film to the National Press Club (which part did not include the Bush years), Clinton attorney Richard Ben-Veniste spoke out harshly against the film and its producers. Another Clinton attorney Bruce Lindsey wrote directly to Disney president Bob Iger to impugn writer Nowrasteh's alleged political agenda. Keith Olberman (remember "The Worst Person in the World"?) interviewed Judd Legum, Research Director for the Center for American Progress and editor of ThinkProgress.org, the latter run by former Clinton Chief of Staff John Podesta, to cast aspersions on the writer. The damning evidence, according to Legum: "[Nowrasteh] admits that he's a conservative". Legum later became Hillary's research director for her 2008 presidential campaign.

More "damning evidence" of a right-wing conspiracy emerged when Rush Limbaugh endorsed the film and called out Nowrasteh personally as "my friend". Little mention was made during this time of Nowrasteh's extensive collaborations with other far-right extremists...like Oliver Stone. Nowrasteh's work with Stone on the Showtime film "The Day Reagan was Shot" had previously earned him charges of *liberal* bias.

Senators Harry Reid, Dick Durbin, Charles Schumer and others wrote to Disney's Bob Iger, threatening legal and legislative sanctions which included jeopardizing ABC's broadcast license. Max Blumenthal, son of Clinton ally Sydney Blumenthal, wrote of a subversive conservative conspiracy, with David Horowitz as its godfather, infiltrating ABC.

Then they went after director David Cunningham for his shocking ties to a -- gasp! -- evangelical Christian ministry founded by his father. Apparently Youth with a Mission, or YWAM, in between digging wells and running schools and orphanages in the third world, had been a major financier and shadow director of the movie. YWAM had an auxiliary film institute which had once stated somewhere its hope to "have a positive influence on Hollywood movies". To Keith Olberman, "The Path to 9/11" was nothing less than "a stealth attack in the culture wars".

According to Carol Felsenthal, author of Clinton in Exile, Bill Clinton personally phoned Bob Iger to demand the suppression of the film, and asked former Senate Majority Leader George Mitchell, then chairman of the board at Disney to do the same. Another Clinton attorney (how many do they have?), Floyd Abrams, demanded that references to Clinton's impeachment and other scandals be edited out.

Samuel ("Sandy") Berger, the National Security Advisor to Bill Clinton who had been convicted in 2005 of stealing classified documents from the national archives by stuffing them into his underwear for the express purposes of preventing them from being seen by the 9/11 Commission, was given 30 minutes on CNN to denounce the movie and question the producers' honesty, in an interview with Wolf Blitzer. Berger was an advisor to Hillary's presidential campaign.

One of the most colorful and yet chilling demonstrations of the left's spirit of censorship came from New York congresswoman Louise Slaughter (a major Hillary Clinton ally) in an outdoor press conference:

221

"We demand! that ABC run a disclaimer in every single frame. Saying up front 'this is not true' is not good enough. It's gotta be in every frame, 'don't believe this!'"

Very few of the Clintonite critics had actually seen the film. As a result, while making the charge that the film was historically inaccurate for depicting scenes that never happened, many of them were reduced to making straw-man arguments against scenes that didn't exist in the movie.

No free-speech, civil libertarian or professional guild organization came to the producers' defense; not PEN America (even though Nowrasteh was a 2-time award winner) not the Director's Guild of America, nor the Writer's Guild of America nor the Screen Actors Guild, nor the ACLU. Participant Productions, producer of the anti-McCarthyism movie "Good Night and Good Luck" and others, posted a letter in support of the miniseries on its website, but quickly took it down under pressure from ex Vice President Al Gore.

All of the above happened within the last two weeks before the planned air dates of September 10th and 11th, 2006. Prior to that time, no one, including the executives at ABC and Disney, the attorneys that had vetted every scene of the heavily footnoted script, and the many liberal Democrats and Clinton voters who had senior roles in the production (this is Hollywood, after all) had expressed anything other than the greatest enthusiasm for the project and for its prospects as an annual commemoration broadcast. Members of the Bush administration, who didn't come away much less scathed than the Clintons in the movie, never protested.

In the end, all of this pressure may have been overkill. Bob Iger and the Disney political action committee were donors to Hillary Clinton's campaigns for several years. Iger forbade his employees from talking to anyone and pulled the plug, putting political considerations above his fiduciary duties to the Disney shareholders, going so far as to refuse to sell the film to prospective buyers. (Incidentally, if a corporation takes a $100-million loss for the sake of a political candidate, does that count as a campaign contribution for purposes of campaign finance laws? Just asking.)

Nowrasteh, Cunningham and their crew have done an adequate job of responding point-by-point to their critic's more rational challenges to the film's historical accuracy, including explaining the obvious point that squeezing 70,000 hours of historical time into a 5-hour movie requires some amount of compression and amalgamation. It's doubtful that the Clintons would have been happier if the producers, instead of condensing ten missed opportunities to take out Osama bin Laden into one composite "scene that never happened", they had presented every episode in exhaustive detail, extending the film's duration to 10 hours, of which a much greater percentage would have been focused directly on Clinton's failures.

But the bottom-line reason this film should be released is not because it is accurate, fair or true, or least of all because conservatives like it, but because we are a free society of mature adults governed, among other things, by the First Amendment to the Constitution of the United States, in letter, in principle and in spirit. Conservatives who are sick of Michael Moore's Sicko are free to make their own documentary on health care starring Paul Ryan and Ted Cruz. Those who find "*An Inconvenient Truth*" to be mendacious are at liberty to produce their own blockbuster "*Climate Change Is Just Hot Air*" flick starring Senator James Inhofe, geologist Ian Plimer and indicted denier Mark Steyn. No one is saying that Nowrasteh's and Cunningham's Path to 9/11 has to be the last word—unless, on the merits and in the marketplace, no one else is able to do a better job. Competition? Bring it on!

So when Hillary is finally out of the running sometime in the next three to nineteen months, will Bob Iger or his successors at Disney finally relent and release the film? (Or will they persist for Chelsea's sake? Follow the money.) Maybe if they feel enough heat in a different direction, including the direction of their own self-respect.

The suppression of this film is only one example of the latent effects of the Clinton intimidation machine. To combat it we will need the courage of Barbara Olson, author of "Hell to Pay: The Unfolding Story of Hillary Rodham Clinton", who died in American Airlines flight 77 on that fateful day. Once the fear is lifted, there's no telling what other revelations may be made to the American public. We might yet be able to shine a brighter light on how much of HillaryCare, thought to have been defeated in 1994, actually made it into the Clinton-Gingrich budget act of 1997. Price controls, caps on the number of medical student residencies (already under the bureaucratic control of the Center for Medicare and Medicaid Services and never since increased), interference in the patient/doctor relationship, backed by the full might of the tax and criminal justice system, were all piled on. The resulting healthcare market dysfunctions contributed to renewed calls for the government to solve problems of its own making via a socialized medicine scheme in 2009.

But that's a topic for another article. As with everything else Clinton, the horror stories never seem to end. Until now? We can only hope.

Conservative Fundraising: What Me Worry?

[Published March 10, 2015 on AmericanThinker.com]

In the popular consciousness as successfully twisted by the progressive Left, it is axiomatic that the Republican Party is the party of the rich, especially rich, old, white patriarchal Christian men; and that the Democrats are the party that defends and protects the poor, the downtrodden, women, and minorities. From there it follows that in the Darwinian struggle to raise funds for political campaigns and to influence public opinion, it must be a completely unfair fight, with conservatives outraising and outspending progressives from top to bottom. Something must be done to level this grossly imbalanced playing field, lest Republican cannibals eat the poor.

Reality, of course, paints a very different picture.

Adding up the total assets of the 115 left-leaning foundations (as of 2009) yields a figure of $105 billion (with a 'b'), which as it happens is ten times greater than the combined assets of the 75 top conservative foundations.

Not one conservative foundation had assets exceeding one billion dollars in 2009; fourteen progressive foundations did. The Bill and Melinda Gates Foundation's endowment is a whopping $33 billion, by itself more than 3 times the combined assets of the top 75 conservative foundations. The Koch brothers have nothing on George Soros and his machine.

And here's the maddening kicker: most of these "progressive" groups were founded by industrialists and capitalists who must be spinning in their graves witnessing the socialist agenda being promoted with their hard-earned money: Ford, Rockefeller, Kellogg, Heinz, Carnegie, Mellon, ChevronTexaco, and many others. Clearly, these pots of gold have been commandeered to serve purposes which are 180 degrees counter to their founder's intentions.

One conservative group, in order to avoid the fate of so many of its predecessors, deliberately closed and went out of business in 2005: the Olin Foundation. Better to die on the battlefield than to risk capture by the enemy.

And don't think that Republicans get a counterweight to all of this from their living fat cat friends on Wall Street; that's another whopper of a myth. The impoverished CEOs and/or seconds in command at JP Morgan Chase, Goldman Sachs, Lehman Brothers, Bear Stearns, Blackrock, Merrill Lynch, and others collectively raised over $100 million to elect Barack Obama in 2008.

In spite of these facts—or perhaps because of them, since $105 billion can buy an awful lot of P.R.—Democrats get away with posing as champions of the underdog, even as underdogs themselves. The personal net worth of the Clintons, John Kerry, John Edwards, Al Gore, and their cohort run into hundreds of millions of dollars. Of the wealthiest twelve senators and congressmen in 2009, nine were Democrats. Yet with a straight face, Al Gore's 2000 election slogan was "The People vs. the Powerful". John Edwards spoke of "Two Americas", by which he meant rich and ruthless Republicans on the one hand with their boots on the necks of the poor masses on the other.

This posing is nothing new. It is a successful strategy stretching back from Diane Feinstein to Jimmy Carter and from Franklin Delano Roosevelt to Andrew Jackson; all men and women of aristocratic wealth.

The Democrat party is the home of the rich. 8 of the top 10 per-capita income congressional districts are represented by Democrats. 7 of the top 10 wealthiest counties in the U.S. voted for Obama. 19 of the wealthiest 20 ZIP codes in the country gave more money to Democrats than to Republicans in 2012; 10024 on Manhattan's Upper West Side gave 86% to Democrats.

And if all of that is not enough, liberals, progressives and socialists dominate of our public, taxpayer-funded education systems, from pre-K-12 to the universities. At least 80 percent of the professoriat is left, and teach their captive audience from that perspective.

It becomes clear then that the money machine arrayed against conservatives, Republicans, and constitutionalists amounts to hundreds of billions of dollars, including a substantial quantity of funds extracted from ordinary conservative citizens via taxes, tuition, and union dues. From foundations and think tanks to public employee unions and colleges, progressives expropriate the fruits of capitalism to finance their anti-capitalist agenda. In that context, it's a miracle that conservatives and Republicans are viable at all.

So, what do we do about this? Well, if I suppose if were smart enough to know the answer, I'd be a billionaire. But let me toss out a couple of ideas: we're going to have to get creative, entrepreneurial, and risk-taking. Capitalism and the fortunes it creates along with general prosperity isn't dead yet. We need to identify the current crop of millionaires, billionaires, and ordinary pro-capitalists who want to promote limited government and free markets in their own lifetimes and beyond. We have to found a new generation of pro free-market foundations and think tanks with charters, bylaws and constitutions that guarantee that they will act according to their founder's wishes and not get hijacked by the left; or that each one, after a period, should close before it gets taken over, as the Olin Foundation did. Requiring in the bylaws—amendable only by supermajority if amendable at all— that officers and executive directors *not* be recruited from Harvard and the ranks of existing foundations, and that they have a minimum of ten years private-sector employment, or better yet, business ownership experience, would go a long way toward guaranteeing the orientation of such organizations. We will need to take as much care in crafting the charters of these organizations as the Founders did composing the United States Constitution (read *Miracle in Philadelphia* by Catherine Drinker Bowen).

And where do we find such people? We find them... in America: in the Midwest, the South, the rural states, Texas, and yes, Silicon Valley, Hollywood, Seattle, Berkeley, Harvard, and Manhattan 10024.

The opportunities are here, and now. God knows the urgency is. 2016 is yesterday.

Part V: Global Warning

Overpopulation
Famine
Pollution
Resource Exhaustion
Radioactivity
Acid Rain
Urban Sprawl
Soil Erosion
Deforestation
Alar
Running out of Oil
Oil is bad and must be suppressed
Species extinction
Incipient Ice Age
No, Global Warming
No! Climate Change.
No! Climate Chaos!

Here we go again. Strap in. This is the biggest one they've tried so far.

Why do conservatives and Republicans reflexively oppose well-meaning liberals on environmental issues? Apart from the track record of repeated fraud and "wolf-crying", there is the minor detail that the liberal's villain is ALWAYS capitalism, and their solution is ALWAYS more government control, higher taxes, more regulation by unaccountable agencies with expanded powers: socialism. In 100% of cases.

It's almost unnecessary to examine the alleged problems and threats as presented by the Left on the merits. Just take a look at what the proposed "solutions" are, and you will have all you need to know.

Don't say you weren't warned.

Climate Change: Where is the Science?

[Published June 11 2015 on www.AmericanThinker.com]

Climate Change skeptics (or "deniers", as sometimes pejoratively characterized) must be prepared for the possibility that the climate change alarmists could be right; that the Earth is in a hazardous, uncontrolled, hyper-warming phase that is being caused by the unprecedented carbon footprint of industrial human activity.

Almost by definition, Climate Change thus qualified is a possibility. But it is also a possibility that the same human factors are actually setting up the Earth for a catastrophically rapid descent into next ice age. And it is a possibility that human activity has had, and will continue to have, a negligible effect on the Earth's climate, overwhelmed by a hundred other much more consequential natural forces.

The question before us is to adequately estimate the relative probabilities of these different outcomes, and others. Are they all roughly equal? Is it twice as likely that the Earth is cooling than that it is warming? That humans and fossil fuels have nothing, or everything to do with it, or somewhere in between? Or is it over 99% certain that anthropogenic carbon burning-induced warming is the course we are on, with all other possibilities combined being less than one percent probable?

The only way to find out is through the most rigorous and critical application of the scientific method, in practice and in public discourse. Anything less than that increases the risk that the economic, political and social impact of the "solution" may be more catastrophic to humans than the physical results of climate change.

Don't these premises vindicate the IPCC, Al Gore and the warming warning community? After all, the scientists have spoken, and definitively, right?

Have they? Let us examine what the climate change alarm community has done and how they have done it, and see if it qualifies as the rigorous and unimpeachable science that its proponents claim it is. We'll walk it back from results to first principles.

First, *results*. Nothing defines science so well in the popular mind than the predictive power of scientific theory. "If the conditions, materials and/or forces A, B, C, and D come together in such-and-such a way, then the outcome WILL BE 6.7294874X. If variables P, Q, and R are substituted for A, C, and D, then the outcome will be 2.1 milligrams of tetrahydrocannabinol in combustion." Awesome.

So, how is that predictive power working out so far? And more to the point, what effect have those results had on the public's confidence in the supposedly infallible science and scientists? In 1999 they said that warming would wipe out the Great Barrier Reef. In 2000 they said that Britain would no longer see snow during winter. In 2001 they predicted starvation from failing grain crops in India. From 2003 to 2005 they concluded that the drought then occurring in Australia would be permanent and city dwellers would have nothing to drink. In 2006 they predicted unprecedented severe cyclones and hurricanes. In 2008 they said that by 2013 there would be no more arctic ice cap; that we would be swimming with the otters at the North Pole.

None of these predictions have come to pass. The Reef is still there, as is the arctic ice. Children make more snowmen than ever in Britain and the rains returned to Australia with a vengeance. Thanks to the instantaneous and ubiquitous communications made possible by our smartphones and social networking, there is much greater awareness of the severe weather events that do occur than there was before, but in absolute terms, these are no greater than they have always been.

The computer-based climate models have been demonstrated to have no reliable predictive power. The mother of all predictions, that global warming was inexorable, has been debunked by the past seventeen years of actual measurement, sending the climate change community into a mad scramble to explain it, deny it, "correct" the earlier data, explain why it doesn't disprove their theories, or explain it away.

Even so, none of this proves that global warming isn't happening or won't happen, or that excess carbon dioxide from fossil fuel burning won't send us over the brink, right? Of course not; how do you prove a negative? But the persistence of politicians with a vested interest insisting that Climate Change is a greater threat to humanity than ISIS, Iran, North Korea, unemployment, burning American cities and negative economic growth combined, in spite of the failures of any of the predictions to come true, suggests that something is wrong at a deeper level with the way we are practicing and discussing science.

Scientists, strictly speaking, should have no agenda whatsoever other than the discovery of truth; truth of which no human being is the ultimate arbiter, but only Nature. Albert Einstein famously did not want his theory of Relativity accepted until its predictive power had been proven. Scientists who have come to believe that a certain theory is closer to the truth than any known alternatives have the right, indeed the duty, to defend that theory against any and all challenges. But the true scientist must always, without exception, maintain intellectual honesty and be prepared to abandon a theory if its predictive power cannot explain empirical data that does not fit and/or when a rival theory that seems to do a better job of explaining the subject phenomena (often in simpler terms) arises. Skepticism and openness to change is the fundamentalist creed of the true scientist.

A theory that does not contain within it the terms of its own falsification is not a valid theory. If the planet Mercury's orbit did not vary by the number of degrees that Einstein's theory said it would, then Relativity would be unproven and Albert would have had to admit failure, as he indicated he would be willing to do. A weasel-word term like "Climate Change", where any drought and any flood, any heat wave or cold wave, any storm or any clear sky, any melting or freezing, anywhere at any time, can be cited as evidence of industrial humans' culpability, and there are no defined criteria that would exculpate us, is not a valid theory; it is meaningless Catch-22 Heads-I-Win-Tails-You-Lose political propaganda.

The climate change alarm scientists have lost credibility because too many of them have behaved not as scientists but as politicians. They will regain the trust of the people when they rediscover their principles and comport themselves accordingly, to wit:

- They debate each other honestly and respectfully, including the skeptics and "deniers", with no recourse to ad hominem attacks, defamation lawsuits [or RICO prosecutions[37]].

- Instead of firing, defunding and/or persecuting scientists with whom they disagree, they advocate for funding for research into alternate theories by those same rival scientists on a comparable scale as their own results-oriented research.

---

[37] Senator Sheldon Whitehouse (D-RI) has called for climate "deniers" to be prosecuted under statutes designed for going after the godfathers of organized crime syndicates.

- They express their honest scientific opinions in terms of relative probabilities. "100% certainty" should be looked upon with the utmost suspicion.

- They rebuke any and all meteorologists or news readers who ascribe any significance whatsoever to transient local weather events as proof, or even evidence, of anthropomorphic climate change.

- They discontinue all scare tactics and sensationalism, and stick to objective reporting of measurement and rational hypotheses.

- They discontinue all recourse to consensus or authority, and rely only on facts, logic, and the demonstrated track record of their predictions over the long term.

- They stop papering over the differences of opinion within the alarm community in order to present a unified public front; keep the discussion transparent.

- They publicly disclaim any among them who make anti-scientific claims such as that "The debate is over" or "The science is settled". Yes, that means Al Gore and anyone else. Anyone asserting such a thing should take the statement to its logical conclusion by resigning his or her position and/or returning any unspent research grant money and forswearing any continuance of the same. If the world is round not flat, we don't need to fund research and deploy hardware to ascertain the shape of the earth. If the debate is over, then go home.

In short, we will restore to them the trust and respect to which science and scientists aspire when they demonstrate that they are worthy of it.

Lay persons are easily intimidated from taking on scientists on their turf. But when supposed scientists behave anti-scientifically and demand that we surrender our civil liberties, our private property rights and our prosperity, that's our turf. Giving up the cheapest and most plentiful energy sources available (fossil fuels and Nuclear, the latter which does not contribute to greenhouse gasses) can cause a great deal of poverty, hunger and death by exposure to the hostile elements of a poorly understood climate.

It doesn't take a PhD to know what science is and isn't; climate science as practiced by the IPCC, Al Gore and their fellow travelers does not qualify.

Back to the Future

and the Solution to Climate Change

[Published June 4, 2015 on FrontPageMag.com]

The United Nations Intergovernmental Panel on Climate Change or IPCC, together with former Vice President Al Gore, President Obama, Pope Francis, and their colleagues in the government-funded scientific research community have made extraordinary claims about Climate Change, going so far as to say that it represents the single greatest threat to all of our lives. In spite of their computer models failing to predict or explain the absence of any measurable average warming now for the past seventeen years, among many other failures, they are doubling down on this narrative undeterred. Congressman Ted Lieu, D-CA (district 33) who succeeded Henry Waxman and who co-authored California's Assembly Bill 32, the "Global Warming Solutions Act" when he was a member of the California Assembly, has made combating Climate Change the defining theme of his service, introducing to the House the "Climate Change Solutions Act".

We skeptics have many reasons for doubting the validity of the alarmists' claims. But perhaps the most damning evidence of their disingenuousness is that they don't just solve the problem and be done with it. For solving global warming, like solving any problem—a raw material shortage, a faulty architectural plan, a bug in a software program—does not depend on convincing everyone that you are right; it just depends on BEING right and taking the appropriate action. That is exactly what entrepreneurs do, at their own expense, risk and reward, for all of our benefit. Why won't the bureaucrats who are determined to take over our lives do the same?

Remember that 1980's time-travel movie Back to the Future Part II? Our young hero Marty McFly travels instantaneously from the year 1985 to the far distant, uh, 2015 (yeah, it's been that long!) where he encounters flying cars and an antique store featuring an original Apple Macintosh computer (cutting edge of consumer technology at the time the film was made) and a sports almanac—a printed magazine listing thousands of scores from popular athletic contests—spanning 50 years of (future) historical time. Long story short, the almanac falls into the hands of the Bad Guy Biff Tannen, who steals the time machine, travels back 60 years to 1955 to deliver the almanac to his younger self. The rest as they say, is... "history". With all the future sports scores in hand, young Biff becomes the richest man in the world by betting on events whose outcomes are foretold in the gift from the future.

The climate change alarmists are effectively claiming to be young Biff Tannen, future climate almanac in hand. THEY KNOW. Armed with their hard-science PhDs (or at least M.A.s in English Lit) and supercomputers, they know what is going to happen to the climate tomorrow, next year, ten years from now and 100 years from now. They know where the seas are rising and where the ice is melting. They know where the droughts and floods will be, what species are going extinct and where the forests are dying. They even know where bumper crops will thrive and where forests will grow where before there was only desert; even the IPCC concedes that not all change is negative everywhere.

Very well then, let the IPCC climatologists act on that superior knowledge and reap the benefit as Biff Tannen did. After all, what are we talking about when we say Climate Change or Global Warming? We're talking about the future. And what happens to the one who knows the future? He or she wins every bet and gets rich. If the IPCC scientists and Al Gore & Assocs LLP were honest, they would stop wasting resources on lobbying and just get on with it. They know the future, so they can bet on it, pocket their winnings, and make the rest of us do as they please, not by force but through voluntary incentives.

The IPCC climatologists are the ultimate insider traders, hiding in plain sight; all they have to do is leverage their presumed superior knowledge into perfectly legal and ethical voluntary market transactions facilitated by the capitalist system. Buy the undervalued assets, sell the overvalued ones. Sell Malibu beach front property and buy all of the available adjacent land at 10 to 100 feet higher elevation. Amplify winnings through leverage: short the overvalued, borrow cheap to buy the undervalued. Buy the most valuable commodities from where they will be abundant and reap the higher prices caused by shortages elsewhere. A billion here, a trillion there, and pretty soon you're talking about real money. In short order, the Ones Who Know will be richer than the Forbes 400 combined, easily accumulating the 1% to 10% of GDP that they say it will cost to forestall environmental disaster.

Some readers may take this for satire. But if this is not realistic, the jokesters are the climate change alarmists themselves. Listen again to their conceit: THEY KNOW! The debate is over. The science is settled. They are infallible. The computer models are irrefutable. Anyone who disagrees with them is not just wrong, but as evil as a person who denies that the murder of six million Jews during the World War II Holocaust ever took place. And to prove that all true scientists agree, they'll defund, terminate and assassinate the reputation of anyone with or without a PhD who differs. Seriously?

Never mind the repeated failure of the computer models to predict what actually happened for the past 17 years. Suspend your disbelief that a system far more complex than the stock market, with a thousand variables from solar cycles to volcanoes and from deep ocean currents to earthquakes to variations in the Earth's orbit to water vapor, can be reduced to just one overarching evil, carbon dioxide, previously thought to be the greatest boon to green plants. Forget that the Earth has been warming and cooling, warming and cooling in cycles measured from decades to millennia ever since the planet first cooled some forty million centuries ago. Perish the thought that Greenland could be Green again as it was 1,000 years ago, to the great benefit of the farmers and grazing cows there. Disregard the insecurity belied by the very weasel words "Climate Change" (is it warming, or isn't it? or is it an oncoming ice age, as the consensus of all respectable scientists thought during the 1970s, just because that was in fact the trend-line at the time?). Pay no attention to the utterly anti-scientific phrases like "consensus" and "authority" with which they bully any dissenters (what significant advance of science was ever made by those means?). Turn a blind eye to the leaked emails from the Climate Research Unit at East Anglia exposing the extreme bias against dissenting scientists, and allegations of falsified readings of primary data by the U.S. government's Global Historical Climate Network (GHCN). And above all, trust their impartiality, their utter lack of political bias. The fact that all the solutions proposed amount to restricting freedom and emasculating capitalism are necessary strictly from a scientific basis having nothing to do with anti-capitalist ideology.

Who is engaged in satire here? We'll believe them when they sell refrigerators to the Eskimos, polar bear fur coats to the Kuwaitis and break ground on their tropical vacation resort investments in Canada. Let them put their own money (instead of ours) where their mouths are.

Regardless of whether the Earth is warming or cooling, whether CO_2 is a factor or not, or even whether or not it is the fault of fossil fuels, the solution is not the suppression of freedom and of the cheapest and most plentiful energy sources available. To the contrary, voluntary cooperation and competition, informed as to the relative scarcities and abundances by the price system, with wide latitude for individual action not pre-approved by any authority, enjoying the full complement of the fruits of our age's unprecedented wealth, are what will enable us to solve the challenges that we are confronted with. It is the great genius of free markets that the greatest prosperity for the greatest number is achieved by tapping into diverse talent without respect to birth, race, class or credentials; and without prior agreement or consensus as to what any collective "we" should do in every instance. Capitalism, not socialism, is the solution.

The climate change alarmists should put up or shut up. In the meantime, all legislative, punitive taxation and/or privileged subsidy schemes and education curricula that are derived from fraudulent environmentalism and the assumption that only government can save us from ourselves and from fossil fuels, must be defeated and/or repealed.

We have a lot of weather today!

Transcript of Interview on "The Larry Elder Show," June 12, 2015[38]

Larry Elder: Howard Hyde is an ex-liberal, sociologist [sic], progressive Democrat from Berkeley. He edits a website called CitizenEcon.com. He's also a columnist with FrontPageMag; also, he writes for WesternJournalism.com and AmericanThinker.com. In fact, in American Thinker is where he published his article called, "Climate Change: Where is the Science?" And Howard lives in Southern California, out here, but for the past couple days he's been attending the D.C. climate change conference sponsored by the Heartland Institute, the think tank that I told you about in Chicago. Howard, are you there?

Howard Hyde: I am there. Thanks, Larry. It's great to be here.

LE: Howard, thank you very much for joining me and taking the time. This is the twelfth annual conference?

HH: It's the tenth annual.

LE: And over those ten years, how's the climate been? [laughs]

HH: [laughs] Well, it's been pretty much flat, actually. It's a pleasant, warm day. You know, nothing much to report.

LE: Howard, I got up yesterday morning and I was watching a woman give the weather report and she said, "We have a lot of weather today!" and I— [laughs]

HH: [laughs] Well, how much weather did you have yesterday?

LE: I have no idea! So, Howard, first of all, I'm sure you heard that exchange between Rick Santorum and Chris Wallace of Fox, where Santorum criticized the pope for the pope talking about climate change, and he said he hoped the pope would kind of stick in his lane. Turns out, the pope has a degree in chemistry; Rick Santorum does not. And so, that raises the question of whether or not somebody who's not a scientist can talk about climate change. Obviously, you can, but what Santorum was basically saying is that the pope was a spiritual leader and ought not be talking about climate change when,

---

38   Available at: http://www.larryelder.com/programhighlights?date=20150612

in fact, he's got a degree in chemistry. Question, Howard: what's your background? Do you have a degree in sciences?

HH: I don't. I have a degree in music and I work in information technology. But that's kind of the point. As I wrote yesterday in AmericanThinker.com, ordinary people like you and me, Larry, are easily intimidated from entering into debates with scientists.

LE: How dare you call me ordinary? [laughs] I'm sub-ordinary!

HH: [laughs] Well, you're extraordinary, Larry—

LE: That's right!

HH: But you don't have a PhD, and you don't speak in incomprehensible charts and graphs and equations and data—

LE: That's true.

HH: —so you've got nothing whatsoever to say about climate.

LE: I got nothing, yeah.

HH: But the fact of the matter is that what's going on in the climate change debate has nothing to do with science and everything to do with politics and power. Scientists who want to investigate alternate theories of climate do not get the research grants.

LE: Howard, there's a 90% consensus! Ninety percent of all climate change scientists say that man is trashing the planet! We've got to do something about it!

HH: And that's why, out of 12,000 published papers, only forty-one of them actually said that human-induced, carbon dioxide producing, fossil fuel burning, is the cause of climate change. You know, there's credible evidence that the *actual* number is 0.3% as it was presented by Lord Christopher Monckton this morning at the conference.

LE: Mmhmm.

HH: 0.3% versus 97%.

LE: All right, Howard, the question, of course, people are going to have is: how does somebody as smart as Obama, as smart as John Kerry, both argue that climate change is a bigger threat to us than even ISIS? They can't be idiots!

HH: Yeah [laughs], well, I mean, first of all, of course, it's grotesque for Obama to declare climate change worse than ISIS taking over the Iraq that he abandoned, worse than the economy that's on life support while he's strangling it, while the cities that are run by the Democrat's welfare state have become kill zones and so on and on—I mean, there are so many other *real* problems that we have. But the fact is, Obama and Kerry and Al Gore and all the rest of them, they're politicians;

they're not scientists. They're not after a disinterested pursuit of the truth with open debate and falsification and all that; they're after an agenda. And their agenda is control, power, the dismantling of capitalism, of fossil fuels, and frankly, the dismantling of our constitutional process of government.

LE: I'm talking to Howard Hyde, he is a[n] editor of the website called CitizenEcon.com, also a columnist with Front Page Magazine, and he just attended the tenth annual conference on climate change, sponsored by the Heartland Institute. You know, Howard, did you see—I'm sure you saw an American, I mean, "An Inconvenient Truth."

HH: [laughs] Actually, I missed that.

LE: [laughs]

HH: I think I was watching the latest *Jurassic Park* movie at the time.

LE: Anyway, as you know, he brags and brags and brags, does Al Gore, about the fact that he was inspired by a Harvard professor named Roger Revelle. Roger Revelle was the one who warned him about manmade activity, anthropogenic activity, and all the CO2 in the air. It turns out, Roger Revelle, in the waning years of his life—as you probably know, Howard—renounced Al Gore and said Al Gore was an alarmist, he didn't believe any of the stuff that Al Gore was saying, and then Al Gore said that he was senile. Now, it seems to me if I'm a climate change guy and Al Gore is bragging about the influence of Roger Revelle and Roger Revelle trashes me, it would cause me to rethink my assumptions. But apparently Roger Revelle didn't even exist!

HH: [laughs] Well, you know, this whole thing kind of makes for strange bedfellows because, you know, Michael Mann, the author of the infamous hockey stick graph, has been suing Mark Steyn for exercising his freedom of speech under the First Amendment to the Constitution for the last couple of years, and this lawsuit's going on much longer than it ought to—I mean, it should've been laughed out of court on the first day.

LE: Mmhmm.

HH: But in spite of the fact that, you know, the *Los Angeles Times* and the *New York Times*—I forget the exact list, but it's a list of not-at-all right-wing organizations, including the ACLU, are on Mark Steyn's side in this case because they recognize the threat to free speech and the First Amendment. It's ludicrous.

LE: You know, Mark Steyn has spoken out against the science that allegedly supports climate change and as Howard pointed out, he is literally being sued. Literally being sued. And this is where we are, right here. I even read about a senator from Rhode Island who suggested that using the RICO statute to go after oil companies the way the RICO statute was used to go after tobacco companies because they're engaged in a conspiracy to deceive the American people. My goodness! A sitting senator suggesting going after CEOs, oil companies, for lying about climate change and using the RICO statutes to do it?

HH: Yeah, I mean, it's truly frightening what, you know, the descent into persecution that we're having. You know, many years ago in the Soviet Union there was this agronomist, this scientist, named Lysenko, and he curried favor with Joseph Stalin and he had all the scientists who disagreed with him either sent off to Siberia or literally executed, killed, OK? So, for forty years or something like that, there was one theory of agronomy which was the politically correct theory and if you disagreed with it, you were in deep doo-doo. And the problem is that the theory, in fact, turned out not quite to agree with the laws of Nature and as a result, millions of Russians starved to death because the way they were planting their crops just didn't work. And, you know, that's the slippery slope that we're heading down with this encroachment upon our civil liberties, the First Amendment and this insane rhetoric that you just described.

LE: I'm talking to Howard Hyde, again, editor of CitizenEcon.com, also is a columnist for a number of publications including Front Page Mag. Howard, I've been on the air now twenty years, you're the first one who's ever used the word "doo-doo" on my show.

HH: [laughs]

LE: I'm impressed.

HH: Well, yeah, OK, that slipped out.

LE: Howard, OK, take the next couple of minutes and tell us, what is the truth? What is the truth about the science? What is the truth about climate change?

HH: Well, the truth is, first of all, that you can't take something as huge and as complex as the climate, particularly over the next hundred years, and simplify it down to just one variable that happens conveniently to be the thing that the Left is against, which is to say fossil fuels and capitalism and prosperity. Carbon dioxide, as we all learned in kindergarten, is plant food; it makes the plants turn green. As a matter of fact, plants that get more carbon dioxide need less water in order to thrive. Carbon dioxide is a good thing, it's something we want more of, and there is not a correlation between the rise of carbon dioxide and the rise of heat, there's just—in the geological record—there's just as much evidence of the inverse, of carbon dioxide going up and the planet cooling. And, by the way, a cooling planet is a lot more to be feared than a warming planet. Mark Steyn pointed out that 90% of the population of Canada lives within 100 miles of the United States border, and the reason is, it's so bloody cold up there!

LE: [laughs]

HH: OK? So it would be a good thing for Canada and Greenland, where, you know, Greenland used to be green, right? I mean, that's how it got its name.

LE: That's right.

HH: Now it's kind of iced over. So, you know, carbon dioxide is not one element that controls it all, water vapor is the dominant greenhouse gas, and water, to my knowledge, by itself is not a pollutant, OK? But neither is carbon dioxide a pollutant. These are not pollutants. So, it's a lot more complex than that and there's a great deal of doubt expressed by all the PhDs at this conference and the 9,000 PhDs who find the petition expressing a dissenting opinion that CO2 really has very little to do with it and human activity probably has a slim chance of affecting the climate the way the alarmists are describing.

LE: Mmhmm.

HH: And even if it were so, it would probably not even be such a bad thing. I mean, the Earth has been a lot warmer than it is today, and in the recent geologic past, like a thousand years ago, there was a medieval warming period where, you know, you could grow wine in Great Britain.

LE: Right.

HH: You know, that's not a bad thing.

LE: I'm talking to Howard Hyde, he edits the website CitizenEcon.com, just finished the tenth annual conference on climate change sponsored by the Heritage Foundation [sic; meant to say Heartland Institute]. Howard, here's the difficulty that we have: there's a man named Freeman Dyson, I'm sure you know who he is—

HH: Yes, I've been a fan for thirty-five years, actually.

LE: Freeman Dyson is arguably one of the smartest people on the planet. He is a physicist, he's well liked, he voted for Obama twice, he's not a right-winger the way Howard and I are, but he has gotten

244

involved in the climate change issue and he says it's B.S. And when I said this is where we are, Howard, so Freeman Dyson goes to see this movie, "An Inconvenient Truth," with his wife. His wife comes out and turns to him and says, "You've lied to me all this time. You've lied to me about this." Now, if Freeman Dyson cannot convince his wife that climate change is crap, how can we?

HH: [laughs] Well, you know, Senator Inhofe was here, he opened the breakfast keynote yesterday, and he pointed out he's got something like twenty children and grandchildren, and one of his granddaughters came up to him and said, "Grandpa, how come you don't understand climate change?"

LE: [laughs]

HH: You know, Senator Inhofe is author of a book on climate change.

LE: Right.

HH: He's *the* leader in the Senate, you know, opposing the climate taxes and carbon taxes and "Cap and Trade" and all the other schemes. You know, you'd think he, you know, if anything else, he at least knows something about it.

LE: Right.

HH: But his granddaughter, because she's going to the schools and this is what they're teaching, they're not teaching them how to think, they're teaching them—they're telling them *what* to think and how to *emote* about it.

LE: Mmhmm.

HH: And that's a scary thing. As you say, Freeman Dyson is not some right-wing, Tea Party nutcase like you and me, OK? [laughs]

LE: [laughs]

HH: My father was a PhD research scientist and he instilled in me the importance of intellectual honesty, of being open to debate, of weighing the evidence, of not publishing your conclusions before you're certain and before they've been peer reviewed and all of that. And I just think, you know, he was a Democrat, he was a John Kennedy Democrat, but he was also a staunch supporter of nuclear power and I'm sure he would be appalled at the collapse of the true pursuit of science and the scientific method that we're seeing going on today.

LE: Well, Howard, as you probably know, a John Kennedy Democrat could probably get you arrested in seven states nowadays.

HH: [laughs] John Kennedy could never win the nomination of the Democrat Party today.

LE: Not today, not somebody who runs on the campaign of cutting taxes, are you kidding me?

HH: Exactly.

LE: Howard, before you go, you used to be an ex—you used to be a liberal, sociologist [sic], progressive Democrat from Berkeley.

HH: Did I spell that incorrectly? It's "socialist."

LE: Socialist, yeah.

HH: Liberal, socialist, progressive Democrat from Berkeley.

LE: Right. And what the hell happened?

HH: [laughs] Well, I was all of that, I was immersed in that climate of Berkeley in the 60s and 70s, with all the radicalism and the Vietnam War protests and the marijuana and everything else, you know, but as I said, I did get something of—about the value of intellectual honesty. And so, I applied that. I wanted to understand these problems about poverty and wealth and pollution and the environment and everything else, and in the process of honestly evaluating alternate theories of how this all works, I came to radically different conclusions. Now, Milton Friedman was an influence with his "Free to Choose" series on PBS—

LE: Right.

HH: Julian Simon of the Cato Institute was a strong influence with his book, "The Ultimate Resource," and by the way, this is very apropos because Julian Simon debunked 200 years of environmental scares. We're running out of this, we're running out of coal, we're running out of that, we're running out of oil, we're running out of food, we're running out of everything, we're—you know, we're all gonna die. But what actually happened was, all these commodities and resources got cheaper and people got wealthier and even though we had a higher population, the people were living better than ever before.

LE: Howard Hyde has been my guest. Website—CitizenEcon.com. My brother Kirk is up next. Howard, thank you very much for taking the time. I appreciate it.

HH: Thank you, Larry.

LE: You got it.

Part VI: America

Some thoughts on the beginning and end of our great civilization.

Día de Independencia

In July 2011 I hosted a lecture-screening of the second episode of HBO's series on the American Revolution, "John Adams" (this episode showing the events and debate leading to the Declaration of Independence), in Spanish, at *La Iglesia en El Camino* (Church on the Way) in Van Nuys, California. There were about fifty in attendance. During the same week I had been an in-studio guest on a political commentary talk radio program on Univision, guest-hosted by a man who would become a close personal friend and Republican candidate for Congress, Pablo Kleinman (the regular host would have been the center-leftist Fernando Espuellas).

I chose HBO's "John Adams" because it is one of the best American Revolutionary War films ever made, presenting in intimate detail the struggle for the founding of our unique nation, as seen through the eyes of a heroic but not larger-than-life couple and their family. I highly recommend it to anyone, immigrant or native, who wants to understand the origins of our nation (another unpaid endorsement).

Below is the translation, back into English, of the lecture[39]. I offer this as a simple introduction to anyone unfamiliar with the story of America's founding, which, thanks to the corruption of our education

---

[39]   Speaking of (North) American history in Spanish, one of the best lectures ever given on the Founding Fathers of the United States, the Declaration of Independence and the Constitution was in Spanish, presented by José Piñera at the Universidad Francisco Marroquín in Guatemala in 2010, to an audience of students from all over Latin America. Piñera is a former finance minister of Chile who, inspired and advised by Milton Friedman, reformed the Chilean social security system into one of individual, privately owned accounts, thereby banishing forever the pyramid scheme which corrupts our own system, whose success has been imitated around the world from Mexico to Poland. His reform bill was passed on November 4, 1980, the same day that Ronald Reagan was elected President of the United States, and implemented beginning on May 1 (May Day, a.k.a. "Communist Day"), 1981, as a poke in the eye to the Leftists of Latin America. Piñera speaks of our founding generation and principles, Declaration of Independence and Constitution with a passion, reverence and depth of knowledge that puts many of our own ostensible statesmen to shame.

How do you say "We hold these truths to be self-evident" in Spanish? "Sostenemos que estas verdades son evidentes en si mismos."

http://www.elcato.org/special/cato-univ-guatemala2/videos/lunes2.html

system by the Left, now includes most native-born Americans under the age of 40. (Write to me if you are interested in the Spanish version).

I describe in [square brackets] a few of the visuals from the slide show that accompanied my talk.

- - - - - - - - - - - - -

John Adams and the American Revolution

Good morning and thank you for joining us today.

In anticipation of our great patriotic holiday, Independence Day, which is the Fourth of July, with its festivities and fireworks, we are going to get to know better the men and women who have given us the gift of this day, through the HBO film, "John Adams."

[One-dollar bill] You may know George Washington. Well, it was John Adams that nominated Washington to be commander-in-chief of the Continental (Revolutionary) army and years later became President Washington's vice president.

[Two-dollar bill] Perhaps you know Thomas Jefferson, author of the Declaration of Independence. Well, it was John Adams that nominated Jefferson to write this document, since Adams did not have time while conducting the verbal debate in the Continental Congress in favor of independence.

[100-dollar bill] Perhaps you know Benjamin Franklin. Adams worked together with Franklin for independence and later in France to get the indispensable support of the French in the war against the British.

For all this I call Adams "the greatest of the founders who never got his mug on a dollar bill", or, the greatest lesser-known founder.

[Circa 1770 map of British colonial America] Two hundred and fifty years ago, in the eighteenth century, there were, on the east coast of North America, thirteen colonies ruled by King George III of Great Britain (or England). The colonies were not proper states, nor were they by any means united. There did not exist at that time any "united states."

The subjects of the British crown who lived in these colonies were already well-accustomed to govern themselves without interference. But the king and the British Parliament tried to force the colonies to comply with an increasingly intolerable regimen of taxes, prohibition of trade outside of the British Empire, the obligation to get official stamps and approvals for the most minor articles of commerce and to accept that British soldiers should be quartered in any American's house that the British might order (soldiers whose numbers grew ever larger). All that without the colonies having a voice or rights or American representatives in the British Parliament. For that, the cry "No Taxation Without Representation" was heard with increasing frequency, and tensions between the colonies and Britain increased.

In 1770 John Adams lived in Boston, capital of the colony of Massachusetts. Humble lawyer, son of a farmer, family man, Christian of confession and conviction, Adams became known when he defended in court a group of British soldiers accused of murder in what the colonists called the "Boston Massacre", but what Adams judged to be a riot or mob disturbance in which the soldiers had acted in self-defense. His defense of the despised soldiers did not at all please the colonists, least of all his own cousin, the political activist Samuel Adams. John Adams hoped that his demonstration of justice would be recognized and appreciated by the king and that the heavy hand of the empire would have been lightened. But George III decreed that any trial of British officers accused of capital crimes in America in the future could not take place in the colonies, but only in Great Britain, on the other side of the Atlantic Ocean.

The disappointments and provocations continued, and the frequency and intensity of protests and disturbances increased, the most famous being the "Boston Tea Party", in which tons (or 'tonnes', as they spelled it in those days) of English tea were thrown into the waters of the Port of Boston in protest against restricted trade with England.

You are going to share John Adams' experience of all of these events. You will also get to know John Adams' family, his wife and his

253

children. You will see Abigail advising her husband with wisdom, balancing his character defects, such as his vanity, his stubbornness and his inability to keep his mouth shut when he should. By John Adams' own admission, if not for Abigail, instead of becoming one of our most important leaders, he never would have amounted to anything.

In 1774 the good faith between the colonies and the king and Parliament had deteriorated to such a point that Adams, together with his cousin Samuel Adams and representatives of all the thirteen colonies, began to meet at the Continental Congress in Philadelphia, capital of the colony of Pennsylvania, 400 miles from Boston (traveling days and weeks by horse, not minutes by Continental Airlines) to discuss their common defense against British tyranny. Such an assembly was unprecedented in the prior 150 years of the colonies.

The citizens of the colonies and their delegates to the Continental Congress were by no means united on the question of how to respond to the tyranny of the king of England, and much less on the question of independence. Some advocated an armed rebellion for separation; others felt, as loyal subjects of the king of England, that they did not want to break with the mother country, or considered that a military confrontation against the most powerful empire in the world, which was Great Britain at that time, was destined to fail catastrophically. And so, the contentious debate dragged on for more than two years.

Reconciliation between the colonies and the king became less and less possible after military battles between the rebels and the British forces broke out in Lexington and Concord in Massachusetts in 1775, followed by the Battle of Bunker Hill and the Siege of Boston. In October of that year the king declared before Parliament that the colonies were in rebellion and that he was sending a military expedition sufficient to suppress the rebels (which is to say, massive; more than 400 ships).

At that time Adams' family lived on his farm in the town of Braintree, just south of Boston. During the Battle of Bunker Hill and the siege, the thunder and flashes of the cannons could be seen from his property.

His wife Abigail managed the farm and cared for their four young children during the frequent absences of her husband in Philadelphia. The Adamses were not rich and life was not easy. Because of the blockade of Boston, outside trade was interrupted and the most necessary goods for daily life were in short supply. To make matters worse, infectious diseases were killing many citizens and soldiers, and threatening even Adams' own family. So, while John was debating independence in Philadelphia, Abigail was having herself and her children vaccinated against the smallpox, which, in those days consisted of scooping pus out of an infected patient and applying it to an open, bleeding cut, suffering the disease itself during a few weeks and risking death (vaccines today are a bit safer and more effective).

When it became apparent that there were no doubts about the intentions of the king to impose his will without mercy or compromise over the colonies, Congress united over the question and elected Thomas Jefferson, a wealthy thirty-three-year-old landowner and representative of Virginia, to write the Declaration of Independence.

The document that Jefferson delivered surpassed all expectations. The Declaration not only separated the American colonies from the king of England; it proclaimed universal ideals of human rights, principles that would threaten any despot or tyrannical regime in any country, in any time.

Lamentably, the institution of slavery survived the American Revolution not only in the Southern states but in the very estates of Thomas Jefferson and George Washington and other prominent American revolutionaries. Even so, the Declaration in effect established a civilization irreconcilable with slavery. The full cost of this incompatibility would be paid in full, eighty-seven ("four score and seven") years later, in the Civil War under President Abraham Lincoln, at a cost of 650,000 lives, twenty-five times as many as died in the Revolutionary War.

The Declaration of Independence is more than 1,000 words long. But there is one phrase that has become immortal that summarizes all of its meaning. It begins: "We hold these truths to be self-evident. . ."

What was so powerful in these simple words was the fact that no head of state in those days—no king, nor aristocrat, nor Emperor—in any way considered such ideas to be "self-evident".

It continued: "We hold these truths to be self-evident, that all men are created equal, that they are endowed by their Creator with certain inalienable Rights, that among these are Life, Liberty and the pursuit of happiness."

This was, and continues to be, the creed of the United States, an imperfect country but among the most free, most prosperous, most just and most enduring that has ever existed in all the world and in all of human history.

[Screen Episode 2: "Independence"]

Yearning to Breathe Free: Immigration Redux

The Only Resource That Counts

Among the strongest influences for me to discard my liberal-socialist "default factory setting" for a conservative free-market worldview were Julian Simon of the Cato Institute, Milton ("Free to Choose") Friedman of the University of Chicago and various members, past and contemporary, of the *Wall Street Journal* Editorial Board. Again, Simon demonstrated that the most indispensable resource of all is not oil, coal, or uranium, but *human beings* living under liberty and the rule of law with private property rights. In addition to his magnum opus, "The Ultimate Resource (2)", Simon also wrote essays, studies and treatises such as "The Economic Consequences of Immigration"[40]. In this work, he concluded that immigration is a benefit to the U.S. economy on net balance. The essence of Simon's analysis that the free flow of labor to where it finds its most useful application in the world is as essential to economic health and general prosperity as the unimpeded flow of raw materials, intermediate producer components and finished consumer products; free international trade, as advocated by most economists since Adam Smith. For his part, Friedman highlighted the stories of immigrants to America, including his own parents, starting at the bottom and moving up the economic ladder by the grace of hard work under laissez-faire government. Ronald Reagan famously welcomed immigrants in his radio broadcasts of the 1970s, before he was President, and in his "Shining City Upon a Hill" speech at the end of his presidency. More recently, Jason Riley of the *Wall Street Journal* makes a compelling case for liberal immigration policy in his book, "Let Them In: The Case for Open Borders; Six Arguments Against Immigration and Why They are Wrong"[41].

---

[40]   Simon, Julian. *The Economic Consequences of Immigration: Second Edition.* Ann Arbor, MI: University of Michigan Press, 1999
[41]   Riley is also author of "Please Stop Helping Us: How Liberals Make it Harder for Blacks to Succeed." Not exactly a left-winger.

I have long felt that conservative talk radio hosts like Mark Levin and Michael Savage, and political leaders, pundits and candidates foaming at the mouth in public over illegal immigration were needlessly alienating Hispanic and other immigrant voters, shooting ourselves in the collective foot and handing the Democrats free ammunition with which to demagogue the issue and paint Republicans as intolerant and hostile, if not racist. For about five recent years, I spent more time and energy studying and practicing Spanish than economics or any other subject outside of my rent-paying professional work, in part because I wanted to be a part of a sincere and effective Republican outreach to the Hispanic community. I produced a sister website to CitizenEcon.com, *HHCapitalismo.com* [note the 'o']: *El Informe Capitalista con Howard Hyde: Un foro internacional para la defensa de la Libertad y de los Mercados y Pueblos Libres,*[42] where I published my pro-free-market economics and conservative-libertarian Republican immigration articles in Spanish. These initiatives culminated in the Univision radio interviews and lecture-screenings of American Revolutionary War films in Spanish churches mentioned previously.

When I began speaking to Republican clubs a few years ago, I was in complete alignment with the Tea Party on such issues as taxes, the IRS, constitutional governance, Obamacare, Agenda 21, Common Core, etc., but on immigration I cut against the grain. Gathering statistics from various sources, I presented, consistent with the aforementioned influences, the following facts and opinions:

- Immigration as a proportion of population today is about half of what it was in the peak years a century ago.

- Immigrant workers *complement* the native population more than they compete directly, with greater numbers at the low and high ends of the skills and education spectrum, while natives are concentrated toward the middle.

- Net immigration from Mexico in 2010-2012 was approximately zero, due to the diminished opportunities of the Great Recession (which suggests an absurd and perverse "solution" to the immigration problem: destroy the economy so that no one will want to come here anymore).

---

[42]   The Capitalist Report with Howard Hyde: An International Forum for the Defense of Liberty, Free Markets and Free People.

- New immigrants are more concentrated than are natives in the youthful labor force ages when people contribute more to the public coffer than they draw from it. The average age is 28[43].

- Putting aside the Great Recession and non-recovery, our economy still creates hundreds of thousands of jobs each year that only require minimal training. The supply of native-born workers without a high school diploma is shrinking by about 300,000 per year. All of Obama's unemployed college graduates are not pining to pick lettuce.

- Cities with high immigrant populations have lower prices for child care, house cleaning, gardening, dry cleaning and other services essential to permitting, for example, middle-class college-educated women with children to pursue professional careers. It's not just the greedy super-rich and multinational corporations that benefit from "cheap labor."

- Illegal immigrants who use fake Social Security numbers to get "legitimate" jobs pay into the system through payroll deductions but will never be able to collect benefits. This is a windfall for the U.S. Treasury and a life-extender for our embattled entitlement programs.

- Social Security and Medicare are by far the most expensive transfer payments made by the government, and these payments go almost entirely to natives. Immigrants typically arrive when they are young and healthy, and older immigrants do not qualify for Social Security for many years after their arrival.

- We need a policy that makes it more difficult for criminals and terrorists to hide among the masses of otherwise honest immigrants who come for work and opportunity.

- Offering and accepting employment at mutually agreeable wages is not fundamentally immoral, even if the letter of many laws prohibits it, from legal residency requirements to

---

[43]   The "youthful labor force age" is also when men have the highest propensity to break the law, a fact that has materially impacted the crime statistics. This point will be explored in detail later in this chapter.

minimum wages. Going after employers for the "crime" of hiring willing workers who are not engaging in murder, robbery, theft, fraud, assault, rape, persecution or conspiracy, is among the least effective or morally justified solutions to the acute problems associated with illegal immigration.

- Many politicians and candidates in both parties have had their careers or campaigns derailed when it was revealed that they had hired domestic help that was—say it ain't so!—illegal (Meg Whitman comes to mind). Meanwhile, many local and state government agencies are actively expanding services intentionally targeted at "undocumented Americans," effectively legitimizing them in contradiction to federal law. We need to declare a truce in which we do not punish people for acting in accordance with de facto reality[44].

- In terms of public health and security, a more open immigration policy that permitted workers to enter through the front door without fear would provide the opportunity to perform screenings for infectious diseases, as well as criminal background checks.

- Hostile ideological infiltration and agitation, such as Communism, is a homegrown issue, not an "immigration" problem. The battleground of radical Leftism is in the public schools and universities, in labor union policy and unaccountable administrative agencies, not the border.

- Narcotraffic is also not an "immigration" issue, but an issue of international crime and terrorism. Putting aside "Fast and Furious,"[45] it is native-born American drug *consumers* who furnish guns to gangs via their market demand expressed in dollars.

---

[44]   See also Three Felonies A Day: How the Feds Target the Innocent by Harvey Silvergate (Encounter Books, 2011) and Go Directly to Jail: The Criminalization of Almost Everything by Gene Healy (Cato Institute, 2004).
[45]   Not the movie. The botched scheme in which arms supplied by the Bureau of Alcohol, Tobacco and Firearms ended up being used by Mexican cartels to kill U.S. Border Patrol agents. See: "Barack Obama ATF Scandal: 8 Facts About Fast and Furious You Might Not Know" by Jerry Shaw (Newsmax.com, December 28, 2014), http://www.newsmax.com/FastFeatures/barack-obama-scandal-atf-fast-and-furious/2014/12/28/id/613434)

- We say we want people to get in line behind everyone else, but we haven't provided any line at all for millions of potentially legitimate people to get into.

- In summary, immigrants make more positive contributions to our society than they impose negative costs, and we should liberalize and streamline the process of allowing people to enter and stay in the U.S. legally.

I further argued that mass deportation was not a realistic option and that a pathway to legal status (NOT fast-track to citizenship or "amnesty") for the estimated 12 million illegals residing in the United States was in America's, and the Republican Party's, best interest.

Needless to say, this appeal to Republicans in favor of a liberal (small "l") immigration policy didn't go over well with all of them. The response was about 50-50 for vs. against me, some telling me "Hell no!" and a few telling me that they had changed their point of view as result of what I had said.

These positions have become increasingly difficult to defend, not just in the overheated political arena, but on the merits. In a nutshell, the erosion of liberty, of the rule of constitutional law and private property rights that has been creeping for decades and accelerating since 2009, is wearing away the benefits of immigration and exacerbating its inherent worst social, political and economic hazards. Free-for-all immigration combined with a socialist welfare state that invites fraud and devalues both the host culture and citizenship itself, while neglecting the protection of native-born citizens and dishonestly accounting for the threats to the same, is a recipe for disaster. Libertarian advocates for open immigration policies cannot dismiss the arguments of restrictionists out of hand, especially as the issue heats up under a regime that has become daily by degrees less libertarian and more arbitrary and capricious.

The Case for Closing the Border: Real and Present Dangers

For purposes of exposition and analysis of the hazards of uncontrolled or erroneously managed immigration, we can group the arguments for and against restricting immigration under the categories of:

- Unfair/harmful economic competition
- Crime and demographics
- Media and government corruption
- Economic collateral damage
- Cultural challenges
- Partisan gamesmanship
- Invasion ("La Reconquista")
- Islamic fundamentalist Sharia law

There are valid arguments on multiple sides of each of these categories, some stronger than others. The point is not to rush to a simplistic conclusion, but to inform and possibly provoke deeper thought about perspectives not previously considered. In some cases, I will simply play Devil's Advocate in lieu of expressing a dogmatic opinion.

Unfair Competition

Intra- and inter-national competition is a fact of life that we can't stop; to attempt to do so would be to ensure that we slouch toward the type of stagnation that is currently gripping the Eurozone and Japan and to allow China and other rivals to surpass us in both prosperity and international clout. Protectionism run amok precipitated and exacerbated the Great Crash of 1929 and the ensuing prolonged 25% unemployment of the Great Depression (see "Why We Don't Need a New New NEW Deal" earlier in this book). We should tread very carefully upon that path.

Just the same, this doesn't mean that we have to fling the door wide open with no control whatsoever.

Proponents of open immigration often claim that immigrants aren't substantially hurting Americans by their competition, as they are mainly doing jobs for which there are insufficient numbers of native-born Americans. This argument is more convincing when the economy is strong and growing, with full employment achieved. While it may not be the fault of immigrants that Americans can't find jobs, the fact of the matter is that our economy is currently (from 2009 through 2016) in the worst employment condition in nearly forty years. And while it may be true that most Americans do not aspire to fruit-picking for their careers, it is a fallacy to say therefore that no Americans can or should do manual labor for some part of their careers, or that it would be harmful to the American economy or character if they did.

Nobody is born with a PhD in astrophysics. All of us progress through levels of education, physical strength/fitness and experience, to reach peaks sometime in adulthood. Like anyone else, all native-born Americans pass through a stage in their lives—like age 18, or 15, or even 12—when they are fully qualified and fit for work requiring minimal training and not much else. I worked newspaper delivery routes—an autonomous, largely unsupervised job which actually requires a significant level of responsibility—when I was just eleven. So have millions of other American boys and girls since 1620.

Why not, then, engage young people part-time to do some of the work? It would not in the least hurt native-born teenagers and twenty-somethings, white, black, Asian, "rich" or "poor," to spend a few months or years of their lives doing some real manual labor that Americans have always done throughout history. Learning the responsibility and necessity of real work is probably more valuable than what the average high school senior or college freshman gets from our institutions of politically correct Leftist indoctrination today, with far greater long-term value in terms of economics and maturity. They might even learn to appreciate and have more true empathy for the people who labor with their hands and their backs throughout their lives. The Marxist studies that they resume after a summer of harvesting vegetables or processing chickens might even be more meaningful to them after experiencing first-hand the proletariat's contact with the soil or the factory floor.

If we stopped subsidizing useless Leftist "social justice" and ethnic grievance studies programs, cut welfare for able-bodied Americans and reduced immigration levels, the wages offered for manual labor would eventually rise to the level that poor, unemployed and even middle-class American young people would be given sufficient incentives to engage of their own free will. This would have both economic and moral benefits for the country as a whole.

Just a thought. The unions would probably oppose any such thing.

H-1B Visa Blues

American high-tech workers have to compete with Indians, whether they are here or in India; Russians, whether they are here or in Russia; Chinese, whether they are here or in China. It is plausible that they are a greater benefit to the U.S. economy working here where they generate additional jobs for Americans. In particular, it seems absurd to kick people out of the country after they have just graduated from one of our prestigious STEM (Science, Technology, Engineering and/or Mathematics) degree programs.

But is the H-1B Visa program the right way to do this?

The H-1B Visa program permits highly educated foreign professionals such as computer programmers and engineers to work in the United States for a limited time period. Ann Coulter has likened this program to indentured servitude because the foreign worker is not at liberty to quit a job he or she doesn't like without losing the residency permit with it and having to start over from his/her home country. This essentially fosters a lose/lose proposition for both the foreign immigrant worker and the American who is obliged to compete against him/her; the employers have the employees and prospective candidates over a barrel[46].

---

[46]   Coulter pp. 239-243

Michelle Malkin and John Miano have made a substantive contribution to this discussion with their book *Sold Out: How High-Tech Billionaires and Bipartisan Beltway Crapweasels Are Screwing America's Best and Brightest Workers*, singling out the H-1B program and its advocates for criticism and deconstruction.

As an American IT professional myself with a front-row seat to the issues that Malkin and Miano talk about, I could hardly be more receptive to their point of view. Malkin and Miano are 100% correct to point out that there is not now, nor has there ever been, a shortage of qualified native-born American workers and graduates in the STEM fields. And they have done a first-rate job of investigative journalism, exposing corruption, fraud and abuse in the programs.

Yet Malkin and Miano's analysis and conclusions are not completely satisfactory. There are plenty of factors other than and larger than just immigration or the H-1B program which could be exerting a decisive influence on the outcomes that we agree that we deplore, such as American workers being coerced into training their cheap foreign replacement workers just before being laid off[47]. There are hundreds of regulations that have turned our entire economy into one giant bureaucratic socialist post office, screwing ALL of us, not just techies. But there are no references in the book to Dodd-Frank, Sarbanes-Oxley or TEFRA (about which more below). These are not trivial omissions; to strain for a metaphor, it's like blaming the speedboat wake for capsizing your sailboat while ignoring the tsunami behind the speedboat, caused by illegal offshore nuclear weapons testing.

America Has No Competitive Advantage in Bureaucratic Governance

Persons interested in what public policies have screwed American high-tech workers should take a hard look at Section 1706 of the Tax Equity and Fairness Reform Act (TEFRA) of 1986 (any time you see the word "fairness" in the title of any legislative project, be afraid; be very afraid). It was this act that put corporations under threat of having their independent contractors reclassified as employees by the IRS, with all the back pay and benefits that that implied, unless they met very stringent multi-point criteria of independence. As a result,

---

47   Malkin and Miano Introduction p. x

corporations cut back severely on engaging cowboys like me and my colleagues unless there was a third-party agency buffer in between (taking a cut of between 10% and 33% of the hourly rate), driving a wedge between the cost to the client and the benefit to the consultant. That, probably more than foreign competition, killed the independent American programmer. Insane geniuses may break through, but mere "A-minus" techies are toast.

This one law has had a devastating impact on this sector of the economy, yet few prominent people have written about it, Steve Forbes (in 1998) being one notable exception:

> Congress should repeal a particularly pernicious tax law that was enacted in 1986. The statute makes it unnecessarily difficult for computer programmers to operate as independent contractors because Congress and the IRS felt these contractors have more opportunity to cheat than individuals who are employees of regular businesses. The IRS thus treats these individuals as if they were engaging in tax scams and tries to shut them down. Corporate employers figure it is cheaper in the long run for these freelancers to become full-time employees than it would be to fight the IRS over whether they "qualify" as independent contractors.
>
> *Why were programmers singled out over a decade ago for this extreme treatment* [my emphasis]? Because in those days they lacked the lobbying clout of doctors and lawyers. Talk about discrimination. This prohibition aimed at high technology should go the way of Prohibition.
>
> In this high-tech age—when computer programmers are in short supply (don't forget the Year 2000 problem) and when Congress may liberalize immigration laws to lure foreign programmers to our shores—this ban on programmers' becoming individual entrepreneurs is absurd.
>
> More and more Americans are getting the entrepreneurial itch. Why won't Congress let them scratch? Operating on their own, many of these programmers would be more productive and inventive. The wealth of the nation would increase—and, as a result, tax receipts would be higher[48].

---

[48]   Steve Forbes. "Fact and Comment," Forbes Magazine, October 12, 1998

New York Times journalist David Cay Johnston nailed it when he wrote in 2010:

> The law, known as Section 1706 of the 1986 Tax Reform Act, made it extremely difficult for information technology professionals to work as self-employed individuals, forcing most to become company employees.
>
> Many software engineers and other such professionals say that the law denies them the opportunity to become wealthy entrepreneurs and that it makes it harder to increase and refine their skills, eventually diminishing their income.
>
> Harvey J. Shulman, a Washington lawyer who represented companies that supported the desires of software engineers to be independent contractors, estimated that the law currently affects at least 100,000 such people.
>
> "This law has ruined many people's lives, hurt the technology industry, and discouraged the creation of small, independent businesses critical to a thriving domestic economy," Mr. Shulman said in an interview Thursday. "That the law still exists—even after its original sponsors called for its repeal and unbiased studies proved it unfairly targeted a tax-compliant industry—shows just how dysfunctional and unresponsive Democratic and Republican Congresses and our political system have been, even on relatively simple issues."
>
> The law was sponsored by Senator Daniel Patrick Moynihan, Democrat of New York, as a favor to I.B.M., which wanted a $60 million tax break on its overseas business[49].

Their dead hands live on.

What terrible economic harm, what gross injustice, what egregious violation of the civil or private property rights of Americans has been remedied by this legislation (or, for that matter, 99% of the 1.5 *million* pages of the Federal Register)? All it has done is make the market less flexible, less creative and more regimented. Thousands—perhaps millions—of Americans have had their opportunities to become

---

49   "Tax Law Was Cited in Software Engineer's Suicide Note." David Cay Johnston. *The New York Times*, February 18,2010.
http://www.nytimes.com/2010/02/19/us/19tax.html
    Let us praise the *New York Times* when they do something worthy.

entrepreneurs cut off at the knees by this single law, yet no one seems even to know that it exists.

In other words and more broadly than just one clause buried in a single 30-year-old statute, what is probably more consequential to American high-tech workers—or any other Americans, for that matter—than immigration and the H-1B program, is the unprecedented burdensome and counterproductive regulatory environment under which businesses, especially banks, operate in the United States today.

In a free market, companies compete against each other on the basis of satisfying customers with the highest quality products and services at the lowest cost, which they can only accomplish by the most effective deployment and management of productive and satisfied employees and contractors. Companies that engage in myopic business practices, like hiring two "cheap" workers at $30 per hour only to discover that they are less productive *combined* than a single "expensive" worker who commands $50 per hour, will be severely punished in the marketplace and go out of business if they don't change their practices. Put another way, the $50-per-hour worker is the one who provides the lower labor cost to the employer or client if he or she is more than twice as productive as two workers who "only" demand $30 per hour apiece. And multiple studies have demonstrated actual differentials of up to ten times the productivity between seasoned master programmers versus rookie coders. Such a dynamic would tend to reward American technologists who pioneered virtually all of the technologies that we depend upon today and are known for their creative initiative, risk-taking and out-of-the-box thinking.

But in a market where companies are forcibly focused on compliance with government regulatory agencies, such market dynamics and feedback mechanisms diminish to the vanishing point. The autonomy and decision-making authority of smaller organizational units is curtailed in favor of obedience to protocols and pre-established rules and workflows. Decentralized autonomy gets crushed by centralized autocracy[50]. Softer multi-dimensional

---

[50]   BB&T was a small but growing regional bank based in North Carolina. It had a decentralized business model that gave wide latitude of autonomy and accountability to its local managers and participated in the mortgage lending industry. In spite of being in the

qualitative distinctions, like English communication skills, personal initiative, cultural affinity with colleagues and customers, willingness to take risks, creativity, etc., get overwhelmed in the management calculus by one-dimensional metrics such as hourly wage rates. Customers, contractors, managers and employees alike all see their range of options shrinking along with their incomes.

If we were to terminate the H-1B program tomorrow without addressing the destructive force of government interference in the market, the worst economic injuries to American high-tech workers— as well as all other American workers—will yet remain. Greater interference in the market by government agencies like the Department of Labor, to scrutinize companies' hiring decisions and wage rates, will almost certainly do more harm than good. In any case, arguing for more government intervention, as Malkin implicitly does when she says such things as, "The toothless Labor Department has little authority to stop them," is not a conservative, free-market position[51].

Freemen Can't Compete with Slaves, so Maybe We Should Free the Slaves

A counterintuitive improvement to the H-1B program's corrupting effects might actually be to give visa holders *greater* freedom than they currently have to quit or change employers without losing their residency status. Workers who have more choices are not as captive to their current employers and therefore exert less downward pressure overall on market wages, salaries and benefits. Giving them greater freedom might even liberate their repressed creative and risk-taking energies, making them more like what Americans pride themselves on being.

Ending indentured servitude in America doesn't necessarily mean turning foreign workers away.

---

black, it was forced to take TARP money in 2008 in order to help provide cover for the larger, more centralized and politically-connected banks that had made bad loans and fallen into the red. See: Allison, John A. [President of BB&T for 25 years and more recently President of the Cato Institute]. *The Financial Crisis and the Free Market Cure: Why Pure Capitalism Is the World Economy's Only Hope.* New York, NY: McGraw-Hill, 2012.
[51]   Malkin p. 56

"Big business just wants cheap labor," say some immigration critics. Well, that's news, isn't it? Actually, *everyone* wants cheap labor, at least when they are paying for it, and everyone wants their own labor to be as expensive and in high demand as possible. Indeed, from time immemorial it has been the classical art of the politician to simultaneously promise high milk prices to the dairy farmer (the seller) and low milk prices to everyone else (the buyers), while hoping nobody notices the inherent contradiction.

"Greed," as I have argued many times against liberals, Democrats and Marxists, is a meaningless condemnation unless it is accompanied by evidence of actual force, fraud and/or coercion. By that measure, the most egregious exemplars of greed are government officials, followed closely by political party bosses and special-interest lobbyists.

Sayonara, California?

Ann Coulter is one of the most articulate critics of immigration—legal and illegal—in America today. For this reason, in this chapter I will quote extensively from her book *Adios, America! The Left's Plan to Turn Our Country into a Third World Hellhole*, and will follow-up on her sources and references, in order to gauge how well they substantiate her claims.[52] Put another way, this chapter is largely an extended review

---

[52]   To put it mildly, Ann Coulter is not everyone's cup of tea. She has been characterized as an extremist by some, even a race-baiter if not a racist, and not only by liberals (for example, see "Coulter-Sharpton vs. Kemp-Ryan", by Robert L. Woodson, Sr., in *The Wall Street Journal*, October 30, 2015.

http://www.wsj.com/articles/coulter-sharpton-vs-kemp-ryan-1446157241). But it is worth noting that another word for "extremist" is "expert"—someone who has spent exceptional time and energy studying and gaining experience in a certain field or discipline. Michael Jordan may be called a "basketball extremist." Muhammad Ali was a boxing extremist, Steve Jobs was personal computer and consumer electronics design and marketing extremist, and Albert Einstein was a physics extremist. Indeed, positive human progress has been achieved by very few individuals who were not extreme outliers by one measure or another.

So, labeling someone with whom you disagree with a nasty name in order to dismiss their point of view is not permissible in honest debate. People like Coulter, or Debbie What's-her-name Schultz, or Karl Marx or anyone else, have to be addressed and/or refuted on the merits, not by means of insults, however much their words may hurt our feelings.

I also picked Coulter, set against Riley, because Thomas Sowell did: "Jason Riley of the Manhattan Institute has written a book titled 'Let Them In' and columnist Ann Coulter has of her book, its ideas, facts, claims and conclusions, in order that the reader may draw his or her own.

Crime and Demographics

Do immigrants exhibit a greater propensity for crime than native-born Americans?

Looking at Bureau of Justice Statistics data, Coulter found that as of December 31, 2011, Hispanics committed about 84% as many murders as whites, 45% as many (reported and convicted) rapes and 35% as many property crimes[53]. Compared to their percentages of the population, however, that means that Hispanics are two and a half times as likely to commit murder, a third more likely to commit rape, and just slightly more likely to commit property crimes. And that is based on a 3-to-1 ratio of whites to Hispanics in the population. If the real ratio is closer to 3.9-to-1, as the low-estimators of illegal immigration would have us believe and as the U.S. Census says, then that makes Hispanics look even worse: 326% as likely to commit murder, 176% as likely to commit rape, and 137% as likely to commit property crime.

However, comparisons between demographic groups do not tell the whole truth if they do not account for age. Due to fertility rates that are lower both in relation to contemporary Hispanics and to the past, the median age of a white non-Hispanic American today is 41, while the median age of Hispanics is 27. Mexicans, the dominant Hispanic ethnicity, average just 25 years. . . Which just happens to be the peak age for testosterone junkies of *any* ethnicity to act out destructively. The crime rate for 40-plus-year-olds ranges from a high

---

written a book on the other side titled 'Adios, America.' Both cite empirical studies." *Documented Irresponsibility*, Townhall.com, July 28, 2015.
http://townhall.com/columnists/thomassowell/2015/07/28/documented-irresponsibility-n2030990/page/full
I suspect that Coulter had originally wished to use the word "sh**hole" in her subtitle, but that's pure speculation.

53   Carson, E. Ann and Golinelli, Daniela. Prisoners in 2012 - Advance Counts. Table 10. Bureau of Justice Statistics, U.S. Department of Justice. July 2013.
http://www.bjs.gov/content/pub/pdf/p12ac.pdf

of two-thirds down to one-third or less of that of 25-year-olds[54]. Adjusting the numbers mentioned previously, then, the likelihood of a Mexican *of a certain age* committing murder or rape, giving wide latitude to margin of error, is not materially higher than that of a white American of the same age committing the same crime. For property crime, the white rate holding age constant may be higher than the Hispanic rate.

This also the context into which we have to evaluate Coulter's claim that "Mexicans . . . have murdered a minimum of twenty-three thousand Americans in the last few decades" in contrast to "only" four thousand killed by Islamic terrorists over the same period, including 9/11[55]. Is it terrorism, foreign invasion, or "just ordinary crime," which we might have with or without immigrants?

The significance that we ascribe to certain deaths, killings and other assaults and tragedies is at least as significant as the "objective" body count. Otherwise, Pearl Harbor and 9/11 could be dismissed as no more disturbing than the aggregated statistics on automobile accidents, heart attacks, cancer, swimming pool drownings or slipping on a bar of soap in the shower. Coulter is making the case that crimes committed by Mexicans in the United States are the equivalent of terrorism or war, not just part of our ordinary and "acceptable" domestic crime rate. Not all Americans have caught up to Coulter's viewpoint.

The problem may not be so much that we are importing people more likely to commit crimes than that the ethnic source of our young people is changing. Put another way, the ethnicity of our murderers and rapists is being transformed, without necessarily altering the overall aggregate rates of crime. If these rates are going up, it may have nothing to do with ethnicity or immigration.

If this is true, then our focus may need to shift from crime to culture. Perhaps if we stop immigration from Mexico, our crime rate may go down, not for any reasons specific to Mexico or Mexicans but

---

[54]   Federal Bureau of Investigation, U.S. Department of Justice. *Age-Specific Arrest Rates and Race-Specific Arrest Rates for Selected Offenses, 1993-2001.* https://www.fbi.gov/about-us/cjis/ucr/additional-ucr-publications/age_race_arrest93-01.pdf
[55]   Coulter p. 125

for reasons having to do with the nature of 25-year-old men of any race. On the one hand, such men commit the most violent crimes, but it does not necessarily follow that we need to rid the country of young men.

Japan has one of the most homogeneous ethnic populations of any country, near-zero immigration, and one of the lowest crime rates in the world[56]. And a median age of 46. Its economy has stagnated for over a decade (in contrast to the expectation during the 1980s that it would soon grow to swallow the world) and its culture has been in serious decline. As Mark Steyn wrote in his demographic bestseller (how many of those exist?) *America Alone*, "Japan offers the chance to observe the demographic death spiral in its purest form. It's a country with no immigration, no significant minorities and no desire for any: just the Japanese, aging and dwindling"[57]. And in an article for National Review Online: "49 percent of women under 34 are not in any kind of romantic relationship, and nor are 61 percent of single men. A third of Japanese adults under 30 have never dated. Anyone. Ever. It's not that they've stopped 'having sex'—or are disinclined to have hot wax poured on their nipples. It's bigger than that: It's a flight from human intimacy"[58].

Also, as Mark Steyn noted, there was no civil disorder in Japan after a tsunami took out several of its cities and thousands of its citizens in 2011, as might be expected following a natural disaster in other countries (like the U.S.). "Looting is a young man's game"[59].

If the crime rate is unacceptable, then we may need to focus on crime as such—crime as a general social problem—rather than as a phenomenon of immigration. And if we don't want to import 25-year-old men, then we'll either have to start producing more of them ourselves (a project which may take up to 25 years and 9 months to

---

[56]   *Crime Index for Country 2015 Mid Year.* Numbeo.com.
http://www.numbeo.com/crime/rankings_by_country.jsp
[57]   Steyn, Mark. *America Alone: The End of the World As We Know It.* Washington, DC. 2008. Regnery. p. 24
[58]   Mark Steyn, *Sex at Sunset.* National Review Online, November 11, 2013.
https://www.nationalreview.com/nrd/articles/362074/sex-sunset
[59]   Mark Steyn, *Earthquake Demographic.* National Review Online, April 4, 2011.
https://www.nationalreview.com/nrd/articles/302573/earthquake-demographic

realize—Perform Your Patriotic Duty Today!) or decide to what degree we want to trade off crime with economic, demographic and cultural stagnation. The looming Social Security crisis offers perverse incentives, as it was always destined to.

But Coulter is not to be dismissed too hastily. We have noted before the hazard of confusing aggregated statistics for truth. In economics, the real meaning is to be found at street level, in the millions of transactions and trade-offs that particular individuals, families, entrepreneurs, consumers and associations make, voluntarily or under duress, with one another, in specific circumstances. The truth about crime and its meaning may likewise lie in the contemplation of actual events as much as, or more than, abstract and/or aggregated numbers. Moreover, it is worth asking whether the nature and character of the crimes committed by foreigners are the same or different than similarly-categorized crimes committed by homegrown Americans.

Coulter says no. To this end she has rendered a vital service, not least consisting of her recounting of hundreds of horrific cases in stomach-turning detail throughout her book.

Let us therefore contemplate the below cases of murder, rape, honor killing, human trafficking, terrorism, and frauds and scams, and consider what role the dimension of immigration plays in each of them. Following that, we'll examine how honest the media and government are in reporting the facts about these crimes, to get a sense of how well we may trust what we think we know.

Murder

Coulter writes, "A Chinese immigrant in New York, Dong Lu Chen, bludgeoned his wife to death with a claw hammer because she was having an affair. . . Brooklyn Supreme Court Justice Edward Pincus let Chen off with probation—for murder—after an anthropologist testified that, in Chinese culture, the shame of a man being cuckolded justified murder"[60].

---

[60] Coulter p. 89. See also: *Baghdad on the Plains*, by Margaret Talbot, The New Republic, August 11, 1997 http://jummahcrew.tripod.com/baghdad.htm

Also: Culture, Cloaked in Mens Rea, by Doriane Lambelet Coleman. The South Atlantic Quarterly,   Fall   2001 http://scholarship.law.duke.edu/cgi/viewcontent.cgi?article=1924&context=faculty_scholarship

Where are the feminists on this case? Coulter provides an answer: "The *female* [my emphasis] head of the Asian-American Defense and Education Fund, Margaret Fung, applauded Chen's light sentence, saying that a harsher penalty would *'promote the idea that when people come to America they have to give up their way of doing things. That is an idea we cannot support* [my emphasis].'"

To which we may fairly reply: WHY THE HELL NOT?

Perhaps this story is a mere anecdote in the bigger picture of American society and aggregate crime statistics. Here are some more samples of Coulter's "mere anecdotes"[61].

- The seven people murdered by Chechen immigrants Dzhokhar and Tamerlan Tsarnaev, who planted a bomb at the finish line of the Boston Marathon in 2013

- The three people, including a fifteen-year-old girl, Ashley Chow, murdered in North Miami in 2012 by Kesler Dufrene, a Haitian immigrant and convicted felon who had already been arrested in the United States nine times

- Sixty-seven-year-old Florence Donovan-Gunderson and three National Guardsmen—Heath Kelly, Miranda McElhiney and Christian Riege—fatally shot in a Carson City IHOP by immigrant Eduardo Sencion in 2011

- The thirteen soldiers killed at Fort Hood in 2009 by Major Nidal Malik Hasan, son of Palestinian immigrants

- The thirteen people murdered by Vietnamese immigrant Jiverly Wong, at an American Civic Association in Binghamton, New York. Wong became a naturalized citizen two years *after* [my emphasis] being convicted of fraud and forgery in California.

- The five people murdered at the Trolley Square Shopping Mall in Salt Lake City by Bosnian immigrant Sulejman Talovic in 2007. Talovic was a high school dropout with a juvenile record.

---

61   Coulter p. 90-92

- The thirty-two people murdered at Virginia Tech in 2007 by Seung-Hui Cho, a South Korean immigrant
- The six people killed in northern Wisconsin in 2004 by Hmong immigrant Chai Soua Vang, who shot his victims in the back after being caught trespassing on their property
- The six men murdered by Mexican immigrant Salvador Tapia at the Windy City Core Supply warehouse in Chicago in 2003 because he was angry about being fired. Tapia was still in this country despite having been arrested at least a dozen times on weapons and assault charges. Only foreign newspapers mentioned that Tapia was an immigrant. Thirty-four American journalists blamed the gun.
- The three people murdered at the Appalachian School of Law in 2002 by Nigerian immigrant Peter Odighizuwa, who was angry at America because he had failed out of law school.

Coulter on Terrorism:

According to the GAO [Government Accountability Office], 27 percent of terrorism convicts in the United States were lawfully-admitted immigrants, on their way to becoming citizens; 57 percent were citizens, naturalized citizens, or *foreigners brought into the United States for prosecution* [and either acquitted or convicted of lesser crimes, entitling them to asylum]…America has even granted asylum to participants in the Rwandan genocide[62].

Terrorism abetted by chain migration/family reunification:

Najibullah Zazi . . . pleaded guilty in a plot to bomb the New York City subway in 2010. Zazi had been born into a tribe in eastern Afghanistan and came to America in his teens. He dropped out of high school and had an arranged marriage to his cousin in Pakistan. His ticket to entry was his father—whose ticket was, in turn, a brother living in Queens[63].

---

62   Coulter p. 94
63   Coulter p. 95

Americans were shocked in 2014 when snuff videos from a group no one had ever heard of before, "ISIS" or "ISIL"[64], beheading its enemies in its blitzkrieg march into the territories abandoned by Obama. But, as Coulter points out, the Mexican drug cartels have been producing "decapitation porn" for years[65].

In July 2010, Arizona governor Jan Brewer publicly claimed that there had been beheadings in the desert of her state. Coulter: "Salon.com cited Brewer's remark to sneer that 'as you can see, Jan Brewer is crazy' . . . Three months after Brewer's claim, Mexicans beheaded a man in Arizona. Within the next two years, a headless body turned up in the Arizona desert, and the dismembered body of a nineteen-year-old American girl was found in Oklahoma. All three dismemberments were believed to be the work of Mexican cartels—confirmed in the first Arizona case"[66].

Frauds, Scams and Rip-offs

Coulter lists twenty instances of criminal offenses, ranging from Medicare fraud to credit card theft to laundering drug money, which she found for the month of September 2014 alone, committed by people with familiar names like Xilin Chen, Khachatur Bislamyan, Azizur Ullah and Javed Sunesra. The sum of the amounts involved in the fraud cases, where she mentions it—which is in a minority of cases and does not take into account law enforcement, court and jail costs—is $300 million. This may be anecdotal evidence, but Coulter insists that these are largely imported, foreign-specialty crimes[67]. A welcome contribution to our "diversity"?

---

64   Islamic State of Iraq and Syria, or Islamic State of Iraq and the Levant—a geographic region that includes the land area of Israel but does not recognize so much as the existence, much less legitimacy, of the same.
65   Coulter p. 121
66   Coulter p. 124. See also: "Expert Says Beheadings in U.S. Look Like Work of Cartels", by Borderland Beat Reporter Buggs, January 18, 2012.
http://www.borderlandbeat.com/2012/01/expert-says-beheadings-in-us-look-like.html
67   Coulter pp. 111-112

But anecdotes aren't scientific, not good enough? Very well; how about some mind-numbing official statistics from the Government Accountability Office then?

> The number of criminal aliens in federal prisons in fiscal year 2010 was about 55,000, and the number of SCAAP [State Criminal Alien Assistance Program] criminal alien incarcerations in state prison systems and local jails was about 296,000 [total: 351,000] in fiscal year 2009 (the most recent data available), and the majority [68% of those] were from Mexico. The number of criminal aliens in federal prisons increased about 7 percent from about 51,000 in fiscal year 2005 while the number of SCAAP criminal alien incarcerations in state prison systems and local jails increased about 35 percent from about 220,000 in fiscal year 2003. . . [I]n 2005, GAO reported that the percentage of criminal aliens in federal prisons was about 27 percent of the total inmate population from 2001 through 2004[68].

Media Disinformation

The stories about crimes committed by foreigners don't end with the crimes themselves. The real story may be seeing to what lengths the media will go, not only to avoid revealing that the perpetrators were not native-born Americans but to completely distract the reader with superfluous imagery like "small town" or "farmers" and references to years-old famous but irrelevant cases of rape involving American rapists. Thus, in 1998 and 1999:

> About three dozen Hmong [Laotian mountain culture] men were indicted for a series of gang rapes and forced prostitution of our girls in the Fresno area, including the gang rape that reminded the *Times* of high school football players in New Jersey a decade earlier. . . Never did the *Times* inform its readers that the Fresno gang rape was committed by Hmong, nor did

---

[68]   United States Government Accountability Office. "Report to Congressional Requesters: Criminal Alien Statistics: Information on Incarcerations, Arrests, and Costs". March 2011. http://www.gao.gov/assets/320/316959.pdf

the *Times* provide the names of the suspected rapists—not through the arrests, indictments, pleas, and convictions[69].

In 1989 in Missouri, a married couple, the wife Brazilian and the husband "Palestinian," stabbed their own 16-year-old daughter to death. The girl's dying screams were caught on an audio tape due to the father already being under surveillance as a suspected terrorist. The parents' grievance against their daughter was that she had dishonored the family, in part by dating a black American boy. According to Coulter, the *New York Times* called this "a family drama involving clashes of cultures."[70] Another case of classification being more muddying than enlightening.

Coulter even cites at length a story of foreign sex trafficking by fraudulent H-1B immigrants from India in—wait for it—Berkeley, California. It seems a team of Berkeley High School journalism students were able to do the job that the "responsible" adult American media just won't do anymore, which is to report the facts without deference to political correctness[71]. Whodathunk that brainwashed Leftist Berzerkeley students would have the chutzpah to do that? The indoctrination machine must be cracking. Go Yellowjackets! Go Daily Jacket!

The *New York Times* in 2008 reported on a new, disturbing category of terrorist: the "American" suicide bomber. The first individual so identified was a man named Shirwa Ahmed, a "Minnesotan." Of Somali extraction[72].

Another disturbing trend reported by the American mainstream media and Democratic legislators is "Americans becoming radicalized," like David Coleman Headley. Headley's real name is

---

69   Coulter p. 133. See also: "Gang Rape of Three Girls Leaves Fresno Shaken, and Questioning". Don Terry. *The New York Times*, May 1, 1998.
http://www.nytimes.com/1998/05/01/us/gang-rape-of-three-girls-leaves-fresno-shaken-and-questioning.html, and: "Indictment Charges 23 Hmong With Series of Rapes".
Associated Press. *Los Angeles Times*, October 21, 1999.
http://articles.latimes.com/1999/oct/21/news/mn-24690
70   Coulter p. 88-89
71   Coulter p. 227-232 "Spot the Immigrant! Case No. 4 | Indian Sex Slaves in Berkeley"
72   Coulter p. 95-96

Daood Sayed Gilani and he is Pakistani with American citizenship by virtue of being an anchor baby, who spent nearly his entire childhood and youth in Pakistan. Gilani was one of the terrorists who went on a murderous rampage in Mumbai, India, in 2008. Coulter: "Of more than fifty articles mentioning Gilani in the New York Times, only five so much as mentioned his real name—dismissing it as his 'birth name' or 'the Urdu name he was given at birth.'"[73]

Coulter also notes that when the Islamic terrorist is in fact, a radicalized Anglo-American, the press has no problem using his "birth name" or "the English name he was given at birth," as in the case of Michael Finton, a.k.a. Talib Isalam, who attempted to bomb a Chicago federal building.

More "American" Jihadists, as noted by Coulter[74]:
- Najibullah Zazi of Afghanistan
- Umer Farooq of Pakistan
- Waqar Khan of Pakistan
- Many Zamzam of Egypt
- Ahmed Abdullah Minni of Eritrea
- Aman Hassan Yemer of Ethiopia
- Aafia Siddiqui of Pakistan, married to nephew of 9/11 mastermind Khalid Sheikh Mohammad
- Anwar al-Awlaki of Yemen

It doesn't help the credibility of the mainstream media in reporting on illegal immigration that their king, the *New York Times*, is 17% owned—the largest single share—by Mexican telecom monopolist and world-class billionaire Carlos Slim[75].

---

[73]   Coulter p. 96
[74]   Coulter p. 97-98
[75]   Is Mexican Billionaire Carlos Slim Becoming The New York Times' Largest Investor Purely Business? Dolia Estevez. Forbes, Jan 15, 2015.
http://www.forbes.com/sites/doliaestevez/2015/01/15/is-mexican-billionaire-carlos-slim-becoming-the-new-york-times-largest-investor-purely-business/
    Also: Coulter chapter 13: Carlos Slim, The New York Times' Sugar Daddy, p. 213-226

But if media reporting on immigrants, crime and terrorism is bad, the American government's misinformation, disinformation or complete lack of information may be worse.

Federal Bureaus of Missing Data

As Goes Media Reporting, So Go Government Statistics

Why should the conclusions of Coulter's research be so much at odds with those gathered, presumably in good faith and with rigorous academic integrity, by researchers who have come to polar opposite conclusions?

The most prominent reason cited by Coulter is the extreme difficulty of getting a straight answer out of government data. The statistics bureaus that we taxpayers are paying for along with all the cops, public defense attorneys, judges, prison guards and social workers who come into direct contact with criminals of all stripes, seem to be not the least interested in counting and categorizing them for objective analysis. Coulter notes that it is easier to get statistics on how many rental units have broken or missing stair railings or mold in the bathrooms, or how many residents of American Samoa have no battery-powered radios in their homes, than how many foreign-born people in the country have committed crimes[76].

For example, reading between the lines of Government Accountability Office (GAO) reports, Coulter writes that:

> In 2011 . . . America was incarcerating at least—the absolute minimum estimate—351,000 criminal aliens: 55,000 immigrants in federal prison and 296,000 illegal aliens in state and local facilities. . . The GAO's estimate of 351,000 incarcerated aliens *excludes*:
> 1. All legal immigrants in state or local prisons;
> 2. Convicted illegal aliens for whom the states did not submit reimbursement requests to the federal government;

---

[76]   Coulter p. 103, 101

3. Prisoners whose country of birth could not be determined;
4. Immigrants who have been naturalized;
5. Children born to illegal aliens on U.S. soil;
6. Immigrants without at least one felony or two misdemeanor convictions;
7. Immigration detainees; and
8. Illegal immigrants who committed crimes after being amnestied by Reagan in 1986.

Coulter continues:

> To be extra opaque, the GAO counted all immigrants in federal prisons—legal and illegal—but counted only illegal immigrants in state prisons and local jails.
> Why exclude legal immigrants? Isn't that worse [*i.e., doesn't that reflect even worse on who we are granting legal status to*]?[77]

Since government data on immigrants and crime is not as transparent, comprehensive or integrated as it should be, independent collection from multiple sources is necessary in order to clarify the picture. Coulter cites the New York State Department of Corrections, who found that "foreign inmates were 70 percent more likely to have committed a violent crime than American criminals." Among those, here is the list of nationalities, together with the number of criminals of each nationality, found in New York State prisons[78]:

- Dominican Republic: 1,314
- Jamaica: 849
- Mexico: 523
- Guyana: 289
- El Salvador: 245
- Cuba: 242
- Trinidad and Tobago: 237
- Haiti: 201

---

[77]   Coulter pp. 101-102
[78]   Coulter pp. 104-105

- Ecuador: 189
- Colombia: 168

What about inmates of European (i.e., closer culturally to American) origin? Here is the 2007 New York State Department of Corrections list, again as cited by Coulter[79]:

- Denmark: 1
- Czechoslovakia: 2
- Netherlands: 2
- Switzerland: 2
- Ireland: 4
- Poland: 27
- Germany: 46
- England: 49

Even these numbers may overestimate the number of ethnic or fully assimilated cultural Europeans, since nationality is not ancestry, and citizenship has been doled out very liberally in Europe (or as Mark Levin calls it, "Yorp") for the past couple of generations. For example, one of those "British" criminals, arrested for pedophilia in Florida, was Shuhel Mahboob Ali.

Government officials scrupulously avoid mentioning the national origin of criminals if they can possibly help it. In 2007, Richard DeLeon Flores sped through a stop sign in Kansas and struck two cars, killing a teenage girl. He required a translator at his arraignment and trial, yet the Leavenworth County Attorney's office claimed to have no knowledge regarding Flores' citizenship status. Apparently, they didn't consider it relevant.

And what they don't find relevant, they don't report, so we can't find out, unless we dig a lot deeper on our own, as Coulter has done.

---

[79]   Coulter pp. 105-106

Economic Collateral Damage

Macroeconomic Muddle

Even if we were to accept the argument that on net balance, illegal immigrants contribute more to the public piggy bank than they withdraw, it has to be acknowledged that there are gross imbalances between and among the sectors of society and government which receive surplus windfalls versus those bearing intolerable burdens. Local communities and organizations—for example, county-run hospitals and municipal school districts—are being crushed by the costs of treating and educating foreigners who are here without permission and who do not pay for the services rendered[80]. Premature babies, for one, cost over $50,000 a pop[81].

If it is true that illegal workers using stolen or fictitious Social Security numbers pay into the federal system without being able to withdraw from it, then there is an obvious solution: channel the surplus contributions to Social Security into a fund to compensate local entities for their undue burden. Did any Democrat ever suggest that? I doubt it, not least of all because it would have neutralized a key argument for the federal takeover of health care.

Such a proposal would doubtless be attacked as an assault on the sacrosanct Social Security system—something people are pretty touchy about these days.

So, it would seem that we have a lose/lose proposition: forego the "illegal" windfall revenue to the Social Security kitty or get ripped off by freeloaders. If the supposed benefits of immigration are prohibited from compensating the manifest costs, then some Americans are having their rights violated and their property plundered by other Americans and by foreigners whom the government has the

---

[80] "In 2003 in Stockton, California, 70 percent of the 2,300 babies born in San Joaquin General Hospital's maternity ward were anchor babies." *Illegal Aliens and American Medicine*, by Madeleine Pelner Cosman, Ph.D., Esq. Journal of American Physicians and Surgeons Volume 10 Number 1 Spring 2005 http://www.jpands.org/vol10no1/cosman.pdf
Hat tip: Coulter p. 39

[81] *Prenatal Care Is Important to Healthy Pregnancies.* The American Congress of Obstetricians and Gynecologists.
http://www.acog.org/-/media/Departments/Government-Relations-and-Outreach/20120221factsareimportant.pdf
Hat tip: Coulter p. 13.

responsibility to keep out. This is not defensible morally or economically.

There is abundant evidence of the uncompensated social costs of immigrants, legal and illegal. Coulter:

> [A] more detailed breakdown of the costs and benefits shows that college-educated Americans pay an average of $29,000 more in taxes every year than they get back in government services. . . By contrast, legal immigrants, on average, get back $4,344 more in government services than they pay in taxes. Those with only a high school degree net about $14,642 in government payments, and those without a high school degree collect a whopping $36,993. . . The vast majority of illegal aliens—about 75 percent—have only a high school diploma or less, so . . . [finish this sentence yourself][82].

Los Angeles (city and county) is a prime example of a place overrun with costs associated with illegal immigration. Coulter writes, "According to the county supervisor [Michael Antonovich], Los Angeles alone spends more than $1.6 billion a year on illegal aliens— $600 million for welfare, $550 million for public safety (mostly jail costs), and $500 million for their healthcare."[83]

Coulter sprinkles comments and anecdotes about welfare use by legal and illegal immigrants throughout her book. The strongest backing for her positions come from various studies conducted by the Center for Immigration Studies, or CIS, which in turn are based on analyses of the Current Population Survey, or CPS, which is a statistical survey conducted by the United States Census Bureau for the United States Bureau of Labor Statistics (BLS). For example, excerpting from the pre-introduction to the report "Welfare Use by Immigrant Households with Children: A Look at Cash, Medicaid, Housing, and

---

[82]   Coulter p. 47. See also: "The Fiscal Cost of Unlawful Immigrants and Amnesty to the U.S. Taxpayer". Robert Rector and Jason Richwine, Ph.D. From the Heritage Foundation's Special Report #133 on Immigration.
http://www.heritage.org/research/reports/2013/05/the-fiscal-cost-of-unlawful-immigrants-and-amnesty-to-the-us-taxpayer
[83]   "Rise in public benefits to children of illegal immigrants in L.A. County has supervisor 'very concerned.'" *Los Angeles Times*, September 3, 2010.
http://latimesblogs.latimes.com/lanow/2010/09/rise-in-public-benefits-to-children-of-illegal-immigrants-in-los-angeles-county-concerns-supervisor-michael-antonovich.html

Food Programs" by Steven A. Camarota, CIS Director of Research, April 2011:

- In 2009 (based on data collected in 2010), 57 percent of households headed by an immigrant (legal and illegal) with children (under 18) used at least one welfare program, compared to 39 percent for native households with children.

- Immigrant households' use of welfare tends to be much higher than natives for food assistance programs and Medicaid. Their use of cash and housing programs tends to be similar to native households.

- A large share of the welfare used by immigrant households with children is received on behalf of their U.S.-born children, who are American citizens. But even households with children comprised entirely of immigrants (no U.S.-born children) still had a welfare use rate of 56 percent in 2009.

- Welfare use tends to be high for both new arrivals and established residents. In 2009, 60 percent of households with children headed by an immigrant who arrived in 2000 or later used at least one welfare program; for households headed by immigrants who arrived before 2000, it was 55 percent.

- For all households (those with and without children), the use rates were 37 percent for households headed by immigrants and 22 percent for those headed by natives.

Or, in Coulter's words, "We're told—as if it's good news—that immigrants use welfare at only at 18 percent *above* the native-born rate. No, the fact that any immigrants are on welfare proves we're not taking the right immigrants."[84]

Culture Matters

Many contemporary philosophers and even economists, from Mark Steyn to Thomas Sowell, have pointed out the primacy of culture over economic determinism. While free markets have the virtue of

---

[84]   Coulter p. 15

permitting individuals the greatest freedom to pursue their own happiness in accordance with their own values, those values are in the main derived from culture, and all cultures are NOT equal; *most* cultures in the world are, in fact, hostile to the traditional American values embodied in our founding documents, free-market economy and Judeo-Christian heritage. It's not a good idea to dilute the culture that produced the Declaration of Independence, the Constitution, the abolition of slavery, the end of Jim Crow segregation, the vote for blacks and for women, an end to the persecution of homosexuals, the rights of migrant farm workers etc., if you consider all of the above to be good things. America could not have achieved the freedom, prosperity and civil rights that it has under any other culture than the one that we inherited from the Founders. Will Hispanics and gays be better off when we are more like tribal Somalia or the Muslim Middle East?

Less than 2 percent of births in the United States are to girls under the age of 16, and of those, the majority are Hispanic. In other countries from whom we are importing people, percentages are much higher; 15 percent in Argentina and 17 percent in Uruguay, for example.[85]

American feminists in particular should be concerned about importing higher degrees of sexual abuse and assault into our country. There has never been a culture and society more considerate of the rights and dignity of women than the Anglosphere, the descendants of Anglo-Saxon peoples now distributed from Britain to the United States and from Canada to Australia. Not even France comes close. Ann Coulter presents an appalling catalog of rapes, sexual molestations, and human trafficking committed against native-born and immigrant women and girls by immigrants from third-world countries, from Mexico to India to the Middle East. Under Islamic culture, it is common for girls to have their clitorises cut out—not necessarily using anesthesia—in a "purification" ritual, failing which they would be considered "unclean." In that same culture, the woman or girl is more likely to be prosecuted for the *crime of having been raped* than the rapist(s). Are these wonderful contributions to our cultural

---

[85]   Coulter p. 189

diversity that we wish to permit, or "better" yet, celebrate and encourage?

Cultural Compatibility and Assimilation

Cultural traits like average IQs, propensity to crime or antisocial behavior, affinity with America's founding principles and documents, etc., are not fixed and immutable; like anything else under the sun, they evolve over time. Thomas Sowell has noted, for example, that Jewish immigrants arriving in the U.S. from Eastern Europe in the late nineteenth and early twentieth centuries had low IQ scores, while black American children in public schools in Harlem during the 1940s scored comparably to those pupils in all-white schools in New York's working-class Lower East Side, and occasionally surpassed them[86]. DNA is not destiny, and to embellish Coulter, Anglo-Saxon culture and polity can be acquired by people lacking a drop of King John the First's blood[87].

But assimilation takes time, measured in decades and generations, and some cultural traits can remain dominant even after centuries, explaining inequalities and disproportionate demographic patterns that are not otherwise explainable by genetics or "environment." The relevant question is, do we have the capacity to absorb and assimilate the people from unlike cultures at the rate at which they are arriving? It is not encouraging when an increasing number of "spokespersons" for foreign groups insist that it is *we Americans* who must assimilate to the cultures of the rest of the world. "Can they?" and "Will they?" are separate questions. If they will not, then we risk committing civilizational suicide.

---

[86]   Sowell, Thomas, *Wealth, Poverty and Politics: An International Perspective*, p. 116-117. See also: Sowell, Thomas. *A Personal Odyssey*. New York, NY: Free Press, 2002. From his description of middle school/junior high school in Harlem in the 1940s, I can confidently say that he got a better education there than I got at the racially integrated Martin Luther King, Jr., Junior High School in the advanced, progressive and affluent Berkeley, California, of the 1970s.

[87]   Coulter p. 59

Post-Constitutional Polity and Culture
(Or, Ellis Island in the Nanny State)

Jason Riley and others in his camp charge that the arguments put forth by immigration restrictionists today are no different than the tired old unfounded rantings of one hundred, two hundred or even three hundred years ago against people of different nationalities or ethnicities moving in, all of which turned out to be much sound and fury signifying nothing. Even Benjamin Franklin had railed against Germans is his time[88]. But there are differences, and they fundamentally change the game.

Up to one hundred years ago, whether they were welcomed with open arms or spat upon, immigrants were expected to pull their own weight along with native-born Americans, learn English, work for a living, and adapt to the culture and civic institutions—in a word, assimilate. There was no entitlement bureaucracy, and the government trod on the economy with a very light, laissez-faire footprint, as Milton Friedman, an advocate of liberal immigration policies, pointed out. What institutions existed to help immigrants were largely of the community church or synagogue self-help variety, where the more-assimilated members of immigrant groups assisted newcomers in adjusting to the culture of the host country.

Before the immigration bill spearheaded by Senator Edward Kennedy in 1965, according to Coulter:

> Seven countries each provided 5 percent or more of the total number of immigrants each year—Italy, Germany, Canada, the United Kingdom, Poland, the Soviet Union, and Mexico. . . By 2000 Mexico was the only country supplying more than 5 percent, accounting for nearly a third of all immigrants to the United States. . . In 1970, there were fewer than 10 million foreign born in the United States, and 75 percent of them were from Europe. By 2010, there were 40 million foreign-born in the United States and only 13 percent were from Europe.

Among countries sending us legal immigrants as of 2013, Canada is in fifteenth place, with 1.3 percent of the total, behind Mexico, China,

---

[88]   Jason Riley, Let Them In: The Case for Open Borders, p. 8.

India, the Philippines, Dominican Republic, Cuba, Vietnam, South Korea, Colombia, Haiti, Jamaica, El Salvador, Nigeria and Pakistan. The United Kingdom is in eighteenth place, behind Ethiopia and Nepal, and is followed immediately by Iran and Burma[89].

Today, in contrast to our laissez-faire past, the combined local, state and federal government footprint weighs in at 40% or heavier, with an elaborate and entrenched entitlement system that is shot through with corruption and abuse. Scores of advocacy and lobbying firms have sprouted up to defend the "civil rights" (read: free goodies) for their clients at the expense of native-born Americans, while insisting upon ever-reduced demands on immigrants that they support themselves and conform to American culture and traditions. This ain't your grandpa's Ellis Island.

Below is a partial list of the organizations which did not exist one hundred years ago which advocate on behalf of various sectors of the immigrant population. Are all of these focused primarily on getting their clients to embrace traditional American values and personal responsibility, learn English and the Constitution and adapt to the host country's values and norms?[90]

- ACLU Immigrant's Right Freedom Network
- The National Immigration Law Center
- The National Immigration Project of the National Lawyers Guild
- The National Network for Immigration and Refugee Rights
- The Office of Migration and Refugee Services
- The American Immigration Law Foundation
- The American Immigration Lawyers Association
- The Border Information and Outreach Service
- The Farmworker Justice Fund
- Grantmakers Concerned with Immigrants and Refugees
- The Immigration Legal Resource Center

---

[89]   Office of Immigration Statistics, Department of Homeland Security. U.S. Lawful Permanent Residents: 2013.
http://www.dhs.gov/sites/default/files/publications/ois_lpr_fr_2013.pdf
[90]   Coulter p. 247.

Made in the USA
San Bernardino, CA
06 May 2017

- The International Center for Migration, Ethnicity, and Citizenship
- The Lesbian and Gay Immigration Rights Taskforce
- The Lutheran Immigration and Refugee Service;
- The National Association for Bilingual Education
- The National Clearinghouse on Agricultural Guest Worker Issues
- The National Coalition for Dignity and Amnesty for Undocumented Immigrants
- The National Coalition for Haitian Rights
- The National Farm Worker Ministry.
- The National Council of La Raza ("The Race")

Democrat Party Political Gamesmanship

¿Cómo se siente, ser mascota?

In 2009, the Democrats, holding both houses of Congress in addition to the White House, could easily have passed comprehensive immigration reform with the cooperation of many Republicans and with goodwill and political capital left over for their other pet projects. The fact that they neglected both immigration and the suffering economy and job market in order to focus like Darth Vader's Death Star on their century-long priority of socialized medicine gives away what they really think of Hispanics and Republicans; the former are just pawns in their political game, to be used and manipulated, and the latter are only useful as whipping boys (and girls) on whom to blame their own failures, not to be seen agreeing with on anything in public.

Nor is the 2009 Democrats' cynical treatment of their captive Hispanic mascots anything new in that party's gamesmanship. As Coulter writes:

> A year before the 1996 presidential election, the Clinton White House worked feverishly to naturalize 1 million immigrants in time for Clinton's reelection. Criminal background checks were jettisoned for 200,000 applicants, so that citizenship was granted to at least 70,000 people with FBI criminal records and 10,000 with felony records. Murderers,

robbers, and rapists were all made our fellow Americans so the Democrats would have 1 million new voters by the 1996 election. In 2013 alone, the Obama administration released 36,007 convicted criminal aliens with about 88,000 convictions among them, including 426 for rape and 193 for murder.[91]

May be good for the Democratic Party, at least in the short term. But good for America?

President Obama's attempts at granting legal status to millions of illegal aliens without consulting Congress have been so reckless and unconstitutional that even the pro-open-borders *Wall Street Journal* had to applaud a Texas court's injunction against the Obama administration's unilateral actions. "The injunction isn't about prosecutorial discretion. It is about granting illegal aliens benefits not allowed by law."[92]

As for the "immigration" crisis of late 2015, the Syrian refugees, and whether we should grant them asylum, citizenship and/or halal meals, Mark Steyn points out:

> According to the United Nations, 49 percent are non-Syrian. As to whether they're refugees, well, usually, refugees flees as families. Yet here, from those UN statistics, is the breakdown of those "refugees": 13 percent children; 12 percent women; 75 percent men. That's not the demographic distribution of fleeing refugees, but of an invading army.[93]

Or Thomas Sowell:[94]

> The refugee crisis in Europe is one of those human tragedies for which there are no real solutions, despite how

---

91   Coulter p. 246. See also: "INS Accused Of Giving In To Politics; White House Pressure Tied to Citizen Push," by William Branigin. *Washington Post*, March 4, 1997. http://www.highbeam.com/doc/1P2-707430.html

92   "Why Obama's Immigration Order Was Blocked." Michael W. McConnell. *The Wall Street Journal*, February 17, 2015. http://www.wsj.com/articles/michael-mcconnell-why-obamas-immigration-order-was-blocked-1424219904. See also: "Obama's Immigration Rebuke." Review and Outlook. *The Wall Street Journal*, February 17, 2015. http://www.wsj.com/articles/obamas-immigration-rebuke-1424220099

93   Steyn, Mark. "Taking it." SteynOnline.com, September 7, 2015. http://www.steynonline.com/7158/taking-it

94   Sowell, Thomas. "The Past and Future of the Refugee Crisis." Townhall.com, Sep 08, 2015 http://townhall.com/columnists/thomassowell/2015/09/08/the-past-and-future-of-the-refugee-crisis-n2049033/page/full

many shrill voices in the media may denounce those who fail to come up with a solution.

. . .

All the new generation [of immigrants] will know is that they are not doing as well as other people in the country where they live. They will also know that the values of their culture clash with the values of the Western culture around them. And there will be no lack of "leaders" to tell them that they have been wronged, including some who will urge them to jihad.

Europeans have already seen this scenario play out in their midst, creating strife and even terrorism. Most of the Muslims may be peaceful people who are willing to live and let live. But it takes only a fraction who are not to create havoc.

No nation has an unlimited capacity to absorb immigrants of any sort, and especially immigrants whose cultures are not simply different, but antagonistic, to the values of the society in which they settle.

The inescapable reality is that it is an irreversible decision to admit a foreign population of any sort—but especially a foreign population that has a track record of remaining foreign.

. . .

Barack Obama's decision to pull American troops out of Iraq, with happy talk about how he was ending a war, turned out to be a bitter mockery when the policy in fact opened the doors to new wars with unspeakable horrors in the present and incalculable consequences for the future.

. . .

Sending money to Middle Eastern countries that are taking in Muslim refugees makes a lot more sense for the West than taking in more refugees themselves. It may even encounter far less political opposition at home. But a real attempt to deal with the underlying causes of this human tragedy will probably have to wait until Barack Obama is gone from the White House.

Republican Demographic Blues

For their part, Republicans are, with reason, concerned about the electoral calculus of their stance on immigration. Many hope eventually to regain the 40% of the Hispanic vote that George W. Bush achieved in 2006, in spite of that being a losing year overall for Republicans in the House and Senate due to perceptions about the Iraq war. But Coulter counters that Republicans are wasting ammunition going after groups that are *never* going to pull the lever for them, like Hispanics and blacks, while neglecting and alienating traditional white Anglo-Saxon Protestant male voters who are the traditional base not only of the Republican Party but of the country as a whole. Conversely, there are others, notably black conservatives like Larry Elder and Jesse Lee Peterson, who say that Republicans can win black votes if they would just 1) show up, 2) engage and 3) tell the truth the same as they do to white audiences, instead of watering down the message with mushy platitudes about Martin Luther King, Jr.; in a word, stop pandering (okay, two words). That might work in the case of Hispanics, too (just substitute Cesar Chavez for MLK in the "do not pander" column).

Coulter also provides some backbone-enhancing encouragement to Republicans:

> In 2011, 73 percent of *California* Hispanics [my emphasis, mostly because I am a Californian] said they'd support a candidate who wanted to "secure the border first, stop illegal immigration, and then find a way to address the status of people already here illegally." In a 2014 Univision poll, 58 percent chose "require border security first" over "pass immigration reform."[95]

Moreover, support for beefing up border security and deporting illegals may be stronger than might be supposed from reading or viewing the mainstream media or poll summaries[96]. For example, in a poll taken by the Field Research Corporation in California in February 2013, in spite of the description, "NEAR-UNIVERSAL SUPPORT FOR ALLOWING LONG-TIME UNDOCUMENTED RESIDENTS TO STAY AND BECOME CITIZENS UNDER CERTAIN CONDITIONS. MAJORITY ALSO BACKS GRANTING CALIFORNIA DRIVER'S LICENSES TO THESE RESIDENTS,"[97] in the fine print it noted that 46 percent of

---

[95]   Coulter p. 8
[96]   Coulter p. 48
[97]   The Field Poll, Release #2349.
     http://www.field.com/fieldpollonline/subscribers/Rls2439.pdf

respondents supported (versus 43 percent opposed) "Continue the policy of having federal immigration agents round up, detain and deport immigrants found to be living here illegally." That number rose to 54 percent if only white non-Hispanics were counted; 24 percent of Latinos agreed.

In a political environment where neither side of an issue can point to unambiguous and unchallengeable support for their position, especially where that support is less objective and fact-based than based on popular perceptions and opinions, the decisive factor is *leadership*: take a stand for what you believe is right, persuade people to your point of view as best you can and let the chips fall where they may. The leaders most sought-after in a crisis are the ones no one would listen to the day before because they were considered crank alarmists. Just ask Winston Churchill.

Invasion: "La Reconquista"

It may come as surprise, but many intellectuals and politicians in Mexico are not huge fans of us gringos. The loss of half the territory of Mexico in the Mexican-American War of 1846-7 remains an open wound at least as fresh in the Mexican intelligencia's and political class's mind as the resentments of some present-day American southerners regarding the outcome of the Civil War.

The difference between *los Mexicanos* and Dixie is that the former have a plausible possibility of winning their lost territory back by overwhelming the southwestern United States demographically. Considering the absolute numbers and percentages of Mexicans swelling the populations of Texas, New Mexico, Arizona and California, this possibility cannot be dismissed as a pipe dream or exaggerated threat in the long term.

Whether this is in the interest of Anglo-, Afro- or Sino-American Texans or Californians—or for that matter, the Mexicans who come across the border for a better life—is another story entirely. It may not be politically correct to say so, but *the United States has been better-governed than Mexico for the past 170 years, or ever.* It has provided better security and economic prosperity for all, including Mexican immigrants, than has the Mexican government.

Mexico does not lack natural resources; it has simply chosen the national socialist model of state control and ownership (see: Pemex) instead of the free-market capitalist model of private property, and the Mexican people have suffered the inevitable consequences. Put another way, the United States does not have a national oil company operating on behalf of *el pueblo*, and we are no worse off for the fact.

Mexico has plenty of technology and smarts; Monterrey is a high-tech hub, the Mexican Silicon Valley from which hails one of my own smartest and closest colleagues and bosses. But in Mexican society and government, business contracts and privileges are awarded on the basis of political pull, most notoriously Carlos Slim's monopoly on the telephone system. Mexicans get substandard phone service in exchange for the bragging rights of having one of the richest billionaires in the world. As for the common people, says Coulter, "In Mexico, every transaction between a citizen and a government official involves a cash bribe."[98]

Mexico had a good president in 1880, a fine upstanding man named Porfirio Diaz. If he had followed George Washington's example, he might yet be remembered as a great president. But in 1910, after *thirty years* in office (almost four times as long as Washington had thought proper), he still wouldn't leave. Like too many tinhorn dictators today, he considered himself indispensable. It took a ten-year bloody civil war to effect a succession in Mexico, the outcome of which was substantially flawed.

Mexican intellectuals blame the United States for many of their ills due to our undue interference in their affairs. I suspect that with respect to the "progressive" president Woodrow Wilson, they may have a case. But we did not force them to organize their political economy along corrupt socialist/statist principles—and that is the single greatest factor holding them back.

It is not in the interest of anyone living in the United States, least of all poor Mexicans, that the government of Mexico, let alone the

---

[98]   Coulter p. 111. See also: "Mexican Journalist Fired for Exposing Government Corruption", by Ildefonzo Ortiz. Breitbart.com, March 18, 2015.
http://www.breitbart.com/texas/2015/03/18/mexican-journalist-fired-for-exposing-government-corruption/

drug cartels, should reign over any part of what is today de facto and de jure the United States of (North) America. To the contrary, if Mexico sends us 25 percent of its population, perhaps it is we who should govern 25 percent of Mexico's remaining territory—percentage as measured by economic value. Ditto any other country that sends us any percentage above 1 of their population.

The desire for *La Reconquista* is real. The tactics are in full deployment today. It will not succeed if we remain true to the principles that made the United States superior in the first place. But there are real and present forces, especially in our universities and political lobbying sector, which are working tirelessly and with the fuel of our own money against us.

We judge this to be an insignificant concern at our peril.

Islamic Sharia Law

Allahu Akbar in the Streets of L.A.

In October 2015, hundreds of Muslims blocked a street in Los Angeles to conduct Islamic prayers, and no authority prevented it or broke it up[99]. This is not an innocent act. It is a calculated, cultural, religious and political assault on our once Judeo-Christian nation—testing, probing to see how far they can go, how much they can get away with, and then pushing ever farther. We don't have to guess as to how far this may go; we have only to observe what is happening in Old, Tired Europe, where the native Europeans have completely lost the confidence of their cultures and socialism has eaten away at their moral and economic strength. The Los Angeles incident is only the furthest Westward push of this movement.

You don't have to be a conservative to have your doubts about Islamic culture being good for America. Bill Maher: "This idea that all religions share the same values is bull***t and we need to call it bull***t. . . If you are in this religion [Islam], you probably do have

---

[99]

http://www.americanthinker.com/blog/2015/10/los_angeles_muslims_block_th e_street_to_pray.html values that are at odds [with American values]. This is what liberals don't want to recognize."[100]

Will the liberals recognize that it will take more than Kumbaya Twitter hashtag campaigns and candlelight vigils of soft and squishy non-committal solidarity after the ISIS attacks on Western civilians in Paris on November 13, 2015 that killed 130, the Jihadi attack on a government agency Christmas Party in San Bernardino, California, on December 2, 2015 that killed 14 Americans, and the ISIS attack on the Brussels airport and subway that killed 31 westerners? I'm not holding my breath.

Choices

The choices we have to make are not between mass deportation on the one hand and complete amnesty on the other. We have to choose between sets of complex and imperfect trade-offs, based on an assessment of reality distilled out of hard statistics, disputed facts and competing claims. Perfection is impossible, but there are huge opportunities for improvement. I will outline the policy suite which I believe holds the greatest promise of improving the economy and reducing both the crime rate and the conflicts among Americans and immigrants, in the next chapter (no fear; it's much shorter than this one just past).

---

[100]   "Bill Maher Criticizes Liberals for Believing That All of Islam is Peaceful," by Justin Holcomb, Townhall.com, November 23, 2015.
http://townhall.com/tipsheet/justinholcomb/2015/11/23/bill-maher-criticizes-islam-gets-slammed-by-liberal-panel-n2084414

Comprehen*sible* Immigration Reform[101]

On the one hand, solving the immigration crisis is inexorably tied to solving our more general economic and social problems. On the other hand, this does *not* mean that the solution is "Comprehensive Immigration Reform." The *last* thing that is needed is another multi-thousand-page, all-or-nothing, take-it-or-leave it omnibus bill that no one can read in its entirety, laden with pork. The political process necessary to achieve a transparent, honest and balanced outcome will be one of incremental reforms; one bill focused on one specific subject area at a time, short enough to be comprehended and debated in the light of day, certainly no longer than the text of the U.S. Constitution, and ideally much shorter than that.

How many pages does it take to say, "Build, staff and administer a security fence"? How many pages are required to propose a new *bracero*-style guest worker program? (Or not?) How much ink is required to decree that municipalities may *not* declare themselves to be "sanctuary cities" in direct contravention to federal law? How many trees have to die to ensure that violent criminals are not given a second, a third and a fourth chance to murder innocent Americans like Kate Steinle?[102]

The Beltway Way of working out all of the competing and interdependent facets of reform in any sector is to shove hundreds of initiatives into a single monster bill and then attach riders, earmarks, favors, pork, "Cornhusker kickbacks"[103] and midnight amendments. This practice needs to give way to a more transparent, bite-sized-piece-at-a-time approach. The mutual dependencies among the many immigration-related bills need to be worked out in negotiations between and among the bills competing for attention, manifesting primarily in the order in which they come to the floors of the House

---

101   For the chapter title, kudos to Michael Medved for coming up with the expression at about the same time that I thought of it.

102   "Steinle family announces lawsuit against gov't agencies in SF murder." FoxNews, September 01, 2015. http://www.foxnews.com/politics/2015/09/01/kate-steinle-family-announce-lawsuits-against-agencies-blamed-for-her-murder.html

103   The Senator from Nebraska, Ben Nelson, was offered $100 million in Medicaid funding for his state by Majority Leader Harry Reid in exchange for his (the 60th) vote for the Affordable Care Act in 2010.

and/or Senate. Assuming a divided house in which neither party can expect to get everything it wants, if Democrats want reform A, B and C, and Republicans want X, Y and Z, then both parties have to figure out which reform they want most and which they are willing to trade away in exchange for bipartisan cooperation. If Republicans say to Democrats, "We'll give you A if you'll give us X," and Democrats agree to vote on A, then Republicans can refuse to discuss B, much less vote on it, before X is passed. However, Republicans holding a majority should not be shy about exercising their majority prerogatives, consistent with constitutional constraints. Democrats have certainly not shown any restraint in recent years.

And so it goes, the difference with current actual practice being that this occurs out in the open instead of in the smoke-filled back room, and each reform is encapsulated into its own separate bill instead of being glued together with all of the others by means of copious ladles of lard. A, X and B don't have to be, and probably shouldn't be, in the same bill.

It's not about comprehensive reform piled into Godzilla bills. Nor is it a soundbyte-sized simplistic choice between "amnesty" versus "mass deportation." It's about the consistent application of the principles that made America the place that used to attract the most immigrants for all the right reasons.

A Bill a Week for a Year

The Coulter-Levin camp may seem to be completely irreconcilable with the Cato-WSJ-Manhattan Institute camp. But there is plenty of opportunity for policy changes which the former could propose, the majority of which the latter should at least not object to. Most arguments within the Right are likely to be over political strategy and tactics more than disagreement over substance. Anyone who is not cheerleading for the Democrat Party, the Socialist States of America, the Mexican Reconquista or a post-Constitutional Sharia U.S.A. should support most of the below proposals, though obviously not in equal measure or urgency.

The astute reader will notice that a number of these are not strictly limited to immigration. This is because many (possibly most) of the problems we commonly associate with immigration do not originate in or remain limited to that domain. Some proposals are specific and targeted while others express more general principles.

These are suggestions, and I'm certain that my readers can come up with enough of their own to double this list, some of which will be more liberal. That is fine; just don't try to shove them all into an all-inclusive horror and call it the "**G**eneral **O**mnibus **D**emocratic **Z**ealous **I**mmigration **L**iberalization and **L**imitation **A**ct."

- Build, staff and administer a physical, electronic and satellite GPS-supported border fence capable of reducing illegal crossings by 90 percent—or 99 percent. Building, technology and security contracts to be awarded on the basis of maximum results at lowest cost, *not* union clout, "prevailing wages," crony favoritism or affirmative action. (Maybe we should hire illegal aliens to build it, and then award them citizenship upon achievement of the required objective.)

- Deport visa over-stayers; enforce the law consistently. If Indian H-1B visa holders obediently return to India when their visas expire (as I have personally witnessed many times), then we should expect no less from our visa-holding friends from south of the border.
  Forty to fifty percent of illegals didn't crawl across the desert in the dead of night; they simply didn't give notice to their landlords and board their return flights when their permits expired. They are "documented." Presumably, we know where they are, and therefore can show them the door—the more promptly, the better.

- For every new law passed, sunset or repeal *two* that have either outlived their usefulness or never should have been enacted in the first place. That is the majority of them.

- Reinstate (at a minimum) the welfare reform of 1996 that was achieved by Bill Clinton and Newt Gingrich and dismantled by Barack Obama. The success of the 1996 reform demonstrated that many able-bodied Americans were better able to take care of themselves than the entitlement bureaucracies. In any case, we cannot permit, and therefore should not tempt, people to come to this country merely to live off the fruits of American citizens' labor. Unplug the moral hazard and fraud magnet.

- Reset the quota system for how many immigrants we take from various countries to its pre-1965 configuration, in order to favor immigrants from countries who are more likely to share our common cultural values.

- Repeal/reverse the "anchor baby" interpretation of the 14th Amendment to the U.S. Constitution. That amendment was put in place immediately after the Civil War for the unambiguous purpose of granting citizenship to black former slaves. Now, thanks to a reinterpretation by a Supreme Court justice that even Harry Reid at one time had called insane, it serves as a perverse enticement, drawing people into our country for illegitimate reasons and imposing direct financial costs on our county hospitals in the process[104].

  And no, we don't need a new amendment to "clarify" the original amendment. Learn to read.[105]

- End English-language proficiency exemptions for citizenship. We currently allow people age fifty or older who have lived for twenty years legally in the country (or fifty-five/fifteen) to acquire citizenship without having to demonstrate English proficiency.

  Why should we admit as citizens people who have been here for twenty years and yet haven't bothered to learn the language? Being here that long without assimilating should be considered a *dis*-qualifier.

  We also allow exemptions "because of a physical or developmental disability or a mental impairment."[106] Why?

  The practice of conducting citizenship ceremonies as well as printing and publishing election materials in foreign languages,

---

[104]   Coulter p. 35-40
[105]   See Coulter p. 34-36, 38-39, 119, 127
[106]   http://www.uscis.gov/us-citizenship/citizenship-through-naturalization/exceptions-accommodations

indicates that the standards we are demanding are too low. These practices should end.

Multilingualism is a source of national disintegration, from Quebec to Yugoslavia (ever heard of?), and it devalues citizenship. Persons who don't speak English are not able to understand the public debates and are therefore not qualified to fully participate in American constitutional democracy. Raise the bar and the true Americans among the immigrants will rise to the challenge[107]. (Individuals, churches, synagogues and political parties are free to voluntarily reach out to non-English-speaking persons and communities to help bring them into the American polity. In fact, they have a duty to do so; Republicans especially must not miss the boat.)

- Stop encouraging foreign immigrants *not* to assimilate, as we are doing in the K-12 schools and universities run by the Left. Bobby Jindal and others are correct when they say that "immigration without assimilation is invasion." No government contracts or funds should go to any organizations whose missions are antagonistic to assimilation, such as The National Council of La Raza ("The Race")[108].

- Stop teaching multiculturalism and "bilingualism" (a.k.a. Spanish as the primary language) in our schools.

- Strengthen the integrity of the electoral process through such measures as voter ID, to prevent so much as the appearance of non-citizens voting.

- Repeal Section 1706 of the 1986 Tax Equity and Fairness Reform Act, or TEFRA (see previous chapter).

- Repeal Dodd-Frank and all other regulations that foist excessive burdens upon business which are not justified by government's legitimate responsibility to prevent and punish

---

107   Coulter p. 27: "By 2010, 60 million people living in America [20 percent of the population] spoke a language other than English."

108   Coulter accuses Marco Rubio of including $150 million worth of earmarks for nonprofit organizations in his bill, "The Border Security, Economic Opportunity, and Immigration Modernization Act of 2013." (Coulter p. 8) As for La Raza's sentiments about America, see: http://www.washingtontimes.com/news/2006/apr/3/20060403-091645-7346r/

murder, robbery, theft, fraud, assault, rape, persecution and conspiracy.

- Whatever reforms are proposed for the H-1B visa program, they should be based on the point of fact that there is not now, nor has there ever been, a shortage of native-born American workers or graduates capable of performing the S.T.E.M. work demanded in the market.

- Restore the Rule of Law. This cuts both ways. If a law is out of touch with social or economic reality, then propose, sponsor, debate and vote on legislation to replace or fix it. But in the meantime, enforce the law as it is written.

- Arrest, incarcerate and deport criminals camping and/or polluting or desecrating our wilderness, deserts, national parks or cities[109].

- Apply the law (including incarceration, deportation and, in extreme cases, execution) without respect to nationality, ethnicity, religion, culture, color, gender or sexual orientation. Contrary to the 180-degree twisted narrative of the Left, this means going after criminal members of favored minority groups *just as severely* as we would criminal white Anglo-Saxon protestant males. You wouldn't let Bubba or Mitt Romney rape girls, block city streets for Jesus-worshipping prayers, murder people, desecrate protected wilderness, practice a profession without a license, stab people, cheat on taxes, run a business in contravention of regulations, violate zoning laws, speed, drive drunk, rob people or jaywalk.

- Give us Truth in Advertising (reporting and data). The government and the media have to restore the trust in the impartiality of the reporting of stories, facts and statistics about crimes committed by immigrants even—or perhaps especially—if they have U.S. citizenship. The American people

---

[109]   If you are like most Americans, you probably had no idea that illegal aliens and drug cartels are camping in our wilderness and national parks, dumping garbage and human waste in the neighborhood of centuries-old natural treasures. Read Coulter chapter 12, "Keep America ~~Beautiful~~ Multicultural," and then call up your local forest ranger or Sierra Club chapter and ask them what the hell is going on and what they are doing about it.

have a right to know what they are getting in return for giving residency and citizenship away cheaply.

- Abolish "sanctuary cities."
- Repeal any and all child labor laws that obviously have more to do with protecting unionized adults from competition than with safeguarding children. That is the majority of them.
- Address, prosecute and eliminate fraud[110]:
  - o In "family reunifications": reduce or eliminate chain migration. Just because we admit one worker shouldn't mean that we admit his entire clan or village.
  - o In the "farmworkers" program. Coulter p. 45: "Within the first three years of the agricultural worker amnesty [of 1986], the government identified 888,637 fraudulent applications, of which it approved more than 800,000."[111]
  - o In the high-tech H-1B Visa program.
  - o In asylum and refugee cases.
  - o In welfare and entitlements.
  - o Anywhere and everywhere in the system that it may arise.
- If a government program is not redeemable, shut it down completely.
- Zero tolerance for Sharia law[112]:
  - o No Sharia Courts *anywhere* in the United States, as it is absolutely incompatible with our Constitution.

---

[110]   See Coulter chapter 14: "Every Single Immigration Category is a Fraud" (p. 233-243) and: "The family reunifications are fraud, the 'farmworkers' are frauds, the high-tech visas are frauds—and the asylum and refugee cases are monumental frauds." (p. 248)

[111]   Coulter's source is *Lessons Learned from the Legalization Programs of the 1980s* by David North for the Center for Immigration Studies, 2005.
http://www.ilw.com/articles/2005,0302-north.shtm

[112]   I happen to believe that it is acceptable for a Muslim cab driver to refuse to pick up a fare carrying alcohol, pork, a dog or anything else that offends his religious sensibilities. It is a voluntary exchange between consenting adults; the fare does not own the cab. Non-Muslim cabbies have a market opportunity, a niche to fill. It is only by defining taxicabs as a "public good"—a socialist/collectivist concept—that interference in the voluntary mutual agreement becomes justified; a weak case, IMHO.

- o No Sharia-derived excuses for crimes such as spousal abuse, child abuse, rape, female genital mutilation, honor killing or disruption of a public thoroughfare.
- End the public employee union domination of pre-K-12 schools.
- Put the public education dollars into the hands of the parents, not the unions.
- End the Leftist indoctrination of children in pre-K-12 schools.
- Abolish Agenda 21.
- De-commission the Department of Education
- Address the absence of diversity among professors in universities; end discrimination against conservative professors and students.
- Repeal, as unconstitutional, state laws and municipal ordinances which infringe upon the rights of citizens to keep and bear arms, as guaranteed by the Second Amendment. Then watch the murder rate go down, and with it, resentment against immigrants.
- Grant a monopoly of database design contracts for immigration, citizenship, health care and crime to the world's leading Oracle Expert, Howard Hyde.

This is not a call to pitchforks, nor to simplistic slogans, but to books, thoughtful discussion, more-than-superficial study, open debate and well-defined and thought-through action.

Let's restore America, for the sake of all Americans, native and immigrant, present and future.

John Henry's America

If you arrived at this chapter by starting on page 1 and devouring every page sequentially until you reached here, I salute you! You are a member of the elite One Percent! You have demonstrated exceptional courage and intelligence.

And patience. While I have tried to make the reading light and entertaining where possible, I acknowledge that I have made significant demands on the left side of your brain. And so I wanted to end on a slightly different note, not as contradiction but as affirmation. For while logic and facts have been my armaments, the true essence of this book is my love for America, a country I was once systematically taught to hate.

This short chapter is included, and concludes the book, for no good reason whatsoever except to express admiration for the unique spirit of America and its greatness in a simple, heartfelt way.

Few countries or cultures in the world have given as much respect and honor to *work*—difficult, back-breaking but soul-ennobling labor—as America. For all the shallow Marxist gripes about America being a land of oppression by rich capitalist fat cats exploiting the proletariat slaves, the fact of the matter is that no country before or since (2009) has offered as much opportunity for social and economic mobility to those who start out as manual laborers. Our CEOs and Presidents of the nation are drawn from such stock more commonly than in any other country. And, at least traditionally, those who live honestly by the labor of their hands and backs have never been as respected or rewarded anywhere in the world as they are in the United States.

Economic progress leading to higher standards of living for all means that machines and computers will, and of necessity must, substitute for human labor in many instances, from the simplest and most brutish to increasing levels of cognitive sophistication and intelligence; we're not Luddites here[113]. But there will always be a place of honor for those who work as most of our ancestors did, those who work as hard as those whose sacrifice made our ease today possible. As expressed in the song lyrics below, America is the land that admires and exalts the spirt of John Henry. His is a spirit we must never lose.

John Henry was a little baby, sitting on his daddy's knee
He picked up a hammer and little piece of steel
Said "Hammer's gonna be the death of me, Lord, Lord
Hammer's gonna be the death of me."

The captain said to John Henry
"Gonna bring that steam drill 'round
Gonna bring that steam drill out on the job
Gonna whop that steel on down, Lord, Lord
Gonna whop that steel on down."

John Henry told his captain
"A man ain't nothing but a man
But before I let your steam drill beat me down
I'd die with a hammer in my hand, Lord, Lord
I'd die with a hammer in my hand."

John Henry said to his shaker
"Shaker, why don't you sing?
I'm throwin' thirty pounds from my hips on down
Just listen to that cold steel ring, Lord, Lord
Just listen to that cold steel ring."

The shaker said to John Henry
"I think this mountain's cavin' in!"
John Henry said to his shaker, "Man
That ain't nothin' but my hammer suckin' wind! Lord, Lord
Ain't nothin' but my hammer suckin' wind!"

---

[113]   Luddites: "One of a group of early 19th century English workmen destroying laborsaving machinery as a protest; broadly: one who is opposed to especially technological change." http://www.merriam-webster.com/dictionary/luddite

Now the man that invented the steam drill
Thought he was mighty fine
But John Henry made fifteen feet
While the steam drill only made nine, Lord, Lord
The steam drill only made nine.

John Henry hammered in the mountains
His hammer was striking fire
But he worked so hard, he broke his poor heart
He laid down his hammer and he died, Lord, Lord
He laid down his hammer and he died.

They took John Henry to the graveyard
And they buried him in the sand
And every locomotive comes a-roaring by
Says, "There lies a steel-driving man, Lord, Lord
There lies a steel-driving man."

The Legend of John Henry[114]

May God bless America, even Berkeley.

---

[114]   Hat tip for the lyrics: www.songsforteaching.com. See also:
https://en.wikipedia.org/wiki/John_Henry_(folklore)

Bibliography

Ajami, Fouad. "Bush of Arabia." *The Wall Street Journal,* January 8, 2008.

An Inconvenient Truth. Directed by Davis Guggenheim. 2006. Paramount Classics.

Allison, John A. *The Financial Crisis and the Free Market Cure: Why Pure Capitalism Is the World Economy's Only Hope. New York, NY: McGraw-Hill, 2012.*

Back to the Future: Part II. Directed by Robert Zemeckis. 1989. Universal Pictures.

Bartley, Robert. *The Seven Fat Years: And How to Do It Again.* New York, NY: Free Press, 1992.

Berkeley in the Sixties. Directed by Mark Kitchell. 1990. First Run Features.

Bowen, Catherine Drinker. *Miracle at Philadelphia: The Story of the Constitutional Convention.* New York, NY: Back Bay Books, 1986.

Bureau of Labor Statistics, U.S. Department of Labor. *The Employment Situation—June 2013* (news release), July 5, 2013.

Buzzell, Colby. "Thank You for Being Expendable." *The New York Times*, May 25, 2014.

Carson, E. Ann and Golinelli, Daniela. *Prisoners in 2012—Advance Counts.* Table 10. Bureau of Justice Statistics, U.S. Department of Justice. July 2013. http://www.bjs.gov/content/pub/pdf/p12ac.pdf

Chambers, Whittaker. *Witness.* New York, NY: Random House, 1952.

Chapman, Graham. *A Liar's Autobiography, Volume VI.* London: Methuen, 1980.

Coase, Ronald. *The Firm, the Market and the Law.* Chicago, IL: University of Chicago Press, 1988.

————. *Essays on Economics and Economists.* Chicago, IL: University of Chicago Press, 1994.

Collier, Peter, and Horowitz, David. *Destructive Generation: Second Thoughts About the Sixties.* New York, NY: Summit Books, 1989.

————. *The Fords: An American Epic.* New York, NY: Summit Books, 1987.

————. *The Kennedys: An American Dream.* New York, NY: Summit Books, 1984.

————. *The Rockefellers: An American Dynasty.* New York, NY: Holt, Rinehart, and Winston, 1976.

Coulter, Ann. *Adios, America!* New York, NY: Regnery, 2015

Darwish, Nonie. *Cruel and Usual Punishment: The Terrifying Global Implications of Islamic Law.* Nashville, TN: Thomas Nelson, 2009.

————. *The Devil We Don't Know: The Dark Side of Revolutions in the Middle East.* Hoboken, NJ: Wiley, 2012.

————. *Now They Call Me Infidel: Why I Renounced Jihad for America, Israel, and the War on Terror.* New York, NY: Sentinel, 2006.

De Soto, Hernando. *The Mystery of Capital: Why Capitalism Triumphs in the West and Fails Everywhere Else.* New York, NY: Basic Books, 2000.

Feinstein, Dianne. Reply letter to Christopher Kepus, October 19, 2012, http://www.opencongress.org/contact_congress_letters/41807-S-J-Res-48-A-joint-resolution-disapproving-the-rule-submitted-by-the-Internal-Revenue-Service-relating-to-the-health-insurance-premium-tax-credit-

Free to Choose (TV series). Performed by Milton Friedman. 1980. PBS.

Gamage, David. "ObamaCare's Costs to the Working Class." *The Wall Street Journal,* October 30, 2012.

Gilder, George. *Knowledge and Power: The Information Theory of Capitalism and How It Is Revolutionizing Our World.* Washington, DC: Regnery, 2013.

———. *Wealth and Poverty.* New York, NY: Basic Books, 1981.

Griswold, Daniel. *Mad About Trade: Why Main Street America should Embrace Globalization.* Washington, DC: The Cato Institute, 2009

Horowitz, David. *Radical Son: A Generational Odyssey.* New York, NY: Touchstone, 1997.

Horowitz, David, and Laksin, Jacob. *The New Leviathan: How the Left-Wing Money Machine Shapes American Politics and Threatens America's Future.* New York, NY: Crown Forum, 2012.

Hyde, Howard. "It's the Constitution, Stupid!" *Citizen Economics* (blog), April 17, 2013, http://www.citizenecon.com/2013/04/its-constitution-stupid.html

———. *Pull the Plug on Obamacare: A Citizen Pamphlet.* Printed by author, 2013.

John Adams (TV series). Directed by Tom Hooper. 2008. HBO.

Kane, Tim. "The Importance of Startups in Job Creation and Job Destruction." *Kauffman Foundation Research Series: Firm Foundation and Economic Growth,* July 2010.

Karlgaard, Rich. "Apple to the Rescue?" *The Wall Street Journal,* January 28, 2010.

Knowledge Products. *The Audio Classics Series: Giants of Political Thought.* Read by Craig Deitschmann. Nashville, TN: Carmichael & Carmichael, Inc., 1985.

Knowledge Products. *The Audio Classics Series: Great Economic Thinkers.* Read by Louis Rukeyser. Nashville, TN: Carmichael & Carmichael, Inc., 1988.

L'Auberge Espagnole (The Spanish Apartment). Directed by Cédric Klapisch. 2002. Mars Distribution.

Luntz, Frank. *Words That Work: It's Not What You Say, It's What People Hear*, New York, NY: Hachette, 2008.

McCaughey, Betsy. *Beating Obamacare: Your Handbook for the New Healthcare Law*. Washington, DC: Regnery, 2013.

Mead, Walter R. "For the U.S., a Disappointing World." *The Wall Street Journal*, June 13, 2014.

Monty Python's The Meaning of Life. Directed by Terry Jones. 1983. Universal Studios.

Murphy, Robert P. "The Social Function of Call and Put Options." *Mises Daily*, December 13, 2006.

Murray, Charles. *Losing Ground: American Social Policy, 1950-1980*. New York, NY: Basic Books, 1984.

Nomination of Judge Clarence Thomas to be Associate Justice of the Supreme Court of the United States, October 11, 12, & 13, 1993. 102nd Cong. Washington, DC: U.S. Government Printing Office, 1993.

Obama, Barack. "Remarks by the President to the Annual Conference of the American Medical Association." June 15, 2009.

Office of Immigration Statistics, Department of Homeland Security. *2013 Yearbook of Immigration Statistics*. Published August 2014. 121 pages. (As of November 2015, the 2014 edition was not yet available.) http://www.dhs.gov/sites/default/files/publications/ois_yb_2013_0.pdf

————. *U.S. Lawful Permanent Residents: 2013*. 6 pages. http://www.dhs.gov/sites/default/files/publications/ois_lpr_fr_2013.pdf

The Path to 9/11 (TV series). Directed by David L. Cunningham. 2006. ABC.

The Patient Protection and Affordable Care Act (H.R. 3590), January 5, 2010. 111th Cong. Washington, DC: United States Government Printing Office, 2010.

The Port Huron Statement of the Students for a Democratic Society. New York, NY: Students for a Democratic Society.

Pipes, Sally. *The Cure for Obamacare.* New York, NY: Encounter Books, 2013.

Rand, Ayn. *Atlas Shrugged.* New York, NY: Random House, 1957.

————. *The Fountainhead.* Indianapolis, IN: Bobbs-Merrill, 1943.

————. *The New Left: The Anti-Industrial Revolution.* New York, NY: New American Library, 1971.

Reagan, Ronald. *An American Life.* New York, NY: Simon & Schuster, 1990.

Reisman, George. *Capitalism: A Treatise on Economics.* Laguna Hills, CA: TJS Books, 1996.

Riley, Jason. *Let Them In: The Case for Open Borders; Six Arguments Against Immigration and Why They are Wrong.* New York, NY: Gotham Books, 2009

————. *Please Stop Helping Us: How Liberals Make it Harder for Blacks to Succeed.* New York, NY: Encounter Books, 2014

Roosevelt, Franklin D. *Letter on the Resolution of Federation of Federal Employees Against Strikes in Federal Service,* August 16, 1937.

Rorabaugh, W. J. *Berkeley at War: The 1960s.* New York, NY: Oxford University Press, 1989.

Rothbard, Murray. *America's Great Depression.* Princeton, NJ: D. Van Nostrand, 1963.

————. *The Case Against the Fed.* Auburn, AL: Ludwig Von Mises Institute, 1994.

————. *Man, Economy, and State.* Princeton, NJ: William Volker Fund and D. Van Nostrand, 1962.

————. "Ronald Reagan: An Autopsy." *Liberty* 2, no. 4 (March 1989)

Simon, Julian. *The Ultimate Resource 2*. Princeton, NJ: Princeton University Press, 1996.

———. *The Economic Consequences of Immigration: Second Edition*. Ann Arbor, MI: University of Michigan Press, 1999

Smith, Adam. *An Inquiry into the Nature and Causes of the Wealth of Nations*. Edwin Cannan, ed. London: Methuen, 1904.

———. *The Theory of Moral Sentiments*. London: A. Millar, 1759.

Sowell, Thomas. *Basic Economics: A Citizen's Guide to the Economy*. New York, NY: Basic Books, 2000.

———. *Conquest and Cultures*. New York, NY: Basic Books, 1999.

———. *The Housing Boom and Bust, Revised Edition*. New York, NY: Basic Books, 2010.

———. *Knowledge and Decisions*. New York, NY: Basic Books, 1980.

———. *The Thomas Sowell Reader*. New York, NY: Basic Books, 2011.

———. *Migrations and Cultures*. New York, NY: Basic Books, 1997.

———. *A Personal Odyssey*. New York, NY: Free Press, 2002.

———. *Race and Culture*. New York, NY: Basic Books, 1995.

———. *Wealth, Poverty and Politics: An International Perspective*. New York, NY: Basic Books, 2015.

Steyn, Mark. *America Alone: The End of the World As We Know It*. Washington, DC. 2008. Regnery

Strassel, Kimberley A. "Big Labor's VA Chokehold." *The Wall Street Journal,* March 29, 2014.

Vanden Heuvel, Katrina. "An Undeserved Win for the GOP." *The Wall Street Journal,* November 5, 2010.

Von Hayek, Friedrich. *The Road to Serfdom*. London: Routledge, 1944.

Von Mises, Ludwig. *Economic Policy: Thoughts for Today and Tomorrow*. Chicago, IL: Regnery, 1979.

———. *Human Action: A Treatise on Economics.* New Haven, CT: Yale University Press, 1949.

———. *Socialism: An Economic and Sociological Analysis.* New Haven, CT: Yale University Press, 1951.

Wanniski, Jude. *The Way the World Works.* New York, NY: Basic Books, 1978.

Whyte, William H. *The Organization Man.* New York, NY: Simon & Schuster, 1956.

Wikipedia contributors. "Mario Savio." *Wikipedia, The Free Encyclopedia,* http://en.wikipedia.org/w/index.php?title=Mario_Savio&oldid=684150205

Wikipedia contributors. "Path to 9/11." *Wikipedia, The Free Encyclopedia,* http://en.wikipedia.org/w/index.php?title=Path_to_9/11&oldid=74198218

About the Author

Howard Hyde grew up in the radical leftist environment of Berkeley, California during the 1960's and 70's. Today he is a passionate advocate for limited government, free markets, private property, the Constitution, a strong America, Capitalism and economic literacy, and is President of the Southern California Republican Women and Men, an independent club established 1935. He is also author of the books "Java Web Database Application Development" and "Pull the Plug on Obamacare".

Howard edits the website www.CitizenEcon.com and is a contributing writer and speaker to AmericanThinker.com. FrontPageMag.com and several other venues, organizations, television and radio programs as diverse as the Association of American Physicians and Surgeons (AAPS) and the Larry Elder show.

Howard earns a meager living designing, programming and tuning enterprise database applications for big corporations.

More Praise for *ESCAPE FROM BERKELEY*

"An uplifting story of Howard's real-life escape from Berzerkeley's lunatic leftist politics. Hyde writes history - but not dry history. He writes a personal story - but it doesn't feel insular in the least, because current readers, absorbing the book's engaging prose, looking around at 2015 America, will be moved to say, "Uh oh, here we go again". But Hyde's most readable book also gives reason for hope that the escape path still exists. It's called freedom."
Bill Saracino, Member, Editorial Board, California Political Review

"Like James Burnham and Whittaker Chambers, and more recently Thomas Sowell and David Horowitz, Howard Hyde has made a transcendent voyage from far left to conservative. Personal and political, his book is ultimately a valuable lesson and political economics and how the left's destructive ideology is killing America."
Lawrence Sand, President, California Teachers Empowerment Network